PATTISON

PATTISON

PORTRAIT OF A
CAPITALIST SUPERSTAR

RUSSELL KELLY

 *Vancouver*

Copyright © 1986 by Russell Kelly
All rights reserved

First printing May 1986
3 4 5 90 89 88 87 86

Canadian Cataloguing in Publication Data
Kelly, Russell, 1949-
Pattison

Bibliography: p.
Includes index.
ISBN 0-919573-54-1 (bound). — ISBN
0-919573-55-X (pbk.)

1. Pattison, Jim, 1928- 2. Businessmen
- British Columbia - Biography. 3. Vancouver
(B.C.) - Biography. I. Title
HC112.5.P38K44 1986   338'.04'0924
C86-091214-0

Front cover photo by Robert Karpa

This book is published with assistance from the Canada Council
and the federal Department of Communications.

Printed and bound in Canada
by Gagne Printers, Louisville, Quebec

New Star Books Ltd.
2504 York Avenue
Vancouver, B.C.
V6K 1E3

For Joan and Kelly

CONTENTS

	Acknowledgements	9
	Preface	13
1	Air Wars	21
2	Luseland	35
3	Big Signs, Big Deals	49
4	Goldfinger	63
5	Recipe for a Conglomerate: Add a Company and Stir	80
6	Flour Power	104
7	The Politics of Greed	130
8	The Most Efficient Concealer	152
9	Hard Core Capitalist	181
10	Expo's Dollar-A-Year Man	215
11	Conclusion	238
	Appendix 1: Further Action on Pornography	243
	Appendix 2: Directors of Neonex and the Jim Pattison Group	246
	Notes	250
	Bibliography	253
	Index	256

ACKNOWLEDGEMENTS

One of the many lessons I've learned while writing this book is that I could not have done it alone. The time, energy, money and ideas of many people have made it possible for me to assemble this analytic biography.

I am lucky to have a supportive friend, lover and co-parent, Joan, who not only read the manuscript and suggested many helpful changes, but who endured the frustrations of extended deadlines, and who dealt with my uncertainties about undertaking a project of this scope.

Lee Lakeman and Tom Sandborn first encouraged me to write this book; they suggested many improvements throughout, and also generously let me set up a small office in their home. More importantly, they are my friends, in a way which I think is very rare these days.

Another friend, Don Stewart, was unstinting in his chapter by chapter criticisms and material help. He also steered many useful reference books my way.

The other person who has gone over every word of the text is Lanny Beckman, whose considerable editing skills helped me write more clearly. He also wrote some of the best punch lines. His neighbour and friend, Stan Persky, provided all-important encouragement to a journalist turning his hand for the first time to a book-length project.

A number of friends answered my questions, looked after my son Kelly (McMahon) and fed me ideas and strong coffee. They include Bonnie Agnew, Joni Miller, Jac Hull, Bubbie Polgrain, Shereen Legault, Pam Moody, Michael Renner, Brian Cross, Brian Latimer, Nicole Kennedy, Regina Lorek, Charles Lindsay, Claude Mongeon, Jude Campbell, Diana Allen, George Potvin, Peter Nix, Mike Renner and Rob Hornsey.

The staff at the business department of the Vancouver Public Library, the Law Courts Library, the Law Courts Registry, the Land Titles Office and the Assessment Authority of B.C. offered congenial and efficient help. Combines investigation officer Craig Fulton was especially helpful in explaining the complexities of competition law. A grant from the Centre for Investigative Journalism was helpful during the legal research phase. Thanks to Ian Gill of the *Sun* for his help. And to Donald Gutstein, who showed me many short cuts to sources of public information.

Finally, my thanks to a former CBC colleague, Doug Fraser, for helping me to think.

You know when you play Monopoly with your friends, the objective is to wipe them out. Well, he's doing that every day.
—a former partner of Jim Pattison

PREFACE

The voice on the telephone sounded genuinely concerned.

"No, don't hire a baby sitter. Spend Saturday with your son. I'll make time for you the next morning. Ten o'clock? My office?"

It was the first time in fifteen years of interviewing that I could remember the interview subject putting *my* family ahead of *his* convenience.

I arrive at the Guinness Tower, 1055 West Hastings Street in Vancouver at 9:45 Sunday morning and sign in at the security desk. On the register is Jim Pattison's signature. He came to work at eight o'clock. A few entries above it is Rose Anderson's, the Pattison Group's corporate secretary. She had been on the job since 5:30 a.m.

Although all the offices on the sixteenth floor are open, there is no one at the reception desk (at least someone around here gets a day off). I wander along the thickly broadloomed hallways knocking on doors and calling "hello?" Finally, through an open door I see a bald red-haired man slouched in a chair talking with a tall, older woman sitting at her desk. He glances at me and says he'll be done in a minute. Could I wait in his office?

The office is easy to find. In Vancouver, all important executives occupy the office on the *northwest* corner of the building, offering the best view of the harbour, lush Stanley Park and the steep north shore mountains.

About 170 feet below Pattison's floor-to-ceiling windows a deHavilland Twin Otter eighteen-seat float plane takes off from the calm surface of Coal Harbour. The twin pontoons leave a widening scratch across the surface, as the plane climbs quickly to clear the Douglas firs of Stanley Park. Another cabin full of passengers has just put more money in Jim Pattison's pocket.

The bright light of this clear autumn morning floods the 30 by twenty foot office, but is muted by the tans, beiges and browns of the carpet and furnishings. The paintings harmonize with the decor, and in one distant corner, his polished desk is covered with enough papers to make it look busy.

Pattison walks in, apologizing for the slight delay. He is small, about five feet six, with the pale skin of a man who might be sensitive to the sun and who spends most of his time indoors. The bald pate is covered with freckles, and what is left of the red hair blends with his tweed jacket, white shirt and tan sweater.

He looks and acts less like a billion-dollar businessman than a long-lost rich uncle.

"How many books do you gotta sell to make any money, Russell?" I don't know whether the broken grammar is an affectation or the result of Depression-era schooling added to twenty years of selling used cars. I tell him that 5,000 would be a good start. "Oh, you can sell 5,000 of anything," asserts this man who has bought and sold more in fifteen years than 28,000 average Canadians will in their combined lifetimes.

He slumps into an overstuffed beige couch at the

north end of the sprawling office. I sit across from him, a coffee table between us. Behind me stands a large, very expensive grandfather clock which breaks the hour interview into four neat chunks with its Big Ben chimes.

He answers questions about his childhood and his early work experience in a voice that is high-pitched and soft, qualities that often suggest weakness. He speaks slightly louder than a whisper, yet every syllable is picked up by my tape recorder in the acoustically perfect office. It is easy to imagine the obedience his hushed tones would inspire.

I look for signs of defensiveness or irritation aroused by the flood of interview requests he has fielded since taking over Expo. Yet the only sign of nervous energy is the constant movement of his hands. He either pulls at the loose skin on the backs of his hands or kneads his temples.

But the posture and the bags under his eyes betray a bone-deep tiredness. So do the slurred words. "When I got'nta car business I was nineteen...then from there I star'da sell cars..."

It is not until I ask why, after six months of promises, he still hasn't sold the magazine company that distributes pornography, that the dark blue eyes narrow slightly. "That's a private matter," he says. The avuncular manner disappears. He doesn't move a muscle, yet it's as if he had torn off his mask of charm.

Profits from pornography?

"We don't discuss those matters."

How much business have you lost since women's groups publicly identified you as a major distributor of pornography? He cooly and calmly lectures: "That's a private matter. One of the advantages of being a private company is we don't have to tell anybody anything about nothin', if it doesn't suit us."

Pattison has neatly summarized the paradox. Here is the man in charge of the country's largest fair, in charge of its largest real estate development (B.C. Place), sole owner of the country's eighth-largest private company, a man whose influence is great enough to have spawned the maxim "You can't live a week in B.C. without putting money in Jimmy's pocket," and he is above the requirement of accountability.

This degree of secrecy is permitted by Canadian laws for owners of private corporations, but Pattison carries it over to his public duties. When pressed to reveal how much severance pay he gave former Expo president Michael Bartlett, Pattison said it was "company policy" not to divulge salary figures. And in many ways the Crown-owned exposition has been run like a private affair. Its "public" board is stacked with friends of Pattison and Bill Bennett, and some of its contracts let without public tendering (I will examine these issues in Chapter 10).

Most people can name two or three companies owned by Jim Pattison but few realize how often they buy one of his products or use one of his services.

The Jim Pattison Group, the largest domestically owned private company in British Columbia, has 6,000 employees, assets of $604,198,000, and 1984 revenues of $1,022,985,000. It includes:

• the world's largest electric sign company (Neon Products, Claude Neon and others);

• Canada's largest General Motors *and* Toyota dealerships, which sell over 10,000 cars and trucks a year;

• Berryland Canning Company Ltd., Canada's largest exporter of canned fruits and vegetables;

• Fraser Valley Frosted Foods, a B.C. frozen food processor;

• Trans Ad, which sells advertising space on almost every bus, streetcar, subway car, transit shelter, subway and bus station in the country;

• Air BC, which has a virtual monopoly over Canada's west coast air service and owns the world's largest fleet of float planes;

• Seaboard, Hook and Gould, Pattison's three billboard advertising companies, are, combined, one of only two enterprises with a stranglehold on the national billboard advertising market (until their grip was weakened by an anti-combines conviction in 1985);

• Mainland Magazine, Provincial News and Mountain News: magazine distribution companies located in B.C., Alberta and Hamilton, Ontario. Combined they distribute 100 million copies of publications each year;

• *Beautiful British Columbia* magazine, a 360,000-circulation pictorial monthly, which will also publish the official guide to Expo 86;

• Overwaitea, the largest food store chain in B.C. outside Vancouver;

• Save-On-Foods, which just opened the province's largest supermarket;

• CJOR Radio in Vancouver, which employs ex-premier Dave Barrett as talk show host;

• EDP Industries, western Canada's largest independent data processing company;

• Canadian Fishing Company (Canfisco), commanders of a 91-ship fleet and manufacturers of the well-known Gold Seal brand salmon;

• office buildings and other real estate in Vancouver, Nanaimo, Dallas and Seattle;

• Ripley's Believe It Or Not! (the TV show, the comic strip and the museums);

• Great Pacific Industries, a publicly traded holding company with the same board of directors as the Jim Pattison Group. GPI helps the Jim Pattison Group avoid paying taxes by storing some of its wealth in the vaults of GPI's major subsidiary;

• Great Pacific Capital (of Geneva), a Swiss merchant bank which in May 1984 listed assets of $154,139,000, most of it in cash and most of that belonging to Jim Pattison.

No other individual in Canada owns as many companies with as much revenue as Jim Pattison. The seven private corporations larger than the Pattison Group are themselves owned by corporations (like General Motors) or by families (like the Irvings of New

Brunswick).

In British Columbia, only the forestry giant MacMillan Bloedel and a handful of other companies like B.C. Tel, Genstar and CP Air are larger. Had Pattison not been halted in his attempt to take over Maple Leaf Mills in 1970 (see Chapter 6), his would be the second-largest company in the province.

Nationally his holdings are roughly the same size as the Rothman's tobacco company, Carling-O'Keefe Breweries, or the publishing firms Maclean-Hunter and Southam Inc.

Pattison is not only one of the richest and most powerful men in the country, he is currently one of the best known as well, thanks to his position as head of Expo 86, the first Canadian world's fair since Montreal and the last one in Canada this century.

Pattison took the $1-a-year post, he says, as a way of repaying the province which has been so good to him. If his motives were entirely altruistic, they have been inadvertently tarnished by British Columbia's lax conflict-of-interest guidelines which have assured Pattison Group companies of several lucrative contracts with the fair. Pattison's selflessness was compromised on the international scene as well. As the chairman of Expo he was forced into contact with foreign government officials who would not otherwise have time for an "ordinary millionaire." At least one of those contacts—with the Cuban vice president—may well find Pattison and the Cubans collaborating on a luxury hotel complex at Veradero beach.

Even without Expo, Pattison has hobnobbed with the world's political and business overlords. In Europe Pattison met the former head of South Africa's Anglo-American Corporation, Harry Oppenheimer, and Thomas Bata, the Canadian owner of the multinational shoe manufacturing company (which also has extensive holdings in South Africa). And in the U.S. Pattison has played host to Ronald Reagan, Henry Kissinger and Alexander Haig at his annual "Partners in Pride" gatherings for top managers of the Pattison Group. One of Pattison's neighbours at his Palm Springs, California, residence, Gerald Ford (also a born again Christian) once gave Pattison a friendship gift—a gold money clip bearing the presidential seal.

This is pretty heady company for a boy who grew up in the Depression, hawking carrot seeds in Vancouver's east end. It is the remarkable story of Jim Pattison's climb from poverty to head of a billion-dollar conglomerate and chairman of a $1.5 billion world-class fair that I want to tell in these pages.

At one level this book is biographical, but it is not an authorized biography, nor has it been sanctioned or funded by Pattison. If it had to be placed in a category, the most accurate would probably be "investigative journalism."

Like most investigative journalists, I have a low tolerance for injustice and a suspicion that things are rarely as they seem, and almost never as they should be. I also believe that people who see injustice have a responsibility to use their skills and time to do something about it. When looking for the cause of injustice, I have learned to look to the most powerful figures in our society, who, as Lord Acton noted a century ago, tend to become corrupted in proportion to the power they wield.

This book, then, is about power, about one who wields it by one who watches it, and tries to challenge it by exposing some of the truth to the disinfecting light of day. While I readily admit my bias against abusers of power, the facts uncovered here are all documented, right down to the wind velocity and temperature on a given day.

The idea of writing this book first came to me in the spring of 1984 when it was revealed that Jim Pattison's magazine distribution company was reaping profits from the sale of pornography. As the father of a young child, what stuck in my mind, and in my throat, was the publicity given to one magazine article with the chilling title "How to Seduce Your Seven Year Old."

Like many, I believed that pornography profits flowed through the hands of sleazy downtown merchants and back to some organized crime headquarters. I was shocked to see a prominent businessman and self-proclaimed Christian with close ties to the provincial and federal governments pocketing profits from tales of torture and rape of women and children.

Once friends convinced me of the usefulness of a book such as this, and soon after I had begun preliminary research, my curiosity about Pattison quickly broadened out from concerns about the moral contradictions in peddling pornography. The questions piled up: Who is Pattison and how did he become so rich so quickly? Did he do it alone? Who are his backers? What do other millionaires think of him? And Expo—why did he really take that on and what is the fair's significance for B.C.? What are Pattison's real religious beliefs and how do they fit with his secular enterprises?

This book may be about Jimmy Pattison, but its goal is to take the mystery out of how he got to the top, and therefore to shed light on how anyone accumulates wealth and power in this society. This narrative, therefore, uses Pattison mainly as a framework to examine the forces that ultimately affect all of us.

It is no exaggeration to say that the intriguing story of Jim Pattison's rise to the top brings into focus almost the whole range of basic issues facing British Columbia and Canada in the 1980s.

R.K.
May 1986

1 AIR WARS

> *It is difficult to do business in B.C. without dealing with one of Jim Pattison's companies.*
> —Claude Richmond,
>   minister responsible for Expo 86

It was an unlikely place to find a chief executive officer on Hallowe'en, 1982.

The rain, whipped by mild, southerly winds, slapped against hangar windows. Outside, pilots pulled their peaked caps lower as they walked briskly to the Air BC hangar at the south end of Vancouver International Airport. Inside, mercury-vapour lamps pierced the darkness and reflected off the gleaming surface of the aging twin engine DC-3. Next to the airplane's starboard wing, mechanics erected a small, impromptu stage and steadied a wooden podium on it.

The mechanics, pilots, flight attendants and ground crew of Air BC, numbering about 100, were already in the Hallowe'en spirit. The one thing haunting all of them was the spectre of unemployment. Rumours had already flashed around the airline offices and flight decks that this last-minute meeting between staff and the owner was to be a showdown. Someone said that the cardboard box beside the podium contained layoff notices for all employees.

The murmuring stopped as the small man with the florid complexion mounted the stage. His high, often squeaky voice echoed eerily off the galvanized tin walls. His gloomy message was that the airline faced certain financial disaster. It had lost money since it was formed two years earlier by the merging of a gaggle of small, independent airlines into a single west coast carrier.

The jittery crews already knew the dimensions of the financial losses. The airline, in a fit of public disclosure rare among privately owned companies, told newspaper reporters that it had lost betwen $2 million and $3 million in 1982 against revenues of $11 million, a ratio which one Air BC executive labelled with grim understatement as "significant." The same executive also told the reporters scribbling in their notebooks that the losses could be turned into profits only if the company's unionized workers agreed to a no-strike guarantee, large pay cuts and other concessions.

Union leaders, contacted for their reaction, remained defiant and insisted that the membership would not vote to give back any wage increases or other benefits. But on this night the membership was silent. Most of them, if they had seen their boss at all, knew him as a jovial and friendly man who called even the lowest-paid staff by their first names. He radiated the kind of charm common to car salesmen, which he once was, though his act was much more polished now, after years of climbing to the top. Yet those who had crossed this man said doing business with him was like "getting into bed with a buzzsaw." The Air BC employees had crossed him. And tonight Jim Pattison showed up with his blades whirring. Few employers in the province would have said what he was about to say. He leaned forward on the podium, glaring out at 100 anxious faces. If they didn't go along with his demands right now, he said, he would shut down the entire airline the next day, November 1.

Whether Pattison could have done this without permission from the airline's licensing body, the Canadian Transport Commission, or in the face of an outcry from numerous coastal communities with no other links to the rest of the country, is a moot point. He did not close it down.

On the surface it would appear that Pattison got his way on everything. The unions agreed to a wage freeze, there were no strikes and Air BC did well enough in the following two years to purchase three $8 million Dash-7s.

Yet the unions insist they did not emerge the losers from the "eleventh-hour meeting," as the newspapers called it, even though Pattison told reporters he got everything he wanted.

No one kept official records of what happened at the meeting, and the conflicting stories may never be resolved. But the dispute, while not a landmark in the history of labour-management battles, is worthy of closer examination because of what it reveals about Pattison. There are clues to several well kept secrets: how he became so rich in only 25 years; how he deals with adversaries who insist on retaining some control; how he gambles with entire corporations employing hundreds of people in his quest to enlarge his profits. It is a rare occasion when Jim Pattison plays his hand under the glare of mercury-vapour lamps instead of in the hushed privacy of his spacious corporate headquarters on the sixteenth floor of the Guinness Tower in downtown Vancouver.

Jim Pattison assembled Air BC in much the same way he constructed the rest of his $1 billion-a-year conglomerate of corporations in transportation, food and beverage processing, communications, automobile sales, advertising, financial services and real estate. He purchased existing companies.

"Acquisitions," he once said, "are made in dark rooms and strange places...the most important thing is to keep your mouth shut." Most of his acquisitions were in the consumer field, an extension of his youth when he sold garden seeds and magazines, and later, used cars. Whether he was conscious of it or not, Pattison was jumping into a sector of the Canadian economy that had ballooned since the Second World War. Consumer goods and services supplanted steel and railways as major Canadian industries. The growth of consumer goods and services peaked in the late 1960s, just as Pattison went on a buying spree. In an eighteen-month period beginning in 1967 the 39-year-old Pattison bagged a company a month. In the following ten years he purchased over 50 companies. All this happened before Pattison turned his attention to the half dozen west coast airlines which flew single engined Cessnas and nothing larger than an eighteen-seater Twin Otter float plane. Together these airlines, mainly owned and controlled by former bush pilots, linked remote Pacific coast communities like Bella Bella, Bella Coola and Rivers Inlet with the main port cities of Vancouver, Victoria and Nanaimo.

Following his own advice, Pattison kept quiet about his intentions. He commenced secret negotiations, often using intermediaries, to make initial contacts and determine the financial strengths of each airline. Publicity, if any, was kept to a minimum and the owners seldom knew they were being approached by the same buyer.

In a series of carefully timed moves Pattison acquired 100 per cent control of each airline. Air West, West Coast Airlines, Gulf Air, Haida Airlines, Island Airlines, Pacific Coastal and Trans-Provincial all fell into the Pattison fold. Only with Tyee Air was there a hitch. The small airline provided float plane service between Vancouver and a stretch of the mainland to the northwest known as the Sunshine Coast. Tyee sued the Pattison Group for *not* buying it. What really happened is unclear—it seems that where Pattison is involved there are always conflicting stories, which is not surprising given his private and secret methods. Apparently the owner of Tyee was negotiating separately with Pattison and another potential buyer, one of the existing coastal airlines. Pattison outmanoeuvred them both, bought the competing airline and dropped plans to buy Tyee. The small airline launched an unsuccessful suit, claiming Pattison reneged on a takeover deal.

The rest of the takeovers went smoothly. In a matter of months Pattison had complete ownership of the world's largest fleet of float planes. They formed a vital link in the transportation network of B.C.'s number one industry, lumber. The big forest companies depended on the versatile small aircraft and experienced pilots to get their crews and executives in and out of the remote logging camps.

Only after Pattison purchased the last of the companies did he move to amalgamate them into one large airline, Air BC. Along with the record number of float planes, 45-year-old DC-3s, assorted aging aircraft and airport facilities, Pattison acquired about 500 employees. In their capacities as ground staff, cabin crews, pilots and mechanics, they belonged to the Teamsters Union, the Canadian Brotherhood of Railway, Transport and General Workers (CBRT & GW) or the International Association of Machinists (IAM). This added a new dimension to the Pattison Group of companies, which were non-union. Here was one occasion when Pattison, who often boasted that he "never interferes with the day to day operations of the companies I own," jumped headlong into a prolonged tussle with the Air BC unions.

After Pattison bought the airlines and began moulding them into Air BC, the unions struggled for what is known in labour parlance as "successor rights." Some workers, like those in Island Air and Gulf Air, were organized in pre-Pattison days by the CBRT. Others, like Air West employees, belonged to the Teamsters. Now that they were all one big happy family, which union was going to represent them?

The jostling for successor rights broke into a family feud and the Labour Relations Board stepped in to mediate. After many hearings the board copied the practice of the major airlines. It divided Air BC staff into three bargaining units: the pilots, the mechanics and all others, including ground staff and flight attendants. Ground staff, pilots and flight attendants all went with the CBRT, mechanics stayed with the IAM, and the Teamsters Union was voted out.

At first the new arrangement worked well for the crews, especially the pilots, some of whom got hefty pay raises when the existing CBRT agreement came into effect. As they calculated their new take-home pay, Pattison was busy trying to get permission from the Canadian Transport Commission to form Air BC and, in effect, be granted a monopoly over air service on the west coast.

It is not as contradictory as it may seem for Jim Pattison, whom many politicians hold up as an ideal "free enterpriser," to be messing around with monopolies. Pattison is no different from other tycoons. To achieve success at the highest echelons of the corporate world, free enterprise must often be systematically sacrificed. Success at the top depends on achieving monopolistic control.*

Pattison wasn't going as far as asking for government investment in Air BC—he wanted complete ownership—but he was not above asking his friends in the Social Credit cabinet to put in a good word for him at

---

*Free enterprise has never flourished in Canada, contrary to the popular myth repeated by right wing think tanks like the Vancouver-based Fraser Institute. Economists at the Institute always remember to wear their Adam Smith ties, but conveniently forget what the eighteenth century Scottish economist meant by "free enterprise." Smith's vision included "low and flexible prices, intense competition among many small firms resulting in efficient industries and ever-growing national incomes." In short, the buyers would name the price. In Canada, it is the producers—of cars, gasoline or grapefruits—who name the price. The Canadian economy has always been dominated by large firms (a tradition begun by the Hudson's Bay Company) and there has always been extensive government involvement to stabilize large companies at the expense of small entrepreneurs.

the CTC hearings.

Pattison's ties to the Social Credit government of Bill Bennett go well beyond the fact that he has voted Socred since the party, formed by the premier's father, W.A.C. Bennett, entered the electoral arena in 1952. Pattison's fleet of lawyers include high-profile Socred fundraisers. They are often found defending the government in court. When Pattison needed the government's help, he had only to ask. Pattison did not confine his socializing to the Socreds. Among the federal Liberal cabinet ministers he hosted on his $1 million luxury yacht were Marc Lalonde and Lloyd Axworthy—the latter just before deregulation of airfares. To accommodate Mr. Lalonde's tight schedule, Pattison aide Maureen Chant ordered a scheduled Air BC flight delayed so the float plane could land next to the yacht and fly the minister to his government jet at the airport. "Pattison has a lot more influence than is generally known," grumbled one Air BC dispatcher after juggling planes.

The Socreds told the CTC at the Air BC hearings that it strongly backed an Air BC monopoly. This departure from "free enterprise" philosophy can perhaps be explained by the government's reasoning that the risks of unbridled competition are too great in real life. "We wish to avoid the chaos of the early 1970s when a collapse in the forestry and mining sectors resulted in too many planes for business," warned a government brief. Unwilling to saddle B.C. with too many planes again, the CTC handed Air BC its licence. But the spectre of a collapse in the forestry and mining industries would come back to haunt the airline in the not too distant future.

Federal permission to amalgamate his airlines into one gave Pattison the green light to impose his brand of management on Air BC. One union official grudgingly noted, "He is an astute businessman and once he became owner, management improved. The small airlines [were run by] mostly older pilots [and they] were always in a hell of a mess."

Pattison's brand of housecleaning resulted in better

bookkeeping but more layoffs. At Air BC's Campbell River base, the operation centre was virtually abandoned, and only six of the original 75 pilots were kept on staff. The new airline's maintenance crew was cut to one-fifth its original size. A former employee remembers the drastic changes. "We [in Campbell River] became a backwater after being a viable operation. The staff walked off the job for two days to show how the base was being ignored."

Not only were the pilots and mechanics being fired but former executives too, like W.R. (Rusty) Harris and R.H. (Dick) Laidman. Said Laidman, "Pattison intends to operate a taxi service. He has no eye for growth to a regional carrier like PWA." Laidman was in a position to know. He was the former president and general manager of Pacific Western Airlines.

Pattison shrugged off the criticisms and kept paring staff and equipment. In all he fired one-fifth of the employees and sold all the large aircraft. He also scrapped plans to purchase more modern short-range aircraft like the 50-seat Dash-7, which the previous owners were sure would make money on the lucrative Vancouver to Victoria runs.

For a brief period in the summer of 1981 the concern over cutbacks was forgotten. An Air BC float plane crashed near the resource town of Ocean Falls halfway up the B.C. coast, and all six people aboard were killed. An inquiry later named pilot fatigue as a factor in the crash. The inquiry did not find that Air BC was any more accident prone than the previous airlines which had flown the route. If anything, the opposite was the case ("Scarewest" was the nickname given to Air BC's predecessor, Air West). But the accident raised the inevitable questions about Air BC's policy of demanding more work out of fewer staff.

Apart from this tragedy, the main concern of Air BC's owner was how to stop losing money. Although the privately owned airline was under no obligation to disclose its financial position, the business pages of the daily newspapers carried detailed reports of major losses. One story quoted aviation sources as saying that Pattison had spent $20 million to put Air BC together, and that about $17 million of that was borrowed from the Bank of B.C. at very high interest rates. This was at a time when interest on loans topped 20 per cent, a figure that would have been considered usury at other times but was standard in 1981. Pattison insisted that the debt had to be repaid out of the airline's revenue, and not from profits of any of his other ventures—a result of his rule that "every division must pay its own way regardless of size" (at the time, Air BC represented only 3 per cent of all Pattison holdings). One insider blamed this arrangement, and not high interest rates, for the cuts in staff and service. James Wilson, who represented one of the airlines opposed to the Air BC monopoly, said Pattison "paid too much and turned a profitable airline into a loser to pay off the debts."

Whatever the causes of Air BC's woes, the employees who survived the firings felt new effects beginning in 1982. They were warned to expect no wage increases, and perhaps even cuts in pay. Both the IAM and the CBRT, which had negotiated an increase of 14.7 per cent for the current year, said their members would refuse any rollbacks.

Pattison saw red. Ignoring the usual channels of communication between management and union, he organized a series of "educational" meetings with selected, small groups of Air BC staff. Union leaders charged that Pattison was trying the old "divide and conquer" tactic, to which he replied that he was only offering the facts about the airline's financial state.

Pattison's "students" were attending so many classes in airline economics that union officials complained that they couldn't arrange a meeting with their own membership. The IAM's 35 mechanics and the CBRT's 200 members were not prepared for the intense lessons Pattison gave. They seemed as much like a course in neo-conservative economics as a form of low-grade torture. He used the latest in slide show technology and conducted the lengthy classes with his well-known hyperactive intensity. At the end of each course the message was the same: the company would lose big dollars unless current wages were dropped. Even seasoned labour leaders who were tutored individually by professor Pattison were bewildered by the whirlwind of slides and graphs. They were accustomed to meeting owners at Christmas parties and across bargaining tables. "This is not a recognized tactic," one shop steward observed.

Al Craig, an area representative for the CBRT who attended one of these sessions, recalls the antagonistic mood. "They tried to tell us that if we hold the line now the future is going to be rosy. He [Pattison] didn't give us any details...his approach was a salesman's approach predicting doom and gloom. And, yeah, he did get pretty snarky in respect to either 'take it or we're going down, I'm gonna close it up,' and we suspected that was...a bluff...because we knew he had a hell of an investment there and if he closed it down the only thing he'd have for sale is a hell of a lot of Twin Otters which had no market."

Marketing troubles hadn't stopped Pattison from closing down eight other companies in the past year, and knowledge of this made Craig a little nervous as he recommended the membership not accept any rollbacks. He said afterward that he had no choice, because the national union wanted no precedents in Canada for the pattern of rollbacks emerging in the U.S.

Knowing this, Pattison dispatched Air BC general manager Iain Harris to the CBRT's national office in Ottawa to ask the national president, Jim Hunter, to reverse his stand and let the Vancouver local vote for a rollback. Hunter was not ready to compromise, and calmly told Harris to go to hell.

Air BC's problems received scant attention in the B.C. press. Throughout January 1982 news of the airline's union-management dispute was relegated to the back pages, while more brutal fare dominated the front. In the middle of the month, multiple-murderer Clifford

Olson was sentenced to life, and during the sentencing the judge revealed that B.C. Attorney General Allan Williams had authorized the RCMP to pay Olson's family $100,000—$10,000 for the body of each mutilated child that Olson led the police to. For several days this bizarre twist to plea-bargaining shouldered aside the usual news and hot-line debates about 17 per cent interest rates and 12.5 per cent inflation, the highest in 33 years. And when newspaper editorials weren't trumpeting opinions on these issues they fell back on the favourite of the day, the constitutional talks. For a brief moment B.C.ers turned their attention eastward across the Rockies and prairies to witness the queen handing over the rubber stamp with which the British Parliament had approved changes to the Canadian constitution since this colony was founded. Hardly anyone noticed what happened down at Air BC.

Pressure mounted on Weldon Walburg. As Air BC president he answered directly to Pattison, and the question to him was clear: When will you get me the concessions? Walburg knew that Pattison did not tolerate poor performance. The unwritten rule around his companies was "one major mistake and you're out." Pattison's reputation as a manager without mercy could be traced all the way back to the 1950s when he ran the Bow Mac car dealership in Vancouver. Each month he fired the salesman with the worst sales record. "The best salesman hasn't been hired yet," was his cryptic justification.

So when members of Local 235 of the CBRT voted to reject the wage rollbacks, Walburg knew what to do. He "voluntarily resigned"—although company insiders later said he was "sacrificed" by Pattison. Pattison immediately replaced him with Iain Harris, whom some wag on the Air BC staff quickly nicknamed "hard-knuckle Harris."

As Pattison retreated to his Guinness Tower lair, he paused long enough to tell reporters that he would come up with alternatives "that may amount to the same thing" as closing the airline.

Barely another month passed before the alternatives were imposed. Union leaders had just taken another hard line, this time refusing to defer a wage increase due in April 1982. Two days later, eighteen of the company's 35 mechanics were fired. The IAM's Ralph Steeves questioned how safe the aircraft would be. "There will be only ten mechanics in Vancouver to maintain the airline's fleet," he warned. Undeterred, Pattison fired ten pilots the next day. Of the 585 people on the payroll when Air BC was formed, only 185 remained. The fleet of 130 planes had been slashed to 70.

Not only was Air BC taking drastic internal measures to save money, but it employed some unheard of tactics to win new customers. On April 1 the airline offered 99-cent flights to Victoria from Vancouver on a first come, first served basis. In spite of the date, the airline said the offer was genuine. Other airlines failed to see the humour and immediately notified the Canadian Transport Commission. CTC officers, clearly flummoxed by Air BC's brash tactics, took eight months to agree on a suitable penalty for violating price regulations. They ordered the airline to suspend its flights between Vancouver and Victoria for one day, Tuesday, December 21. The unrepentant Pattison immediately asked that the penalty date be changed to Saturday, December 18, so Air BC would only have to cancel four flights instead of seven.

The same soaring interest rates and record unemployment that hurt most people in B.C. in 1982 were blamed by Pattison for his airline's mounting losses. By October the number of planes in service shrank to 35, and fifteen of those were "parked," or temporarily taken out of service. Pattison's original deal to create Air BC, which he now acknowledged cost $29 million, was named as a major cause of the airline's troubles, along with a slump in forestry and mining.

It was against this background that Pattison

convened the Hallowe'en meeting of Air BC staff at the company hangar and delivered them the ultimatum: "Concede now, or we shut it down."

Apparently he overlooked an important third party—residents of the isolated communities served by the airline. He didn't mention publicly the thousands of people along the coast who would be effectively cut off from the rest of the country if he carried out his threat.

Reaction from the communities was mixed. Many were upset at the prospect of losing their mail service until a replacement airline could be found. Others shrugged off the threat. "A lot of people think we're just a tax write-off for Pattison," said Bella Bella teacher John Buston. Over in Bella Coola, probation officer Ann Petersen complained about the airline's bad reputation. "Air BC planes are often empty and appear in poor repair with drips from the ceiling and a mouldy smell."

CTC authorities could smell more than mould and stepped in quickly to say that no airline can arbitrarily drop service without public hearings and permission from the CTC. Iain Harris, Air B.C.'s chastised president, was forced to backtrack for his boss. "We are too responsible to leave the people entirely cut off," said the red-faced executive. "We will continue until others are appointed by the Ministry."

No appointments were necessary. Before there was any shutdown, the unions and management announced a tentative agreement—five years of labour peace. A gleeful Pattison later said, "that one particular night we'd have shut it down. The employees saved Air BC. I didn't. I'd had enough. We had a meeting at the hangar and I went out to shut it down. The employees saved the company...they gave the company the things that it had to have."

Publicly the union said only that "there is going to be labour peace at Air BC." Privately it had agreed not to reveal the actual results of the settlement "so that we wouldn't make Pattison look as if he lost face."

Yet it is hard to determine from the actual signed

contract how he lost face. He didn't get the wage rollback of 10 per cent he sought, but the union agreed to a wage freeze in the first year of a three-year agreement—and with inflation running at 10 per cent it amounted to the same thing. The agreement offered only a slim chance of cost of living increases in the other two years. There was also a five-year no-strike clause. The union pooh-poohed this, saying a five-year clause has no power in a three-year agreement, but it must be noted that Air BC has been strike free for the life of the agreement. Union leaders were exhausted by the unusual round of bargaining. A bewildered Al Craig said, "They [Pattison and Air BC management] pleaded a lack of expertise in negotiations, but if they lacked any I don't know what it was."

It was true that Pattison had little expertise negotiating with unions. He did his best to keep his enterprises union-free. The expertise Pattison brought to the bargaining table was his finely honed practice of winning, no matter what the cost to his opponents. Pattison had fought and won battles with employees before the Air BC showdown, and he would win many after. Each time, the end justified the means—coercion, threats, intimidation, deception. Such are the methods of success.

By adopting these methods, Pattison abandoned all traces of the co-operative tradition which flourished in the community where he was born—rural Saskatchewan at the height of the booming twenties.

2 LUSELAND

He was called a hero.

Born before the new century, and a veteran of many World War I aerial dogfights, Chandos W. (Pat) Pattison was widely admired by the residents of the tiny farming community of Luseland, Saskatchewan. He was an ace. Like thousands of other prairie boys, he sailed for Europe after World War I began. Unlike many of them, he survived the world's largest and most brutal conflict.

He had smelled the poison gas and seen its victims; he had cowered at the staccato bursts of machine guns; he had flown the fragile biplanes. These three weapons had never before been used in all-out war, and they contributed to the staggering carnage: 39 million casualties, including thirteen million killed.

In 1918, when Pat returned to his home province and settled in Luseland, about 300 kilometres west of Saskatoon and an hour's drive by Model-T from the Alberta border, he was regarded as a living link to the unprecedented upheaval on the battlefields of Europe.

His friends don't remember him talking about the war very much. But they remember his love of flying. One day Pat approached his neighbour William McConica, who was then only fifteen but who eventually became Pat's boss, and asked him if he would like to go for a flight. McConica jumped at the chance and raced to the biplane, the kind used by barnstorming pilots in air shows. After McConica climbed into the back seat, Pat lowered himself into the open cockpit, pulled on his leather helmet, and revved the noisy engine. They slowly bumped down the grass airstrip. In another moment they were several thousand feet above the gently rolling fields of barley, flax and wheat. McConica marvelled at the sight. He had never before seen the prairies from the sky. He could pick out the grain elevators, the tallest buildings in town, which looked like matchboxes standing on end. For the first time he saw the carefully surveyed sections of farmland, the dusty dirt roads marking off each square 640-acre parcel. Suddenly the ground was his sky upside down so that the only thing holding them in the cockpit was their seatbelts. Next Pat stalled the plane and let it drop in a "falling leaf" manoeuvre. He took control only a few hundred feet above the ground and glided to a landing.

McConica later wrote in the town's official history that he was "thrilled but not scared" by the acrobatics. Neighbours remember a different version. "The flight scared the hell out of him," said one, "and he was so dizzy when they landed that he fell several times."

Pat Pattison may have been more comfortable than others hanging upside down in a cockpit at 3,000 feet, but like most people in the booming post-war years he was looking for ways to get rich.

For many, prosperity meant farming. At $10 for a 160-acre quarter section, it was cheap to start. The fertile Saskatchewan clayloam yielded number one wheat and oats in abundance. One farmer recorded harvesting one ton of oats and one and a half tons of wheat per acre. He concluded that Saskatchewan in the 1920s offered "great opportunities for any man of moderate means to get a start in the world."

Others, like William McConica's younger brother Tom, opted for higher education, a far less common route. (He obtained his doctorate from the Massachusetts Institute of Technology and eventually found gainful employment on the Manhattan project building the world's first three atom bombs.)

Such a small town could offer only limited job opportunities. Luseland was, after all, only a small supply and service centre for busy farmers. (The town, which by the mid-1920s had a population of about 400, owed its unusual name to a Minnesota businessman, J.F. Luse. He liked the "business of colonization" so much that in the first decade of the century he bought millions of acres of land in Canada, the USA, Mexico and South America. Later he sold off farm-sized parcels for handsome profits.) Pat Pattison, who knew something about machines and liked selling, was hired on as a salesman for the local John Deere outfit. When the distributorship was later bought by the McConica brothers, they regarded Pattison's sales record so highly that they named the business McConica Brothers and Pattison, even though Pat remained only an employee and not a partner.

Crops flourished. Farmers raked in the cash. They were encouraged by the federal government to keep on growing the same crops, with promises that the export market would be there. With some of their surplus money, farmers purchased new machinery.

Soon Pat's dealership was doing so well that it expanded into the glamorous automobile trade. In 1925 Pat Pattison became Luseland's first car dealer selling the new line of General Motors cars. Until then the only car available locally was the Ford "Tin Lizzie." Now the better-off prairie families could try out the comfort of a Pontiac or the luxury of a Buick. Between closing deals, Pattison acted as the town's postmaster, working out of a cramped post office at one end of the dealership's counter. But Pat's boundless energy was not channelled into work alone. According to townspeople, Pat was a man who "worked hard and played hard," a euphemism for a workaholic who drinks too much on weekends.

"Oh, I heard stories about his drinking but I don't want to repeat them," teases Margaree (Mac) Finlay, a retired school marm and friend of the Pattison's. Art Meier, a retired college administrator who lives in the Pattison's old house in Luseland, is more forthcoming about the "stories." "Pat got drunk every Saturday night with Walter Gerard, the barber, and everytime they got drunk Walter beat him up."

Pat also "liked the girls." While not exactly the image of the dashing war ace—he was short, heavy set, and balding—he was popular at the local dances, which he never missed. It was at one of these dances in 1926 that he met Julia Allen, a small, slender, attractive teacher who had moved to Luseland six years earlier. They were married later that year. In 1928 she gave birth to their first and only child, James Allen Pattison.

With marriage and a child, Pat settled down a little. He turned his energy to establishing the town's first Elks lodge and coaching the baseball team. He rented a large house owned by his bosses, William and John McConica, where he and Julia established a reputation as friendly, hospitable hosts. Julia still taught school, and sometimes her colleague Mac Finlay, or William McConica, babysat young Jimmy.

The 1920s are remembered as the golden years around Luseland. The grain elevators, which stand like sentinels above every flat prairie town, bulged with some of the world's finest quality wheat. The earth was bountiful everywhere. The rich land beside the ditches was studded with sweet clover, brown-eyed susans and the large dandelion-like goat's beard. Out in the fields, beyond the dusty dirt roads of Luseland, waved acre after acre of lush green wheat, mustard-coloured rapeseed, flax, oats and barley. Every fall the harvest was punctuated by the wild honking of snow geese flying in formation to a warmer climate. The vast flocks of ducks and geese that stopped to feed in the area gave Luseland a reputation as an excellent hunting ground for water fowl.

Farmers used revolutionary new implements to break virgin grassland. They traded in their cars for newer, larger models. McConica Brothers and Pattison prospered.

Yet, unknown to the farmers, they were rapidly depleting the very source of their income. The pressure to grow single crops for export, and the lack of knowledge about crop rotation, steadily stripped the soil of its crucial organic components. (The organic content, or humus, had very slowly built up over the 12,000 years since the last glaciers scraped the prairies to the subsoil. When the first homesteaders' ploughs turned the grassland in 1904, the rich soil contained about 8 per cent humus. By the late 1920s there was barely half that amount. The soil was less fertile and had less capacity to hold moisture. More rain was needed to raise the same quantities of crops.)

By 1929 the destructive effects of three decades of intense cultivation coincided with the driest years since the turn of the century. In Luseland and almost every other part of the prairies that spring, almost no crops took hold. Fierce, hot winds whipped the dry soil and seeds into clouds of blinding dust. Some days they blacked out the sun completely. When the dust settled again it was driven by the endless winds into desert-like dunes. Those crops that managed to take root were baked dry before mid-summer. (In contrast, there was less rain in the Luseland area in the 1960s than in the 1930s, but the crops fared much better thanks to irrigation, crop rotation and fertilization.)

Compounding the problems of the drought were disturbing trends in the rest of Canada and the U.S. In 1929 the previous year's wheat crop still hadn't been sold. Wheat was overproduced all over the world that year. Inventories of other commodities bulged dangerously. Many company stocks were grossly overvalued.

In October 1929, the stock prices on the New York Stock Exchange fell drastically. The economic system was in chaos. The Americans threw up high tariffs to protect domestic industries from cheap imports; Canada's chief export market collapsed. Without the demand, wheat prices fell from $1.60 a bushel in 1929 to 38 cents by 1931.

The combination of crop failures and market crashes was felt first on the prairies but rippled quickly into Canada's industrial heartland in Ontario. Factories closed and thousands were thrown out of work. Banks called in loans. Hundreds of thousands were forced onto relief. Desperate men rode the rails in fruitless attempts to find work.

The Great Depression had begun. Contrary to modern accounts it did not begin with a crash, except in high financial circles. In Luseland, as in most of rural North America, it began with a slow and steady decline in the standard of living. As wheat prices dropped, so did incomes. As crops became more scarce because of the drought, prices rose. For a while, those who saved some money during the good years lived off savings, but eventually even savings ran out.

Yet outwardly, people in and around Luseland behaved as if nothing serious was happening. The heavyweight boxing match went ahead at the community centre. Children and adults watched the Elks swimming pool under construction and wondered if the new steam engine would ever be able to heat the water. Edith McConica played the piano accompaniment at the silent movies, which included the very first Mickey Mouse cartoon. The town's nursery owner, Mr. Dowling, buried a time capsule containing information about the inhabitants beneath the newly constructed war monument.

People talked about the miserable state of the crops and they talked about the weather, but they believed these were only temporary problems. The McConica brothers were the first to shatter the illusion. They left the country. Saying, "you can't make money where there isn't any money," they moved with their families in late 1929 to California and set up a successful General Motors dealership in Ventura.

The McConicas put their Luseland dealership and houses up for sale but there were no buyers. The Pattison's continued renting their house, and Pat stayed on for another five years trying to sell machinery and cars to an increasingly poorer population. Friends recall that Pat turned again to alcohol—"they were hard times and people dealt with them in different ways," explained Art Meier.

Eventually, in 1934, before Jimmy entered school, the Pattison family packed their Chevrolet and fled Saskatchewan for the nearest large city outside the prairies, Vancouver. Anything to get away from the dustbowl.

What they found beyond the Rockies in Terminal City (Vancouver's ironic nickname, since so many saw in the city a new beginning) was hardly promising. More than 100,000 were unemployed in the province, most of them in the Lower Mainland. Predictably, the miserable conditions led to unrest and even to rebellions. Groups of unemployed, furious at the lack of jobs or welfare, occupied several department stores and the city museum. The Liberal premier, T.D. Pattulo, who, like Vancouver Mayor Gerry McGeer, feared that a socialist revolution was brewing, retreated behind his claim that the unemployed were the responsibility of the federal government. The two men were immensely relieved when they learned that the core of the unemployed had decided to take their grievances directly to Ottawa.

Such was the political and economic situation during the Pattison's first year in Vancouver. Pat and Julia Pattison decided they could do as well on the road. Pat, described as an "idea man and a risk taker" by Luseland's Art Meier, criss-crossed the province on rutted mountainous dirt roads looking for work in town after town. Jimmy often accompanied his father on odd jobs, and some of them were very odd, such as de-mothing pianos for $2 a piece. In the evenings, Julia taught her son the same public school curriculum used by families in remote parts of the province.

The itinerant life has been widely romanticized, but the reality is usually far from glamorous, especially for a family on the road. In 1936 the Pattisons drove their aging Chevrolet back to Vancouver. The city hadn't changed much. The 27.5 per cent of the population who were unemployed were still demonstrating in the streets. In spite of the competition for jobs, Pat found work. He used his credentials as a General Motors dealer in Saskatchewan to land a job selling used Packards at A.B. Balderston's, in the 1200-block of West Georgia (where the B.C. Resources Investment Corporation offices now stand). The family settled into a modest bungalow in the working class district of east Vancouver, on East 49th between Fraser and Main.

Pat found something else, too—religion. He reacted to troubled times by turning to Jesus. Through the medium of the Pentecostal Church, Pat was "born again." Weekday evenings he could be found in front of the Pentecostal Mission at 40 East Hastings inviting passers-by, most of them broke, to come in for a sandwich and a prayer. Sometimes Jimmy, who showed an early talent for music, played the trumpet on the street beside his father. Jimmy credited the church with getting his father off the bottle.

The street riots that marked the Pattisons' arrival in Vancouver in 1935 erupted again in 1938. This time the cause was the provincial government's decision to cut off assistance to unemployed "prairie migrants." The move did little to win popular support, because most people in Vancouver were immigrants, many from the prairies. Laws were hastily passed by the City of Vancouver imposing stiffer penalties for begging in the streets.

Simmering anger broke into direct action as crowds of men stormed the Georgia Hotel, the Post Office and the Art Gallery. Some at the hotel and the gallery agreed to leave soon after they were offered relief vouchers.

But about twenty men in the Post Office refused to budge.

Eventually mounted police swung batons and hurled tear gas at the crowd of supporters surrounding the building. They forcibly removed all the occupiers. Thirty-nine people were injured, including five police, and 22 were arrested. The number of occupiers was not large, but the action won wide sympathy because of the government's harsh treatment of the unemployed.

Anti-government sentiment translated into a 1941 election victory for the CCF (forerunner of the NDP). However, the CCF did not form a new government. Liberals and Conservatives agreed to bury their differences and form a coalition government. The CCF was elbowed into the opposition benches.

While politicians in Victoria were getting in and out of bed with each other, Jimmy Pattison was preoccupied with school and a succession of part-time jobs. He peddled carrot and pea seeds door to door. He flogged the *Saturday Evening Post* and *Ladies' Home Journal*. He took up an after-school and weekend job as a page boy at the Georgia Hotel. By 1942, when he turned fourteen and had graduated from General Brock elementary to John Oliver high, he was taking the streetcar downtown every day after school to the hotel, where he worked from 4:30 to 8:30. He managed to find enough time during his shift to wolf down a supper packed for him by his mother.

In his scant free hours, Jimmy honed his musical skills. He played the trumpet in the Pentecostal Church orchestra, the Vancouver Junior Symphony and the famous Kitsilano Boys Band. In the Kits band he tuned up beside Ray Smith, who much later cast his trumpet aside and became the president of B.C.'s lumber giant, MacMillan Bloedel.

In 1945, Pattison left the hotel to work for the *Province* newspaper as a swamper. Hurtling 50-pound bundles of newspapers off the rear end of a truck soon gave way to a better job with the city's other daily newspaper, the *News Herald*. Now Pattison was driving the delivery truck.

By this time he had enrolled at the University of British Columbia in arts and commerce. During the long summer breaks he worked for the CPR, making salads and crushing ice in the dining cars. One job led to another. After working on the trains, Pattison got a job washing cars and in 1948, at the age of nineteen, he landed his first job selling used cars. It is said that he would drive a used car to class in the morning, sell it that day to a student, take the bus home and repeat the process the next day.

The post-war years were very prosperous, not only for used car salesmen but for most Canadian and U.S. industries as they peddled their wares in the new, accessible markets of western Europe. But not all companies fared well. One that experienced deteriorating sales was the Consolidated Motor Company—the Packard people. Pat Pattison, who was by now a sales manager at his Packard dealership, was experiencing poor physical health, aggravated by the pressures of a declining business. The auto business had broken him financially in Saskatchewan and now physically in B.C. He took Jimmy aside one day and advised him to get out of the car business and into something more stable, like advertising. He steered his son to a widely respected firm that leased advertising signs, Neon Products Ltd. Pat liked the fact that Neon didn't sell signs but leased them for five-year periods and dealt only with corporations.

Jimmy agreed to give them a try. At the age of 21, he applied for a job at Neon. They read his application, looked him over and turned him down with a curt, "you're too young and you're too short." It was back to selling used cars.

In the following year, 1950, he met and fell in love with another Saskatchewan native, Mary Hudson of Moose Jaw. They were married in 1951.

The pressure to settle down and the lure of money to be made selling cars led Jimmy to quit university nine credits short of his degree. He applied for a job at a large General Motors dealership on West Broadway in

Vancouver, Bowell-McLean Motors. His job at "Bow Mac" was to sell the whole line of cars, from the cheaper Chevrolets and Pontiacs, the mid-range Buicks and Oldsmobiles up to the prestigious Cadillacs—all products of the world's second-largest corporation that builds one-quarter of all the cars in the world. So impressive was Pattison's sales record that by 1955, the same year his father retired, he had become sales manager at Bow Mac.

He established a reputation as a risk-taker. A former lawyer for Bow Mac, Bryan Williams, recalls that when Jimmy took over, the dealership was faced with "a flood of liens." In other words, customers traded in old cars for new ones, but lied about the amount of money owing on the old car. The lawyer pressed Pattison to check more carefully with the Registry of Motor Vehicles before closing the deal. But Pattison, who took one look at his customers and decided on the spot whether they were honest, did not always check out the car. Besides, most sales were made on Saturdays or weekday evenings, and Pattison wasn't going to let his drive to build the city's number one dealership be jeopardized by losing a sale because the customer had twelve extra hours to think it over.

"I'll stick to selling cars, you stick to practising law, and we'll both make money," snapped Pattison.

As sales manager, Pattison was also responsible for organizing meetings of the sales staff. One morning he called the meeting for 8 a.m. which was an unheard of hour in the car business, where salesmen have a reputation of working late and then hitting the town.

At the first meeting only a handful showed up on time. Pattison locked the door. As each late-comer knocked, he opened the door a crack, told them the meeting began at eight sharp and slammed the door. By the third meeting, no one was late.

Late or not, the salesman with the lowest sales each month got worse than a lecture on punctuality. He got his walking papers. Pattison's philosophy was as simple as it was brutal. Deal first with the worst performers.

Clean out the bottom. Make room for someone new. "The best salesman hasn't been hired yet," he would say. Even if the new person did perform worse, Pattison felt the change was worth it, "to give someone else the opportunity."

Pattison rapidly became a dominant and widely admired salesman in Vancouver's cut-throat auto sales field. He even looked the part. A typical day would find the diminutive Pattison striding into the dealership wearing a black, blue and white striped jacket over a black and blue checkered shirt, accented by a blue and white polka-dot tie.

Much more conventional than his attire was his idea of a family life. By 1956, when the second of Jimmy's and Mary's three children was born, the family roles were firmly set. Mary stayed at home with the children, cooked meals and kept house. Jimmy was the breadwinner, period. His idea of "helping out" was going out on his own to a diner, leaving Mary to feed the children. By 1950s' standards, the marriage would have been called a success.

In Victoria the marriage of convenience between the Conservatives and Liberals was in the process of fizzling. The former rival parties fell to bickering over such issues as assignment of cabinet portfolios and spending priorities.

One of the most disgruntled members of the coalition was a Kelowna hardware millionaire who had taken a couple of unsuccessful runs at the provincial Tory leadership in the 1940s, William Andrew Cecil Bennett. Relegated to the backbenches, he gambled his political career at the height of the inter-party squabbling. He abandoned both the coalition and the Tories, and ran for the leadership of the Social Credit party, an offshoot of the Alberta-born, fundamentalist, "funny money" outfit.

After a few ups and downs his opportunism paid off and, in 1952, W.A.C. Bennett became leader of the Socreds and premier of British Columbia.

With his raspy voice, jerky delivery and endless optimism, the beefy, grinning Bennett presided over an economy giddy with what one economist called "hyperactive growth." It was the heyday of the post-war boom and the private sector was taking its rightful place in the order of things. The day the Socreds took power, bank clearings in Vancouver hit a record high. Alcan's $120 million project in Kitimat neared completion while Shell announced a $30 million refinery for Burnaby, then the fastest growing suburb in Canada. Oil for the refinery would be pumped through a new trans-mountain pipeline from Edmonton, and on the drawing boards was another pipeline to bring Alberta gas to Vancouver and U.S. cities in the Pacific northwest.

Nowhere was growth more exuberant than in forestry, the province's largest industry. Through amalgamations, the once diversified sawmills and logging operations passed into the hands of a few large corporations. The process was crowned in 1951 by the merger of two giants, the H.R. MacMillan Export Company and Bloedel and Stewart.

The feverish pace of expansion required enormous sums of money and most of the investment came from the United States. The majority of the province's foreign ownership had passed from British to American hands. By the mid-fifties, over one-half of all money invested in sawmills, pulp mills and forestry operations of all kinds was American.

A newspaper editorial noted that "no other incoming government ever had it so good." But to stay in power in the long term, the Socreds would need a well-financed party machine. They needed more than dimes and nickels dropped into hats at local meetings. They needed large donations, which only corporations could afford. The party turned to the big company men, and few of them refused. They knew that "Wacky" Bennett's party was to be the new dispenser of large favours.

In public, Social Credit was the populist party, the party of the small, devout businessman who pulls himself up by his bootstraps. Those who succeeded were held in high esteem. To the Socreds, no one could be more virtuously employed than in getting more money.

This philosophy appealed to the energetic, 24-year-old Jimmy Pattison. In 1952 he voted Social Credit and he's voted for no one else since.

3 BIG SIGNS, BIG DEALS

The wheel turns and everybody pays for what they do in life. But so far not Jimmy.
—a disgruntled critic

He called it the tallest free-standing sign in the world. Jim Pattison, a 30-year-old supersalesman and now, in the summer of 1959, general manager of Bowell-McLean Motors on West Broadway, told awed reporters that the dealership's new front lot sign would put Vancouver on the map. Pattison handed out press releases with all the usual statistics and comparisons: it took six months to construct; each of the "BOW MAC" letters was eighteen feet high, and the entire sign was over ten storeys tall; inside the sign's shaft were two elevators used for changing the lightbulbs; it was built for the unprecedented price of $120,000 by Neon Products Ltd.

Pattison went all out to publicize the unveiling. He had the dealership's lot painted in large black and red checkerboard squares and hired members of the B.C. Lions football team and cheerleaders to act as "pieces" for a game of human checkers. Pattison's lot was packed with spectators. They spilled out on the sidewalk and into the street. In Pattison's eyes, they were all customers. Bow Mac was by this time the country's second-largest volume auto dealer, and for years Pattison had cast a jealous eye along Broadway where, just a few blocks away, Dueck Chevrolet was situated. They were "number one." "We tried to outdo 'em, of course... that's one reason we built the sign," chortled Pattison later.

Outdo 'em he did. The month he put up the sign, Bow Mac sold 1,046 cars, a record high for any dealer in Canada. The sign was more than paid for before the month was out. And Pattison, whose philosophy of selling cars closely matched that of GM's chairman, Thomas A. Murphy ("GM is in the business of making money...not cars"), was very happy.

The following year, 1960, brought the birth of Cindy, the third of the Pattisons' children. The family she joined was conventional, middle class and conservative. Pattison's attitude toward family life was very traditional, though it included at least one unusual quirk. He vowed that no matter how rich he became, he would never hire his own children. That was the point of principle he formed during his ten years at Bow Mac. Because Bow Mac was the only Cadillac dealer in town, Pattison saw many children of the rich driving their parents' Caddies around. "My job was to serve those people, and the more I saw of them the less I was impressed..." He complained about children who got jobs not because they were competent but because of "an accident of birth" and decided then that when his children were older he would tell them they would have to fend for themselves. That way, he reasoned, they would learn the virtues of hard work, humility and the value of a dollar.

Pattison allows that there are exceptions to the rule against joining the family business. The Bentalls of Vancouver are one—"the boys are being a much greater success than their father"—and Henry Ford II is another. But by and large Jim Pattison is unimpressed with inherited wealth. (Regarding the disposition of his own wealth, Pattison told *Canadian Business* magazine that his board of directors would take over and appoint an able replacement. He hinted that some of his personal wealth might be left to Glad Tidings Church.)

Ten years in the car business had taught Pattison something else about wealth. Although he had catapulted Bow Mac to the top-selling dealership in the country, the people who benefited in terms of hard cash were the owners. Jim Pattison was ready to strike out on his own.

Over the following year, 1961, he hunted for an opportunity to open his own business. He spotted a small, struggling General Motors dealership and gas bar at Cambie and 18th that was up for sale, and approached his Royal Bank manager for help. The bank demanded that Pattison sign over his house (worth $7,000), the cash surrender value of his life insurance policy ($15,000), and all the shares in the new business in return for a $40,000 loan needed to buy the dealership.

Pattison eagerly accepted the conditions and purchased the Pontiac-Buick dealership with its two-car showroom and three-pump gas bar. Jim Pattison Ltd. got off to a shaky start. It sold only 25 cars the first month, losing $13,900. The next month was slightly better: 37 cars sold, but still the balance sheet was in the red by $12,000. The friendly bank manager began hinting that Pattison would not last long at this rate and should consider cutting his—and the bank's—losses. Pattison convinced the bank to hold off, and the next month sales volume increased and the company showed a modest profit of $2,000. From there he sold enough cars to pay off the $40,000 loan in just over a year. The shares were signed over to Pattison, and he experienced the first heady delights of private enterprise. He was on his own.

His timing for opening the new dealership could not have been better, coming as it did just as the economy emerged from the first post-World War II economic slump. In the early 1950s Canadians and Americans bought cars in unprecedented numbers, so encouraged were they by rising wages and government promises of an even brighter future. Suddenly in 1956 the rhetoric changed. Investment in resource extraction—the primary engine of the B.C. economy—slowed due to a decline in world markets. Investment in forestry, mining, steel and other major industries dropped from the white-hot levels of the early fifties and by 1959 stood at only three-quarters of the investment level of 1956. Jobs in the private sector declined too, depriving government of taxable income and adding to welfare and unemployment costs.

Between 1957 and 1959, W.A.C. Bennett reacted in an unexpected way: he fired thousands of public servants, and simultaneously cut spending on a wide range of social service programs like education, welfare and mental health. His actions were in direct opposition to a bit of folksy wisdom he had shared with the voters before he was elected. Managing a provincial economy, he said, was a little like driving a car over hilly terrain. "Going downhill, you don't need much gas. On the level, you need a bit more. Going uphill, you need still more, and, if the hill's very steep, you have to press down hard." (Bennett did not talk over the people's heads.)

As he took his foot off the accelerator and even applied the brakes, he was assailed by cries of outrage, even from his supporters. One magistrate charged that Bennett's cuts amounted to "something approaching criminal mismanagement." The premier's next move was to dazzle unhappy B.C.ers with an expensive sideshow: a proposed $2 billion development in northern B.C., complete with new towns, sawmills, power dams and even a 400-mile high-speed mono-railway. This was to be Bennett's number one fall-back strategy—when problems arise, throw asphalt at them.

Investment and jobs were again on the increase as Pattison dedicated himself to the new business. His 1962 goal was to put $25,000 in his own pocket—a tidy sum in those days when the annual average gross pay for a B.C. worker was $2,280. He reached his goal and doubled it for 1963. When he reached $50,000 in 1963, he set $100,000 as his target for the following year.

At the same time as Pattison prospered, his father's health deteriorated rapidly. The years of hard living had taken their toll on Pat Pattison. Ill health forced him to retire as the sales manager of Balderston's Packard dealership in 1955, and then, in 1963, the heart of the former World War I fighter pilot failed him, leaving Julia a widow.

Aside from this family loss, Jim Pattison's fortunes soared. As the provincial economy again warmed up in the early to mid-1960s, so did his sales. Each year's doubling of income was accomplished with the hard-nosed, kill-thy-neighbour tactics that marked Pattison's years at Bow Mac. He brought to his own business the hallmarks of his success over the years: 8 a.m. meetings, aggressive advertising, and of course firing the salesman with the worst performance each month.

Yet almost everyone who then dealt with Pattison remembers him as a charming, pleasant man. Customers and others remarked that Pattison's greatest quality was his "exceptional talent in relating to people." The irony of that comment was not lost on some of the many sales people he unceremoniously dumped. Said one, "I wanted to dislike him. To my dismay I still found myself attracted to his [manner of] speech...he is a very likeable person."

He was also a very single-minded person. "When you start from scratch, as I did, you can't afford distractions," he said. "I made a commitment when I started out in 1961 that absolutely no outside activities would distract me from making my business survive and grow."

By 1963 the small dealership on Cambie could no longer contain the rate of growth imposed by Pattison, so he sought larger quarters. To his delight, another GM dealer only six blocks east, Jack Marshall Pontiac on

Main, was for sale. Pattison ploughed some of the profits from the previous three years into the new premises, which take up an entire city block at 18th Avenue and Main. He called the new dealership "Jim Pattison on Main" and commissioned Neon Products to erect a 40-foot lighted sign outside the showroom bearing his name in six-foot-high red letters. Viewed from seven or eight blocks to the south, the sign is superimposed on the snow-capped mountains that make up the impressive backdrop to Vancouver's skyline. The brassy young entrepreneur had begun to make his indelible mark on Vancouver.

Pattison's new showroom could hold at least ten cars, eight more than the old one, and he expanded his inventory to carry the full line of General Motors cars, including the top-of-the-line Cadillac, that fan-tailed gas-guzzler named after the French explorer who founded the motor city of Detroit in 1701.

Pattison's goal was to make more money every year, not for its own sake but "because business is fun, and money is a way of keeping score." Along the way this man, who in the words of columnist Allan Fotheringham, "looks like Mickey Rooney's undernourished brother, dresses like Nathan Detroit and thinks like J. Paul Getty," proceeded to make his new dealership the largest in Canada, overtaking his former employers across town at Bow Mac.

During the first half of the 1960s, this slight-statured man with the frenzied schedule mirrored the frantic pace of activity throughout the province. The heavy capital investment in resource industries of the previous decade began to pay off, and there was a new, even larger round of construction. The hub of activity was B.C.'s Interior. Prince George got a $50 million pulp plant; Kamloops was chosen for a $15 million pulp and paper mill; Fraser Lake got a $20 million molybdenum mine. And the electricity, highways and railways needed by the new industries were provided in abundance by a grateful provincial government. So quickly did plans roll off the drawing boards for new hydro-electric projects that Bennett's administration became known as "big dam government."

As usual, most of the investments and most of the profits were associated with forestry. In 1965 the net value of the B.C. forest industries was $980 million, almost double the 1952 figure. Average personal income was up too: higher in B.C. than anywhere in Canada; unemployment stood at 4.2 per cent.

Nowhere was the hectic growth more readily measured than at the Vancouver stock exchange, which in the month of July 1964 registered the highest volume of trading in its history, with 27 million shares worth $18 million changing hands.

All this commotion beyond the Rockies attracted the attention of a *Wall Street Journal* reporter who flew out in the summer of 1966 to tell the story of the minor league premier with the major league statistics.

Then *Time* magazine editors decided to get into the act. Outfitted in hip-waders, *Time* reporters fanned out across the country in search of resource industry statistics that could no longer go ignored. The issue was titled "Canada Today—The Boom No One Noticed" and devoted the entire fold-out cover and a good part of the story to W.A.C. Bennett and his province.

Time had nothing to tell Pattison; quite the opposite. Everywhere, it seemed, profits were crying out for shrewd entrepreneurs. The question was, which business or businesses to go after first? Pattison began showing up at the Vancouver stock exchange some mornings before work, dabbling in stocks. He also began searching for a "seed" company or industry to invest in, one that would provide him with a base from which to expand into many business ventures.

He had already narrowed the field considerably. Resource industries were out, partly because they were already dominated by a handful of giant corporations. He wasn't interested in real estate, either, because he lacked knowledge in that area, although that didn't seem to intimidate some speculators. (Ben Ginter, a highway contractor, was poised to reap enormous profits through speculation. He had been hired to clear sites for the new Prince George pulp mills, and at the same time he quietly bought up large tracts of land on the surrounding hillsides. "When those pulp mills start producing," he told a *Time* correspondent, "that stench is going to sit right down there in the valley. And people are going to start scrambling up the hills to build their homes. And they're going to build them on my land.")

Pattison wanted something closer to home and closer to his area of experience—dealing with the public, selling consumer goods and advertising. So in 1965, sitting comfortably atop a money-making dealership, he began to spread his wings and made a bid for one of Vancouver's most solid radio stations, CJOR. Within a couple of months it was his.

Pattison knew next to nothing about broadcasting but he knew plenty about advertising, which is how commercial radio stations generate income. However, it soon became apparent that radio stations were complex businesses, dependent as they were on "ratings," and the whims of the listening public were too volatile ever to make the station a solid financial base for Pattison's business ambitions. CJOR was to remain a sideline. For Pattison to satiate his hunger for more acquisitions, he would have to look elsewhere, for a rare find in the business world: a company with a good reputation, a steady income and a potential for growth which was not being exploited by the present management.

Even if the kind of business Pattison sought was available, it would not likely be sold to anyone just because they had the cash. The buyer would have to meet the approval of the board of directors, themselves members of that dim and distant entity called "the Canadian establishment," a group that was almost unknown until 1975. It was then that the 1,000 men who are Canada's economic aristocracy began to suffer the indignity of having their personal and financial secrets spilled to the very curious public. Their exploits and exploitations were first chronicled in detail in Peter C. Newman's *The Canadian Establishment*. Newman pointed out in the mid-seventies what Jim Pattison had learned the hard way a decade earlier: that B.C. was run by about 100 companies, some the size of empires. The men behind these formidable institutions were secretive, tough-minded, and, above all, determined to preserve the status quo. That meant, among other things, making financial and other donations to the ruling political party to ensure that legislation favourable to their companies' continued operations in the province could be counted upon.

Among the men who pioneered in the exploitation of B.C.'s "undeveloped depository of fabulous resources" but whose power was waning by the mid-1960s were: Harvey Reginald MacMillan, the timber explorer who laid the foundations for the province's largest corporation, MacMillan Bloedel; Frank McMahon, who made his millions piping Peace River natural gas to the Lower Mainland and the Pacific northwest of the United States; Gordon Farrell, of B.C. Telephone and Ocean Cement; Fred Brown, with directorships in twelve corporations; and Charles Bentall, founder of Dominion Construction.

What Pattison faced as he contemplated nabbing one of the establishment's companies was the current list of men who were B.C.'s "captains of industry." As befits an established upper class, they either inherited their power and wealth, or took control because of their well-established connections. Very few outsiders joined the club. At the head of the class was John Valentine Clyne, chairman of MacMillan Bloedel. It was Clyne who, while studying maritime law in London in 1926, skipped classes and joined the British Police "flying squads," whose duties included swinging billy clubs to disperse groups of strikers.

Other prominent names (and their companies) included Samuel Belzberg (First City Financial Corporation); Clark Bentall (son of Charles, head of Dominion Construction); Graham Dawson (Dawson Construction); Forrest Rogers (B.C. Sugar); Edgar Kaiser (coal and oil); Jack Poole (Daon Development); C.N.W.

"Chunky" Woodward (department stores); and Maurice Young (Finning Tractor).

These men and their fellow captains were as much at home in the elegant surroundings of the Vancouver Club as Jim Pattison was on a used car lot. About the closest Pattison got to them was when they wheeled their $20,000 Cadillacs around the wide curving boulevards of Shaughnessy and over to Main Street to have them serviced at his dealership. Most often it was their chauffeurs Pattison rubbed shoulders with.

Pattison decided to shelve until later the problem of *how* to break into the exclusive ranks of the rich and powerful, and concentrate on *where* to make his entry. After the bitter experience with CJOR he decided to do more homework before deciding where to strike next. He attended a series of "acquisition seminars" conducted by fast-talking lawyers from the United States whose favourite buzzword was "conglomerates." Technically, a conglomerate is a company that grows by buying other companies in unrelated industries. For example, Gulf and Western is a major American conglomerate, controlling a variety of consumer-oriented companies ranging from Paramount film corporation to Hertz rent-a-car.

The seminars taught Pattison to buy a strong base company on which to build. The qualities of this company should include conservative but flexible management, widely held shares and a steady market value showing a modest but steady profit, few debts, and plenty of "underutilized" assets—business parlance for a company whose cash, machinery, land, buildings or inventories are not earning as much as they could.

Another trick that Pattison gleaned from the seminars is that building conglomerates generates money faster than any other business venture. The key was to embark on a series of rapid acquisitions and wherever possible pay for the new companies with shares in the original company, not with cash. Shares in the base company would be rising rapidly with the new acquisitions, so each new purchase would cost "less," or so the reasoning went.

What the seminar leaders didn't say was that in most cases the conglomerate accumulates large debts that can be paid off only if earnings continue to rise. And they will rise only if more people buy more of the conglomerate's products—clearly a short-term strategy since every market is finite. There comes a point when either there are no more customers for a particular product, or a competitor is selling the same thing cheaper. If the conglomerate hits this wall, and if it also paid too high a price for some companies, it could land deep in debt with no quick way out.

But gloomy scenarios are not the stuff of seminars, especially when participants pay good money to hear how they can get rich quick. And, indeed, there are examples in the U.S. of conglomerates that have successfully diversified by purchasing a wide range of businesses and have shown significant jumps in earnings year after year.

Nothing exactly like this existed in Canada. There were conglomerates, of course, including some of the biggest companies in the land, like the Canadian Pacific Railway, Hudson's Bay Company, Brascan, Power Corporation and Argus Corporation. But they had built their portfolios slowly (in the case of Hudson's Bay, over centuries), and the diverse range of holdings usually bore some relationship to the central purpose of the company, whether transportation, selling furs or mining copper. The seminars disregarded this integral component and seemed to propose that a company go on a buying spree for other companies, guided only by the profits the larger company would contribute to the parent company, regardless of the products sold.

More to the point, west coast business empires were built only around the resource industries, in timberlands or mining ventures. In the far reaches of Lotus Land, where most businessmen were pretty staid conservatives, Pattison was preparing to build an industrial empire without hewing wood, drawing water or mining molybdenum. He planned to walk out of the jungle a rich man without ever having walked into it at all.

His next step was to hire experts from the brokerage and accounting community. Together they drew up a list of twenty target companies and then narrowed the field, applying the same criteria outlined in the seminars. When they came up with a short list, the leading possibility was the same company that Pat Pattison had thought so highly of, the same one that had bluntly turned down Jimmy's job application many years before, the same one that he subsequently hired to build the record high Bow Mac sign, and later the Jim Pattison on Main sign: Neon Products Ltd.

Besides having the basic qualities of conservative management, solid assets, few debts and a healthy cash flow, Neon had a host of other attractive features. It was national in scope, serving B.C. and Alberta from its Vancouver headquarters and the rest of Canada from its Toronto plant. It leased and did not sell signs, so at a given moment the company could count on another $17 million income over the next five years without signing another contract.

Very important to Pattison was Neon's fixed position in the establishment firmament. Ever since the late George Sweny had started the company in 1928 out of the back of a Granville Street store, the company's board of directors list read like a who's who in B.C.: W.C. Woodward of the department store chain; Gordon Farrell of B.C. Telephone; J.D.P. Malkin, the wholesaling pioneer; Harold E. Molson; and E. Buckerfield of the feed company.

When Sweny died in an air crash near Moose Jaw in 1956 his shares were acquired by Arthur B. Christopher, a high school dropout who made his fortune with Nelson's, the national chain of launderies. By the time Christopher became chairman, some of the original directors had died or retired, and one of the new ones was Alan Eyre, president of Dueck Chevrolet and Pattison's arch-competitor.

Neon also had some profitable subsidiaries, notably Seaboard Advertising, a billboard company which had been granted a virtual monopoly by the Outdoor Advertising Association to operate in the Vancouver and Victoria markets. (See Chapter 8 for more details on Pattison's conflicts with Canada's anti-monopoly laws.)

So conservative was Neon's management that critics called it complacent. The company's earnings in 1967 were barely higher than 1964, and little new growth was expected. But president Harvey Smith, who joined Neon after twenty years of building everything from dams to railway cars for Kaiser Steel, blamed the low growth on fierce competition. Smith said that although Neon was the largest sign company in Canada and the billboard segment was protected from competition, his competitors in the neon sign business, like Claude Neon Light Company of Toronto, were privately owned. "That means we operate with little knowledge about our competitors," he complained, "because private companies do not have to issue annual reports." Claude Neon, of course, had full access to Neon Products' annual reports.

By analysing the back issues of Neon's annual reports, as well as insider trading reports and other publicly available documents, Pattison and his associates found that in 1967 Neon was "extraordinarily liquid"—it was rich in cash or in assets that could be quickly converted into cash. There was $1 million in the bank, another $3.8 million income guaranteed in the next twelve months, a long-term debt of only $3.7 million, and unused lines of bank credit.

"Neon Products was made to order for a guy like me," chuckled the 39-year-old Pattison as he banged the table with joy. His ambition to become a millionaire before he was 40 was within reach. He wanted to build a Canadian growth company and Neon was the vehicle. It didn't matter that Neon made signs—it could have made flowers or jawbreakers—making money was what counted. Here was a company with money, and Pattison hoped to impose his brand of management on it and redouble that money over and over.

In spite of the availability of documents about Neon,

there were some important facts that Pattison still needed. He couldn't see the company books, which would have told him a lot more about management's skills than the tidy columns of figures in the annual reports. But being one of Neon's best customers, he already knew their management was good. More importantly, he wanted a list of the major shareholders, but no Canadian company is obliged to release those names. (In the United States, the Securities and Exchange Commission used to require large shareholders to disclose their holdings. Using this information, almost anyone could compute the wealth of the super-rich by adding up their shares and multiplying by the current market value. Pressure from the group of men most adversely affected, America's moneyed class, resulted in a repeal of the law just before World War II.)

It was important to Pattison, for obvious reasons, to know who held the largest blocks of shares in Neon. Through questionable means—"I prefer not to tell you how," he later told a *Sun* reporter—he obtained a shareholders' list. To his surprise he found the largest single shareholder was William Anderson, the company's auditor. Pattison's advisers pointed out that although Anderson had only 7 per cent of the total number of shares, his was the largest block; he had almost a controlling interest in Neon. That, they said, could put him in a position of conflict of interest because when he audited the books he would, in effect, be auditing himself. The list showed that the rest of the board of directors held another 7 per cent of the shares.

The "research phase" at an end, Pattison knew that he would have to obtain 14 to 15 per cent of Neon's shares to "neutralize" the holdings of the directors and Anderson and gain control of the company.

The problem of *where* to make his move was solved. The next problem was *how*.

4 GOLDFINGER

> [*Pattison*] *may conform to the gospel and he may tithe and all that shit, but he'll sink you as soon as look at you.*
> —a former Pattison associate

In Manhattan's forest of glass and steel, at 1221 Avenue of the Americas, rises one of the borough's more imposing skyscrapers. On the top floor is the headquarters of the world's largest metals and minerals trading corporations, Englehard Incorporated.

In the late summer of 1967, chairman Charles W. Englehard, son of a German-Jewish merchant who founded the company, received a call from a young investment banker, Michael Dingman of Burnham and Company. Dingman asked Englehard, a man known throughout the U.S. as an influential "checkbook Democrat" who had hobnobbed with presidents Kennedy and Johnson, if he would consider talking to a young Canadian car dealer. This was no ordinary car dealer, Dingman assured the sceptical chairman, but a man who wanted Englehard to lend "seed money" to start a conglomerate, and who predicted he could double Englehard's investment in one year.

Any other multi-millionaire would have laughed at the bizarre request and hung up. But Charles Englehard was not an average business tycoon. Author Stephen Fay, who interviewed Englehard before he died in 1971, descibed him as a "bold, rumbustious spirit...a buccaneer." He was also a very rich man. In 1967, Englehard's fortune was estimated at $300 million, making him one of the ten richest men in the United States. Among his holdings was a fleet of aircraft, villas in five countries and a stable of 250 race horses. He proudly wore the unofficial crown as the "World's Platinum King," bestowed on him because of the volume of the precious metal refined and marketed by his company.

Englehard was a close friend of Ian Fleming, creator of the James Bond adventures. Fleming claimed to have used Englehard's opulent lifestyle as a model for the "non-villainous" characteristics of Bond's arch-rival, Goldfinger. True to the image, Englehard even smoked Old Gold cigarettes.

On this mid-August day, Englehard listened to Dingman explain that the Canadian businessman had really done his homework and could easily double Englehard's seed money in twelve months. Englehard hardly needed the money. For reasons known only to himself, the chairman agreed to meet Pattison.

Jim Pattison was impressed with Michael Dingman from their first meeting. "[He's] a bright young man... my kind of guy," gushed Pattison. Dingman, he noted, was three years his junior, yet had already risen to a position of considerable influence in the New York investment banking firm of Burnham and Company.

Dingman was impressed too. Pattison had come highly recommended by the Toronto investment firm, T.A. Richardson, which told Dingman that Pattison had realistic plans for building a consumer-oriented, diverse empire starting on Canada's west coast. The "target" company destined to become the foundation of this empire was Neon Products, Canada's largest electric sign company.

But there were two problems.

First Pattison needed cash. His car dealership may have been the most successful in the country, but its profits were ploughed right back into the business, and were, at any rate, far too small to buy out a company the size of Neon Products. The Royal Bank agreed to front only a portion of the money, because, according to Pattison, the bank was "afraid of not getting it back fast enough."

The second problem was that Pattison was only a car dealer, credentials enough to win a seat in the B.C. Legislature, but which carried little weight in the staid western Canadian business circles. Pattison was very much outside the establishment. In his own words, "These guys run the town. If I said I'm a car dealer and I want your company, I'd have been thrown out of their offices." To wrest control of Neon Products, Pattison needed a "cover"—a company that had an air of respectability, a good corporate track record and enough cash to do the buying on his behalf.

Dingman's choice of Englehard Inc. as the cover for the takeover attempt was influenced as much by Charles Englehard's wealth as it was by the firm's tight-lipped approach to business. For the takeover to succeed, the identity of the ultimate buyer had to be shrouded in utter secrecy. Englehard Inc., which was virtually unknown to the public—although its earnings were greater than giants like Shell, Du Pont and U.S. Steel—was the perfect choice.

Englehard's secretiveness came with the territory. About half the company's revenue originated from trading in commodities. The traders buy crude oil, plastics, grain, sugar, cement and other products in one part of the world and sell them in another, often the same day, always for a profit. Traders lead quiet lives, often working twelve to fourteen hours a day, and keep their mouths shut about the names of customers and suppliers, or the volume of their trade. The key to their success is market intelligence. They know when to buy in one market and sell for profit somewhere else. The intelligence gathering depends on state of the art communications hardware. The nerve centre of corporate headquarters in New York is laced with telephones, computers and telexes linked with offices and markets around the world. The centre is matched in sophistication only by the communications network of the U.S. Central Intelligence Agency. The book *Everybody's Business* reports that CIA agents and Englehard employees exchange marketing and political information about foreign countries.

Another clue to Englehard's fear of public exposure is apparent to anyone who telephones head office. His is the largest company in the U.S. which lacks a public relations department. Englehard stock can be bought and sold on the open market, but as a Wall Street analyst put it, "They are perhaps the most reluctantly public company in the world."

The other half of the firm's income is rooted in another trading tradition that can be traced back to the fifteenth century Venetian merchants. It involves trading in precious metals like gold, silver and platinum (and more recently uranium). Generally, the corporation purchases metals from mines in South Africa, Canada, Latin America and elsewhere and processes them at its plants around the world. The finished products are used in everything from X-ray film to catalytic converters for automobiles.

The South African connection goes much deeper than the country's famous gold mines. Charles Englehard sat on the board of directors of the Anglo-American Corporation, South Africa's largest firm, and several other South African companies. In turn, Anglo-American's chairman, Harry Oppenheimer, owned 27.6 per cent of Englehard's stock, making him the largest shareholder in the U.S. firm.

Journalists have virtually ignored the strong links between the company that gave Pattison his start, Englehard Incorporated, and one of the world's colossal corporations, Anglo-American of South Africa. In hundreds of newspaper articles and magazine stories written over the past fifteen years, the South Africa link is never mentioned and Englehard's name comes up only a few times. Until recently, a senior Englehard official, Larry Hoguet, sat on the Jim Pattison Group's board of directors.

Englehard's South African connections have brought it into conflict with American laws. On at least one occasion the New York company was subpoenaed by the U.S. government for alleged violations of a 1954 order banning direct purchases from South Africa—this case involved purchases of diamonds from DeBeers.

For a company that cherishes privacy, Englehard often finds itself in the news—the two may be related. Most of the coverage involves allegations of wrongdoing. In 1974, Englehard convinced the Oklahoma Health Board to lower its pollution standards so the company could build a 56,000-ton zinc smelter; two years later, the U.S. Institute for Occupational Health and Safety said the deaths of some Englehard employees may have been caused by exposure to talc dust at the company's plants; in 1977, Englehard was one of thirteen firms named by the Tennessee Valley Authority in a uranium price-fixing case; and in 1982 a sales manager for the company, George Karmi, was sentenced to four years in a Stockholm prison for gold smuggling.

Englehard also had a controversial presence in developing countries. His company established a private bank in Switzerland (in Zug, where Jim Pattison set up a similar bank ten years later) which often lent money to those countries to open new mines. It was understood that the mines' output would be sold only to Englehard.

The most dramatic event associated with Englehard was the great silver scandal of 1979-80 when the super-rich Hunt brothers of Texas cornered the silver market. The price of silver dropped when the Hunts thought it would rise, and they lost hundreds of millions of dollars. Unable to pay off their debts to Englehard, the Hunts were forced to fork over 8.5 million ounces of silver and the oil and gas rights to 3.5 million acres in Canada's Beaufort Sea. Englehard emerged the biggest winner, walking away with an enormous windfall.

Englehard's meeting with Pattison and Dingman was short and to the point. Pattison sketched his plans. He said he could move the value of Neon Stock, which traded around $7.25 a share, to at least double that amount within the year. If Englehard put up between $3 and $4 million, which Pattison figured he would need to buy a controlling interest in Neon, then Englehard could double his money, or get his original investment back and still own stock in Neon. Of course, if Pattison failed, Englehard would lose his money.

Charles Engelhard "asked" Pattison if there would be a place on the board of directors for one or two of Englehard's top men. Pattison naturally agreed. The deal was clinched.

Years later, when Pattison was asked how he, an unknown car dealer from western Canada, persuaded one of the captains of U.S. industry to back him, he said, "That's where my garden seeds paid off. *Saturday Evening Post*. I sold them on what I believed could be done in Canada...they believed in me, and they had the money, I didn't." What he didn't say was that his takeover of Neon Products gave Englehard a foothold in Canada at a time when nationalist sentiment ran high and "foreign investment" was a derogatory term.

On September 12, 1967, Richardson's in Toronto got the call they'd been told to expect. It was from Michael Dingman in New York. The instructions were to buy 200 shares of Neon, then trading on the Toronto stock exchange for $7. A few days later, another call, this time for 300 shares, now selling at $7.25. The following week it was 500 shares at $7.50.

Each purchase nudged the share price up because Neon was listed on only two exchanges, Toronto and Vancouver, and traded only about 100 shares a day. Any greater demand forced up the price. Pattison's agents carefully purchased small orders so as not to attract attention. After several weeks, they had accumulated about 6 per cent of Neon's stock, and the trading price was up to $9.

The members of the Neon Products board of directors looked at each other in puzzlement. Senator John Nichol, taking time away from his duties as the National Liberal Federation president to attend the meeting, said aloud what was on everyone's mind. "Why are the share prices going up?" No one knew.

Facts may have been hard to come by but rumours abounded. The most persistent was that a buyer, possibly a big U.S. company, was after Neon stock. Word was "on the street"—a euphemism referring to the relatively small circle of traders who frequent the stock exchanges—that Neon was about to be "taken over" for $12 a share.

A rush to "buy" orders descended on the stock exchanges. Neon jumped from $9 to $10. Speculators hoped for a quick profit. But Pattison told his people to cut out. "We didn't buy a stick," he said.

Even though Pattison now had 6 per cent of the company shares, his name didn't appear on a single certificate. Richardson's had taken care to distribute the shares among six banks (five Canadian and one in the U.S.) so they wouldn't pile up in one place attached to one buyer's name. Knowing how to conceal the real identity of the prospective owner was just one of the tricks that helped investment bankers like Richardson's and Burnham get where they are.

Pattison had reached the point of no return. He couldn't continue to buy small blocks of shares because the price would rise too high. He had invested hundreds of thousands of dollars of other people's money in Neon stock, and if he tried to sell shares on the open market, the price of the stock would plummet, leaving investors with substantial losses. And if Pattison were to unload the stock at Neon's normal rate of about 100 shares a day, it would take years to sell them.

He decided to gamble. To obtain controlling interest, Pattison needed to buy up the single largest block of shares. As it happened, that block—about 10 per cent of the total—belonged to a small group of men represented by Neon chairman Arthur B. Christopher.

Christopher was no stranger to corporate takeovers. He had abandoned a brief stint as a Victoria bank manager and investment dealer to become a wheeler-dealer in Vancouver financial circles. He made his mark by transforming a struggling laundry outfit, Nelson's, into a national chain. The laundry business, known for its low wages, made a fortune for the stocky, bushy-eyebrowed Christopher. And although the B.C. establishment considered him something of an outsider, he was rewarded for his accomplishments with a host of directorships, including seats at the board room tables of MacMillan Bloedel, the Royal Bank and Neon Products.

He then joined Neon, which had become the largest sign company in the country by acquiring a string of other companies. The first acquisition, in 1946, was Ruddy Duker and Company. Neon changed the unwieldy name to Seaboard Advertising and from then on enjoyed a near-monopoly in the Vancouver and Victoria billboard business.

Ten years later Neon Products established a national foothold with the purchase of Outdoor Neon Displays of Toronto, and the following year, 1957, the company eliminated one of its main prairie competitors by acquiring Baxter Signs of Winnipeg. For the first time, however, the tables were now turned as Christopher and his company became the target of a serious takeover bid. One morning in early November 1967, Christopher received a call at his Vancouver office. It was Richardson's in Toronto. An unnamed buyer was placing a bid on the block of 175,000 shares controlled by Christopher, Neon's auditor William Anderson, and some other shareholders. They were offered $10 a share. Christopher growled, "You can tell your client to take his $10 and go jump." Down the hall, Neon president Harvey Smith knew nothing of the offer to Christopher, but he soon smelled an opportunity to make money.

Smith, a Calgary native, was no stranger to the ways of big corporations and had a resume to prove it. He had worked for some of the biggest, including Kaiser

Steel, where he supervised the construction of portions of the giant Hoover and Grand Coolee dams. During the Second World War he had supervised construction of U.S. air and naval bases in the Pacific. He served a stint as president of Avro Aircraft, the Canadian developer of the ill-fated Avro Arrow jet fighter. Smith knew when major changes were afoot. Exercising his executive stock option, he purchased 10,000 Neon shares at $8.55 each—a below-market price. He did not tell Christopher about the purchase.

Events moved quickly. Pattison called Burnham. He wanted assurances that Englehard money was still available if he offered the Christopher group more than $10 a share. Burnham called Englehard and relayed the answer back to Vancouver: "We'll go with you if you need us."

On Thursday morning, November 9, Christopher telephoned his Toronto broker, coincidentally also at Richardson's, with instructions to make a counter-offer to Burnham. The Richardson's agent flew to New York to meet personally with Dingman.

The next morning, November 10, Dingman called Pattison with the details of the counter-offer. Pattison smiled at the thought of these eastern money men negotiating on behalf of a buyer and seller sitting less than two miles apart in their Vancouver offices. When the word finally came down, Dingman reported that Christopher would sell all 175,000 shares at $10.75, a total of $1.88 million. Combined with his current holdings that would give Pattison about 16 per cent of Neon, making him by far the largest shareholder. Pattison said, "I'll take it." He glanced at his gold watch. It was 11:50 a.m.

Dingman notified Richardson's, who tracked down Christopher at lunch in the executive dining room at the Royal Bank's main branch at Hastings and Granville. His counter-offer had been accepted. (Ironically, Christopher, a Royal Bank director, had no knowledge of the money his bank had lent Pattison to help finance the takeover.) The waiting was over. All that remained was the formality of signing over the shares. Christopher had just sold a controlling interest in his company to an unknown outsider and now he could ask what he'd been wanting to know all along.

"Okay," he snapped, "who is it?"

The reply came through the static of a poor connection. "It's a man called Jim Pattison."

"Jesus Christ," barked Christopher and hung up.

That afternoon, Neon president Harvey Smith also got a call from Richardson's. It was the same offer: $10.75 for his 10,000 shares. Smith accepted. His "profit," though smaller than Christopher's, was still a substantial $22,000.

The atmosphere in Arthur Christopher's living room the following Sunday morning was icy as he and Pattison formally concluded the deal. Christopher was furious that control of his company had been wrested from him by this upstart car dealer, someone completely outside the business establishment who dressed like a circus clown. What he didn't know was that Pattison's "theft" had been masterminded and bankrolled by one of the most powerful multinational corporations in the capitalist world.

Monday morning, November 13, the Toronto stock exchange opened for business as usual at 10 a.m. and traders were startled to see the massive transfer of Neon shares over the weekend, more than three times the total number of shares traded in the previous eight months. Newswires buzzed, and soon the *Globe and Mail* called president Harvey Smith for a comment.

"Yes," he told the reporter who had found him at home in Vancouver, where it was not yet 8 a.m., "we've thought from the increased activity and rising price of the shares in the past couple of weeks that someone was trying to get control of Neon Products." He added that he had no idea who that someone was.

Unknown to Smith, at the same moment Christopher was talking to a Vancouver *Sun* reporter confirming that a New York syndicate "headed by a local investor" closed a deal which made it the largest shareholder in Neon. Christopher said he was "not at liberty to divulge the names of the principals" and that he was assured by the syndicate's spokesman that there would be "no change in the company's management or business philosophy."

When the *Sun* hit the streets later that morning the other directors and some of Neon's shareholders were furious. W.E. Thomson, a Neon director and president of Pemberton Securities, whose clients "held a lot of Neon stock," grumbled that as a director and shareholder he had "no knowledge of the transaction arranged by Mr. Christopher."

None of the other directors or 2,000-plus shareholders (except Smith) had the opportunity to sell their shares for the $10.75 price—$1.50 above market. By the time they found out, Neon had already "crossed the block" (business jargon for sale of a controlling interest in a company) and delivered itself into the waiting hands of Jim Pattison.

On that mid-November afternoon, 63 days after Pattison began gobbling up Neon shares, he marched into the board room at Neon's Clark Drive headquarters in Vancouver. He asserted his control swiftly. The faces in the room, except Christopher's and Smith's, were hostile.

Senator Nichol hurled the first stone. "I strongly disagree with the procedure that has been followed by the shareholders who accepted this offer," he said, an obvious attack on the president and chairman. Others nodded. The unwritten rules of takeovers include an understanding that if a buyer makes an offer, the chairman takes the details to the board of directors, who then recommend to the shareholders either acceptance or rejection of the offer. The final decision, again according to unwritten rules, rests with the shareholders. In this case, the senator pointed out, only Smith and Christopher (and through him William Anderson and some unnamed associates) knew about the offer and they kept the information to themselves.

Immediately Christopher was put on the defensive. "The sale of my shares was a private affair," he replied. "I bought the stock with my own money." Here he was probably taking a shot at Pattison and his still-unnamed financial backers. Christopher's ultimate defence rested on tradition rather than unwritten rules. "I'm old-fashioned enough," he allowed, "to believe that I am free to dispose of [my shares] as I wish."

What alarmed the other directors was that in exercising their freedom, neither Smith nor Christopher knew who they were selling to. They could have delivered the well-established company into the hands of a competitor, or some U.S. giant that would have "killed Neon." While neither scenario was true, they were not happy that Neon was effectively in the hands of a car dealer.

Smith, for his part, used the irrational excuse that he had "no intention of owning shares in a company when I don't know who owns it," as his reason for buying 10,000 shares before "that magic week" and then selling them for a $22,000 profit. Christopher, too, seemed to think the anonymity of the buyer was a good reason to sell. "I didn't think [a new owner] would be bad for the shareholders. But I felt it would be bad for me personally," he said enigmatically, adding that if he had to do it again, he would do "exactly what I did."

The senator was red-faced. Announcing his resignation from the board, he stormed out of the meeting. (Later he sold all his Neon shares for an average price of $9.85.)

W.E. Thomson, the Pemberton president, assured other board members that all the transactions had been technically legal, if questionable. "There is nothing in the Securities Act of B.C. or Ontario which covers things like this," he said, adding, "some shareholders think there should be."

Pattison emulated the conciliatory tone of Thomson's remarks as he consoled the remaining directors. "Takeovers are traumatic affairs," he purred, "[and] nobody likes to have his company taken off him." He assured the board that there would be no major changes. Christopher would stay on as chairman and Smith as president. Once Smith learned that his job was secure, his fears of owning shares in a company whose owner he doesn't know seemed to vanish. He later told a *Sun* reporter, "Really, who holds the shares is of little concern to the company...officials." He went on to cleanse Pattison's motives, saying his new boss wanted only to invest in a sound business, and had no intention of changing the company.

Still open to question was the role played by William Anderson, formerly Neon's largest shareholder. He did well on the sale of shares which he, Christopher and others had inherited from the estate of the late George Sweny, Neon's founder. But he was in an obvious conflict of interest while he owned the shares. His company, Winspear, Higgins, Stevenson and Doane, was the auditor of Neon Products' books.

The Institute of Chartered Accountants apparently forbade a conflict of interest like Anderson's. Its code of ethics stated: "No member shall allow their names to be used in connection with any financial statement in which any of them...have a direct or indirect beneficial interest...unless a full disclosure thereof is included in a report accompanying such financial statement." There was no such disclosure in any of Neon's annual reports.

Anderson said he had never audited the Neon books himself and "wouldn't know the Neon books if I saw them." But when asked if it wasn't unusual to have his firm's name appear on the financial statement of a company in which he was the major shareholder, Anderson retorted, "Just because one or two companies forbid it doesn't make it unusual. I discussed it with the Vancouver stock exchange and there is nothing in the Companies Act which forbids it." (In our society the smallest amounts of money are the most rigidly controlled. Everyone knows the amount of a welfare cheque or an old age pension. They must be disclosed by law. But as the amount of money increases, laws become rules, rules become unwritten rules, unwritten rules become vague traditions, and vague traditions end up being an honour system.)

The ethics committee of the Institute of Chartered Accountants wasn't so sure. They were keenly interested in the role of Anderson in the sale of the $1.88 million block of Neon shares, and launched their own investigation. Even the American Securities and Exchange Commission, alerted to the situation by the outflow of American capital, began an informal investigation.

In August 1968 the Institute of Chartered Accountants found Anderson guilty of professional misconduct and fined him $200.

Even the business community winced at the Pattison takeover. Bill Hamilton, former head of the Employers' Council of B.C.—a provincial lobby group for business, not given to criticism of its own members—made it known that he was very unhappy with the way Pattison bought Neon Products.

What Pattison and his "friendly money" in New York had just acquired was more than just a conservatively managed electric sign company. Although management had been criticized for its "complacent" attitudes in the sixties, the company had a history of expansion and innovation.

The expansion initiated by Neon management that thrust the company to the top of its field in Canada by 1967 carried with it the expected dividends. The *Financial Post* estimated that $1,000 invested in Neon Stock in 1947 had grown to $12,948 by 1967. That is an annual growth rate of 13.7 per cent—pretty healthy in those pre-inflation days.

When examining success stories in the corporate world, it is easy to overlook, in the blizzard of praise for management's conquests, the unsung heroes. They are, in Neon's case, the glass blowers who bend the tubes, the sheet metal workers who shape the sign frames, the printers who produce billboard panels, the delivery and maintenance workers, the office staff and the other workers.

There are some unique aspects to Neon's success. Because it dominated the Vancouver market, Neon almost single-handedly transformed Granville Street. By the 1950s, Neon Products had installed thousands of signs in Vancouver, most of them along the downtown strip on Granville. Vancouver was said to have more gas-lit signs per capita than any other North American city.

The gaudy signs sparked a debate that many Vancouverites took quite seriously and that went on for years.

Neon's executives, who correctly perceived more than aesthetics at issue here, quickly let their opinions be known. At Neon's 1963 annual meeting of shareholders, then-president Colin Martin allayed the fears of shareholders. "Kill the signs on downtown streets with bylaws and you might as well bury the area," he prophesied, making the downtown's demise synonymous with Neon's.

City Hall disagreed. Within three years the council passed a bylaw which forever turned off the vast majority of neon signs. Gone was the giant Coca-Cola sign on the roof of the Coke plant near the Burrard Bridge, a beacon in the night that had been compared to the biggest signs in New York's Times Square. Also extinguished was the Pontiac rooftop sign which dominated the busy Main and Broadway intersection. But the main target of the bylaw was the myriad of lighted signs which hung at right angles to storefronts over the sidewalks of downtown Vancouver.

As the bylaw vote approached, Neon executives scuttled around to get a few more rooftop signs erected. They assumed that the law would apply only to new signs. City council, angered by Neon's tactics, made the bylaw retroactive. And the downtown, contrary to president Martin's dire predictions, did not die. Neither did the company.

About this time, Neon pioneered in another advertising medium. Like most billboard companies, Neon's subsidiary, Seaboard Advertising, had its problems. It faced regular criticism from the "anti-billboard lobby" about the unsightliness of some billboards. And redevelopment of the city snatched up prime billboard locations.

Seaboard found an answer to its dilemma in an unlikely place, the slums of New York. Josep Llobet, a Spaniard who had worked for an advertising firm in Argentina before immigrating to the U.S., had been working on an invention in his cheap tenement flat in New York City. In 1965, Neon president Harvey Smith got wind of Llobet's technical breakthrough. He was so intrigued he flew to New York to track down the inventor. Llobet showed Smith the plans of his multi-faced billboard. In the same space that would previously accommodate only one unsightly billboard, Llobet had made room for seven. Smith was convinced. He flew back to Vancouver with Llobet to negotiate patent rights and to develop the new sign.

The billboards showed seven different ads in sequence, using seven-sided, vertical, rotating posts. Neon manufactured the entire mechanism and sold it throughout Canada. Llobet was to get a share of the sales, but his dreams of making a fortune faded when the orders stopped coming in. The buyers, including Seaboard itself, found the reality of the rotating billboard was less alluring than the conception. The mechanism in the boards broke down too often, and seven separate advertisers rarely wanted to keep their ads up for exactly the same duration.

The experiment was not futile however. Seaboard modified the plans and came up with a three-sided, or "trio" billboard. Their prism-shaped columns stood up better to the constant rotations, and it was far easier to co-ordinate three advertisers than seven. The advertisers seemed pleased with the result. And with two billboards slapped back to back, one location could now display six ads instead of two.

Curiously, Pattison said it was the seven-sided sign which was the key factor in his decision to buy Neon. In an interview with the *Sun* on the Thursday after the stormy board meeting, he said there were several reasons for his investment, but the new seven-image sign clinched the deal. (At the time, the sign had not been tested.) This would seem to contradict his statements on several occasions that the key factors in his decision to buy Neon were the company's under-utilized capital, its lack of major debts and its steady income.

At first, the changes at Neon came slowly. Senator Nichol, the only director to resign right after the takeover, was soon joined by two others, R.H.B. Ker and D.P. Rogers (former president of Union Gas of Toronto). They handed in their resignations on January 31, 1968, at the same board meeting at which Pattison named himself managing director with "the power to acquire new companies." Pattison appointed two new directors: Mike Dingman, the "bright young man" from Burnham and Company, and Larry Hoguet, a senior vice president of Englehard.

If the rest of the directors and shareholders of Neon were edgy about Pattison's plans for their company, they weren't saying. The only clue to "insiders'" thoughts was found in an editorial comment at the end of a story about Pattison's takeover. The editors of *Signs in Canada*, a publication sent only to sign dealers, enthused with chamber of commerce boosterism typical of trade journals that Pattison's achievement was "the most sensational thing that ever happened to the Canadian sign manufacturing industry." Then, reflecting the heightened nationalist sentiment of the late sixties, the article concluded, "For sheer Canadian spirit, we could do with a few more 'Big Jim' Pattisons in Canada!"

5. RECIPE FOR A CONGLOMERATE: ADD A COMPANY AND STIR

> *You can say two things about Pattison's senior managers—they're dedicated and terrified.*
> —*Sun* reporter Gordon Hamilton

Arthur Christopher was sulking.

"I used to be chairman of a sign business. Now they want to make a conglomerate out of us," he sighed, sitting behind his desk at Neon Products one morning in May 1968.

By "they" Christopher meant Pattison and his new "outside" American directors, Dingman and Hoguet. By "conglomerate" he meant the addition of grocery stores and paint manufacturers to Neon's roster, plus the four or five other companies Pattison was dickering with.

Things were not going well for Christopher. Pattison was not fulfilling the promise he had made when he was still flush from victory from his takeover of the country's largest sign maker the previous fall. At the time, he assured shocked directors and shareholders that there would be no changes in company philosophy or management.

RECIPE FOR A CONGLOMERATE 81

The "company philosophy" Pattison vowed to leave intact was a tradition of four decades: to manufacture and lease advertising signs. Period. Pattison altered that in a matter of months with the purchase of the 51-store Overwaitea chain of supermarkets, the largest grocery store business in B.C. outside Vancouver and Victoria, and with the acquisition of Northern Paint of Winnipeg, a manufacturer and distributor of house paints.

The two acquisitions in the spring of 1968 were only the curtain-raiser on a buying spree that would make Neon Products the largest consumer services and transportation company in Canada before the turn of the decade.

In the first two deals, no cash changed hands. Instead, Neon Products simply paid for companies with its own shares. Overwaitea, a large chain which sold roughly $50 million worth of groceries a year, was bought for over half a million Neon shares, worth $12.5 million. Neon Products picked up Northern Paint for $3 million worth of shares. (Some investment analysts scoffed at both transactions, calling them "paper deals." They pointed out that the purchase price could go up or down, depending on the market price for Neon Products shares. For example, when Pattison signed the agreement in principle with Overwaitea, 500,000 Neon Products shares were worth $8 million. When the deal closed three months later, the same shares were worth $12.5 million. They could drop in value just as rapidly.)

From a business point of view, Neon's first two purchases make perfect sense for a company intent on dominating the consumer services sector of the economy. Overwaitea was already the second largest grocery chain in B.C. after Safeway. Owning it gave Pattison a foothold in the Canadian food and beverage industry, the most important manufacturing and retail business in Canada. (In 1971 that industry employed 13 per cent of all workers in manufacturing, and at the retail level, food sales totalled $7.9 billion, over one-quarter of all retail sales in Canada.)

One of the first effects of the Overwaitea purchase was to multiply Neon's paper earnings. Neon's sales of $8 million a year swelled enormously when combined with Overwaitea's annual revenues of $60 million. But the gain in actual profits was far more modest because supermarkets generally make only 1 or 2 per cent profit on sales of groceries.

Not that the new conglomerate was suffering. Through some wily bookkeeping Neon Products was able to wangle four incomes out of every subsidiary. First, there were the revenues from sales. Then dividends were collected, money that previously went to those companies' shareholders. Next "management fees" were collected for services and expertise rendered. Finally—and most interestingly—head office collected interest payments on loans. Neon Products did not let subsidiaries borrow money themselves. It took out the bank loans, then re-lent the money to its subsidiaries and charged another 1.5 per cent interest. Neon management, in effect, turned itself into a mini-bank. Using these standard business practices, the parent company generated more income. On the other side of the ledger, it neatly arranged "expenses" to be deducted from taxable income.

As the infrastructure of Pattison's corporation was starting to gel, he broke the second promise, the one about not changing Neon's management. Harvey Smith, the man with the staggering resume who, when last heard from, was very pleased that Pattison found Neon such an attractive investment, was the first to be fired. No reason was given, although insiders say there was a sharp difference of opinion between the two on basic issues related to the daily running of the company. Others claim Pattison canned the president because he fumbled negotiations with Neon's 40 unionized office employees in 1968 and only narrowly averted a strike. Whatever the reason, it was still a good year for Smith's bank account. In addition to the $22,000 windfall from his quick purchase and sale of Neon stock, Smith got a $35,000 golden handshake from Pattison. It may be only a coincidence that Smith never uttered a word about why he was fired.

The president's chair was filled by Pattison after Smith left, although many of the duties went to a 47-year-old Neon loyalist, Stanley F. Whittle. For the previous six of his 25 years with the firm, he had been the head of Neon's Toronto operation. On March 5, 1968, Pattison appointed Whittle executive vice president and general manager of the Vancouver operation.

Many Neon shareholders, accustomed as they were to tidy little dividend cheques landing in their mail boxes every three months, and to the slow and steady growth of their investment in the sedate sign company, had mixed feelings about recent events. In only a few months, their company had more than quadrupled in sales, and the value of their shares had more than doubled on the Toronto and Vancouver exchanges. But the silver cloud had a dark lining. With the takeover of Northern Paint in May, Pattison cut the dividends to ten cents a share from 40 cents. Instead of passing money on to the company's shareholders, the boss had it earmarked for further acquisitions.

Neon shareholders may not have been accustomed to being part-owners of a conglomerate, Wall Street style, but neither was Jim Pattison accustomed to answering to shareholders. His other companies, which included the GM dealership, a car and truck leasing company and radio station CJOR, were privately owned. The only shareholder Pattison had to answer to was the one he saw in his shaving mirror each morning.

At Neon Products he was compelled by law to issue quarterly reports on the conglomerate's financial state and to compile detailed annual reports revealing profits or losses, any major changes during the year and plans for the future. He was also, in theory at least, required to obtain shareholders' approval before buying new companies or undertaking similar major purchases. The latter requirement posed few problems in practice, because Pattison and his "friendly money" backers owned about 30 per cent of the shares. At shareholders' meetings, democracy is defined as one share-one vote, not one shareholder-one vote.

And if the threat arose, Pattison would have lobbied potential opponents before a critical vote. Should his powers of persuasion fail him in this area, they would still succeed in others. According to a developing pattern, opponents who could not be won over soon disappeared. In the six months following Pattison's takeover of Neon, eight directors resigned. Eyre (Pattison's arch-rival from Dueck Chevrolet), Ker, Brown, Housser, Senator Nichol, Rogers, Smith and Thomson had all stepped down by April 30, 1968.

In their place Pattison constructed a leaner, American-flavoured board. The first appointment was Michael Dingman from Burnham and Company. Next to join the team was Larry Hoguet, the 53-year-old senior vice president and treasurer of Englehard Minerals and Chemicals Corporation. (Hoguet, like Charles Englehard, had direct dealings with South Africa. He was vice president and treasurer of the American-South African Investment Company Ltd.) The two New Yorkers were soon joined by Robert W. Halliday of Boise, Idaho, executive vice president and a director of Boise Cascade, the fifth largest forest products company in the U.S.

These men were more than figureheads. The days had long passed when a directorship was considered an honorary position. Federal and provincial laws had toughened the qualifications for directors. Under new rules, if a company committed an illegal act with the knowledge or consent of the directors, they too could be charged and tried. And if they were unaware that their conduct was illegal, they could be charged with gross negligence for having failed to supervise the company's affairs in accordance with the law. (These laws, however, are very seldom applied. There's no federal cop on the corporate beat.)

Why would directors take on such responsibilities? Money, for one thing. In Canada, directors' fees range from $5,000 to $30,000 a year for attending ten meetings, plus $500 for each committee meeting, plus an expense account that covers travel and accommodation and many other things that money can buy. (One of Pattison's current directors, John H. Coleman, is president or chairman of five companies and a director of at least 24 others. His total director's fees are conservatively estimated to be $300,000.)

But the perks go well beyond remuneration. Directorships are generally granted (cynics would say sold) to people who invest large sums in a given company and then want a say in how that company is run.

The benefits are usually mutual. That is why the boards of directors of Canadian companies are often generously sprinkled with American, British, German, and other foreign directors, whose principal companies invest in and/or buy from the Canadian concern. At the highest levels of the economy, directors sit on the boards of many different companies—a pattern called interlocking directorships—and their paths cross often. A common purpose is to secure advantages for their companies by co-operating to stifle competition in particular sectors of the economy.

The immediate benefit to Pattison from his three outside directors was their expertise. Burnham and Company gave Neon Products access to the major money markets. In return, Burnham benefited by getting business from Neon. Both Englehard and Boise Cascade were vertically integrated concerns, an example that Pattison tried to emulate. Pattison's goals, in his own words, were three-fold: to become "a large diversified company [with] better than average growth"; to "aggressively [follow] an external acquisition program"; and to "integrate vertically those companies so that they can profit and expand by their association with other companies in the Neon organization."

Englehard and Boise Cascade had excelled at all three. Englehard owned the bank which lent money for the purpose of opening new mines. It owned the plants that processed the raw materials from the mines. It owned the firms that wrought from refined metals products ranging from computers to catalytic converters.

Boise Cascade performed similar tricks with wood. It owned the forests and the companies that cut the trees. It owned the pulp mills and the plywood plants. And it owned the stationery and tissue paper companies. In both cases, the corporations pursued diversification through "aggressive acquisition" and then "vertically integrated" their companies so that profits at each level accumulated into super-profits for the parent company.

With experienced hands like Halliday and Hoguet at the helm, Pattison continued his buying spree, pausing only long enough in mid-May 1968 to express his thanks to the Neon board of directors for having appointed him president and chief executive officer (CEO) of the company.

In late May he announced that a preliminary agreement of sale had been reached between Neon and the Van Dee Group, the Edmonton-based parent of Acme Novelty Corporation, a distributor of carnival merchandise and bingo supplies. Pattison acquired the $30 million-a-year business in exchange for $14 million worth of Neon shares.

Suddenly Pattison found himself caught in what financial analysts call "the classic conglomerate squeeze." Although it sounds like an old-fashioned, intimate dance, it actually meant that Pattison could not continue to buy up new companies with Neon shares because they were running out. He took the conventional route out of the squeeze. He stated at the next shareholders' meeting, June 24, that he would seek authorization to issue more shares.

The size of Pattison's appetite for new companies could be measured by the increase in the number of shares he proposed. From the existing 1.8 million outstanding shares, he pushed for an increase to seven million.

Seldom had British Columbia seen corporate action

as fast-paced as events down at Neon. A new company practically every month. Plans for many more "aggressive" takeovers. Vertical integration. Millions of new shares. Yet few asked why this was happening or who, besides Pattison, was behind it. The daily press, explicitly charged with digging for those answers, did a fair job of reporting on Neon's public reports, but seldom went deeper.

One question begged an answer so desperately that Pattison answered it before anyone asked: "I'm fronting for no one," he proclaimed, the first time he revealed the existence of his U.S. backers. He further insisted that the U.S. money which enabled him to wrest control of Neon Products was "friendly money," implying that Englehard and Burnham were disinterested investors looking only for a lucrative opportunity. Yet the two companies took more than a passing interest in Neon's day to day operations.

For example, both Dingman and Hoguet flew 4,000 kilometres from New York to be present at the June 24 shareholders' meeting. (Pattison estimated that he and the Americans together owned about 650,000 shares. On a separate occasion he said that only 2 per cent of the company shares belonged to him personally. Given this, the U.S. holdings would have represented about 34 per cent of Neon shares at that time.)

About 30 shareholders attended the June 24 meeting. Together they represented about 1.26 million sharevotes. Of those, the Americans held more than half the votes. The outcome of the meeting, therefore, was a foregone conclusion—the shareholders approved an increase in the number of shares to seven million. Neon's acquisitions could continue.

The summer of 1968 produced four more prospective members of the Neon conglomerate: Imbrex Ltd., the country's largest carpet and floor covering wholesaler; Reimer Express Lines, a Winnipeg-based trucking firm; the Haughton Group of companies (a deal that subsequently fell through); and Associated Helicopters of Edmonton.

Neon's spectacular track record prompted an increasingly familiar question: How long can Pattison's success story continue? Answers did not come easily. All Pattison and his associates would say is that they would release details about future acquisitions at the company's annual meeting in August. And of the acquisitions themselves—how the company was purchased, what kind of behind-the-scenes haggling was necessary—Pattison said nothing, except on one occasion.

It was in the Supreme Court of Ontario in 1973, during a trial involving Pattison's takeover of Imbrex, although neither Pattison nor Neon were on trial.* The testimony given in court reveals glimpses of Pattison's backroom dealings, and his insistence on absolute secrecy.

The Imbrex takeover five years earlier began with a letter, dated February 29, 1968, from Pemberton Securities of Vancouver to R.G. Godbout, president of Imbrex of Pointe Claire, Quebec. The letter, on Pemberton letterhead and signed by John G. Chaston, vice president, underwriting, politely asked the Imbrex president under which circumstances "all of the shares of your company might be for sale."

"This is a serious inquiry," wrote Chaston, "and there is no question about the financial capacity of our client." But Godbout was on the defensive. "Imbrex," he wrote back, "has never considered...selling outright its shares. Nevertheless I feel that this must be reported to the board...", but before doing so Godbout wanted to know who the buyer was.

Chaston tried to hedge, replying on March 28 that the interested party was a well-established Canadian corporation interested in acquiring "aggressively managed growth situations oriented towards the consumer market." The hint was broad enough for anyone following

---

*Arthur Green, a major Imbrex shareholder, sued several Imbrex directors for $1 million. He alleged that they withheld information about the pending takeover, which, if he had known, would have more than doubled his profit when he sold his 80,000 shares.

the financial news of the day. Godbout immediately told his board of directors that Neon Products was after Imbrex.

Pattison said during the 1973 trial that he never authorized Pemberton to write to Imbrex. Herein lies one clue to the takeover business.

According to Pattison, Pemberton acted alone, writing to Imbrex in the hope that it would earn a finder's fee if Pattison went on to buy the company. Pemberton and Neon had collaborated in a similar fashion on previous takeovers. William Thomson, the Pemberton president who was on the Neon board at the time, knew very well about Neon's plans to buy up profitable companies, and must have alerted his staff to be on the lookout. So convoluted are the wheels within wheels in the business world that it was unnecessary for Pattison to say a word directly to anyone at Pemberton about Imbrex. And the guidelines—to say nothing of the laws—are so vague and elastic in business' upper reaches that it would be hard to identify just what would constitute relevant communication between Pattison and Thomson (a smile, a frown, a wink?).

It was not until early April that the man who wrote the letter, Chaston, called Pattison and arranged a meeting with Godbout. They met in Vancouver, where Pattison outlined Neon's plans for amalgamations and growth. He made no offer to buy Imbrex.

Then on April 29, when Pattison was in Montreal, he called Godbout and invited him to dinner at his hotel. Godbout and another Imbrex executive, Ted Alexander, met Pattison at the hotel bar, then went to the dining room. The talk was light, with no mention of Imbrex. After dinner Pattison invited them up to his room. "What do you think the Imbrex stock is worth?" Pattison soon got around to asking Godbout. Godbout said he wasn't sure. Pattison said he thought it was worth about $10 a share.

Godbout and Alexander were stunned. Imbrex shares were trading at only $4 to $5 on the market at the time. What they didn't know was that Pattison's financial people had worked out a formula for calculating the actual worth of a company, which had little to do with the market value of shares.

The Imbrex men contained their surprise long enough to formulate a reply. The $10 offer, they said, was too low to even bother taking it to the board of directors. "The only price I would think of reporting to the board was $12.50 a share," said Godbout, continuing the bluff.

Pattison asked permission to send his bookkeeping experts to Imprex to study their records, and the request was granted. Said Pattison, "If the arithmetic makes sense, and I think it will, I would like to make an offer before the next meeting of Imbrex directors," to be held on May 16, 1968. Before they parted, Pattison warned the two men to treat the matter with the utmost secrecy.

Godbout raced back to Imbrex headquarters with the news. He was sure Neon was serious, even though he hadn't seen their books and knew nothing about the company except what Pattison had told him. Clearly, Godbout was awed by Pattison's salesmanship, and the prospect of an offer even approaching $12.50 a share thrilled him. In a memo to the board of directors, Godbout barely contained his glee as he outlined Imbrex' potential new owner: "Neon is building a conglomerate [and] it has substantial U.S. backing and a photostat of certain documentation will show you that its U.S. partners and directors are indeed substantial people with substantial firms."

Imbrex directors, however, were not so easily swayed.

As it happened, Imbrex had two directors in Vancouver. Brothers Charles and Trevor Jordan-Knox, chairman and president respectively of Jordan Rugs Ltd., had heard the clubhouse talk about Pattison. Charles told another Imbrex director that Pattison was "not interested in management, he is a promoter...he has never run anything...he [drives] a Chevrolet and [owns] a radio station that is going downhill..." He ended the conversation with the warning, "Watch out."

Other directors echoed the sentiment. One told

Godbout, "You are wasting your time talking to [Pattison]. Neon is only buying companies with paper money [Neon stock] which could be inflated. Everyone is getting an offer."

Pattison got wind of the criticism and invited Godbout to fly with him to New York. There he introduced the Imbrex chief to Michael Dingman. Pattison admitted later that there was no reason for the trip other than to sell Godbout on the idea of selling Imbrex to Neon and using Dingman to impress him.

The tactic worked. Godbout returned to Montreal more interested than ever in dealing with Pattison, and again his directors tried to dissuade him. One reminded him about the Mississippi Bubble (a famous eighteenth century investment disaster) and warned him that he would get only paper stock in exchange for good Imbrex shares.

The angry directors had another merger in mind. They wanted Godbout to agree to merge with Harding Carpets. Imbrex already functioned as a franchised wholesaler of the brand-name carpets; a merger would have made the franchise permanent. But if Imbrex merged with Neon, there was a danger of Harding cancelling its franchise with Imbrex.

With major divisions of opinion inside Imbrex, Pattison was in no position to offer to buy the company. He had to be certain the directors would recommend the deal to other shareholders. To make the offer and have it refused would discredit Neon in financial circles.

No one at Imbrex heard from Pattison for some time. On May 10, he called Alexander and said he wouldn't be able to make an offer before the May 16 meeting of Imbrex directors, and that he was getting cold feet because Imbrex was neither a manufacturer nor consumer of its products—floor coverings. (Pattison's manoeuvre might have been a ploy to convince Imbrex to accept a lower offer.)

The May 16 meeting went ahead with items number 12 and 13 on the agenda reading "Neon" and "Harding Carpets." The bulk of the discussion—about four hours worth—was about Harding Carpets. The unanimous decision was that Imbrex should forget Neon and merge with Harding. A meeting between Godbout and Harding was set for early the following month.

Harding and Godbout met on June 9 in Toronto. Unknown to Harding, Godbout's intention was to take over the larger Harding company through a complicated share-swap deal, similar to the one Pattison had proposed to take over Imbrex. But Harding realized what Godbout was up to and snapped, "I will not add one share to the common stock"—a reference to Imbrex-Harding stock proposed by Godbout—and walked out.

Now Godbout and Harding were in trouble. In trying to gain control of Harding, Godbout had revealed confidential information about the offer from Neon. And if Harding were to go so far as to cancel its franchise, Imbrex would have trouble getting adequate supplies of flooring material. Further, Godbout knew that Harding would be incensed about the possibility of Imbrex selling out to Neon, a company with no experience in the floor covering business. It was only a matter of time until Harding would cancel the franchise. And all because Godbout had bargained in bad faith with Harding, pretending to talk about a merger when really he intended a takeover.

Godbout was frantic. If word got out that Imbrex' contract with Harding was about to be cancelled, Imbrex stock would plunge. As well, Pattison would want nothing to do with the company.

Of course, Pattison knew the Harding contract could be cancelled at three months' notice, but he had no reason to believe it would be. What he did not know was that his acquisition of Imbrex would give Harding a reason to cancel.

The date was June 10. In despair, Godbout telephoned Jim Pattison in Vancouver and offered to sell all Imbrex shares for $12.50 each. Pattison said he would think about it. An hour later he called back and offered to buy them for $12, payable in Neon shares at that day's market price. Godbout, without authority from anyone, agreed.

He furiously dialed the numbers of the other Imbrex directors. "We have no alternative but to go with it," he told each one, imploring them to agree. The Jordan-Knox brothers in Vancouver sent word back to him by telegram, agreeing to sell their Imbrex shares. So did all the others. Not a word was mentioned about the previous objections to Pattison's promoter image, his Chevrolet or his lacklustre radio station.

Relieved, Godbout notified the three Canadian stock exchanges, recommending to all Imbrex shareholders that they accept the Neon offer. Pattison's terms were that at least 90 per cent of the Imbrex shares had to be offered, with a deadline of September 16.

On September 18, Pattison announced that 96 per cent of the Imbrex shares had been sold to Neon. It was one of the largest responses to a share offering in memory. At that moment, the only complaint came from Arthur Green, an Imbrex shareholder who sold his 80,000 shares for about $6 each just before he heard of Pattison's offer. He threatened to sue Imbrex directors for keeping news of the takeover from him.

Imbrex formally handed over control to Neon on September 25, 1968. Pattison was overjoyed. Neon was now the owner of the country's largest distributor of carpets and floor coverings. Imbrex' annual sales of $28 million would put Neon's total annual sales "over the $100 million mark," boasted Pattison to shareholders at a September 30 meeting.

Pattison had every reason to believe that the carpet firm would continue to do well, and he turned his attention to future acquisitions. He dazzled shareholders with statistics. Neon sales in 1968, he said, were twelve times greater than the previous year's, and profits increased six-fold to $3.25 million.

What he didn't tell the shareholders was that all the increased profits would be diverted into a special fund to buy more companies in the transit, consumer and service industries. None would end up in dividend cheques.

But Pattison did not dwell on such matters. The chief

executive talked about "economic activity...picking up," and how Neon Products was going to get a big slice of the estimated $40 billion consumers would spend the next year. "Neon is attempting to squarely position itself right in the centre of the rapidly growing consumer-oriented economy," he chirped, skipping over split infinitives as he boldly predicted nothing short of a revolutionary change in the Canadian economy. "Leading...economists," he said, without naming them, "predict Canada is moving away from its dependence on the export of raw materials [toward] an economy that stresses marketing."

If Canada was on the verge of reversing its centuries-old dependence on export of raw materials, surprisingly few people knew about it. Nowhere was the prediction more inaccurate than in Pattison's home province. It has been calculated that 95 per cent of the companies in British Columbia depend directly or indirectly on exports for their livelihood.

It was true that consumer spending was picking up, but not for the reasons Pattison cited. B.C.'s unemployment rate had dropped below 5 per cent, personal income rose 10.5 per cent, as did retail sales, and housing starts were up 22 per cent to 32,000 units.

Behind the upswing was a renewed demand for B.C.'s raw materials: lumber, minerals, coal and natural gas. Hundreds of millions of dollars were spent on railways, gas pipelines, forestry projects and the new Robert's Bank super-port for exporting Kootenay coal to the giant steel mills of Japan.

Pattison avoided any mention of the wood-hewing, water-drawing nature of the economy as he lifted his sights to that 10 per cent increase in consumer spending. He subscribed to the then-popular notion that technological advances would free people from dirty manual work, giving them better paying jobs and more leisure time to spend their money. His quest was to capture as much of that surplus cash as he could.

Exactly how much he planned to capture was revealed one month later at a speech given by Pattison to the

Toronto Financial Analysts Society. He predicted that in 1969, Neon sales would hit $250 million, two and a half times the 1968 figures.

Pattison was a hit on the speakers' circuit. His was an authentic success story, the kind investment counsellors love to hear. It revitalizes their faith in the system and gives them something to sell to their customers. Soon, financial societies in Winnipeg, Montreal, Boston, Dallas and Los Angeles were clamoring to hear this whiz kid of Canadian conglomerates.

The speeches were more than a sideshow for Pattison. He needed a constant influx of investment dollars to maintain his pace of acquisitions, and the speeches were really sales pitches for Neon. Between the talks he negotiated a deal through Burnham and Company to raise $20 million (U.S.) for Neon. Then he rushed back to Canada and before Christmas announced three more deals.

In November it was Universport, a Quebec sporting goods company. Pattison's confidence in Imbrex at the time is indicated by his willingness to let Imbrex, and not Neon, purchase the company.

In mid-December Neon exchanged nearly 200,000 shares for the Travelaire Trailer manufacturing company. The firm's Woodstock, Ontario, and Red Deer, Alberta, plants produced 2,500 truck and camper trailers a year.

One week later Pattison proudly proclaimed the conglomerate's entry into the "communications field" with the purchase of Provincial News Company of Edmonton. The $1.3 million purchase gave Neon a company which had a sterling growth record over its half-century in the magazine distribution business. Provincial News had mushroomed from a single outlet (the still-popular Mike's News Stand in downtown Edmonton) to become the exclusive distributor of major magazines and books in northern Saskatchewan, northern Alberta, northern B.C., and all of the Yukon and Northwest Territories. In the emerging web of conglomerates within conglomerates, Provincial News was purchased not by Neon but by another Alberta member of the group, ANC (Acme Novelty).

Other deals were pending, including a $4 million takeover of Associated Helicopters of Edmonton, awaiting approval from the federal regulatory authorities.

Pattison's acquisition hunger was not sated, but his appetite was stretching the budget of the conglomerate to the limit. In the new year he would have to negotiate yet more loans. Pattison also recognized that Neon had grown to the point where he would have to spend more time building the empire and less time managing it. Another task for the new year would be finding a manager with experience in running a conglomerate. Finally, the name of the conglomerate would have to go; "Neon Products" no longer captured the essence of Pattison's brainchild.

There was no way that the Neon Products board of directors could have been prepared for their new year's greeting from Harding Carpets. On January 1, 1969, the main supplier of Imbrex' stock announced it was cancelling the franchise in three months. Shocked, Pattison flung himself into negotiations with Harding and came out with a four-month extension to July 1, but no more.

The blow to Imbrex was every bit as serious as Godbout had feared. No other manufacturer could immediately replace the supplies withdrawn by Harding. Pattison turned to another big manufacturer, New York-based Bigelow-Sandford, but their inventories were already sewn up. Pattison's only option to keep the company alive was to build a new carpet manufacturing plant in Canada. Meanwhile Imbrex sales would plummet, and in the circumstances, Pattison stood no chance of selling Imbrex without taking a significant loss.

Not every player in the Imbrex inter-corporate drama fared so poorly. Jordon Rugs' co-managers Trevor and Charles Jordan-Knox sold 33,000 Imbrex shares for prices ranging from $12.50 to $16.25 in one week the preceding summer, when Neon's takeover drove the share price to a peak. They pocketed $253,762.50.

Imbrex president Roland Godbout transferred ownership of his 10,000 shares to his wife, Yvonne, who through a complex set of purchases, trades and sales walked away with a profit of $83,092.50 (minus brokerage fees) by the time she sold all the shares in January 1969.

Much of this information was entered as evidence in a court action initiated by Arthur B. Green, the Ontario businessman who sold 80,000 shares of Imbrex stock for $6 each the week before Pattison offered $12 for every share. He claimed that Imbrex directors knew about the Pattison offer but kept the information from him. The judge disagreed, and Green's lawsuit was dismissed for lack of evidence of any conspiracy to cheat him. The court ruled that he could blame no one but himself for selling his Imbrex shares for $6 when, had he waited a couple of weeks, he could have sold them for double that figure. Still, Green walked away with $470,000 in exchange for his $80,000 shares. (Riches to rags stories seem even less common than the other way around.)

The last word on the Imbrex affair went to the judge who heard the entire case. Reflecting on the role of Pattison, he noted with judicial reserve that "The purchase of that company [Imbrex] turned out to be a very poor venture for Neon."

Imbrex may have been Pattison's first major setback but he never missed a beat as he criss-crossed the continent in search of further deals. By the third week in January he signed a final agreement for the Edmonton helicopter firm. Then he dashed to New York to arrange $15 million worth of loans, and back to Toronto to sew up another $20 million loan package. Combined with the previous year's $20 million (U.S.) loan, Pattison had access to $57.7 million (Canadian) to carry out future acquisitions—a sum so vast that had he placed it in a savings account it would have earned $15,616 a day in interest.

Of course, the money belonged to investors and had to be repaid eventually. But while Pattison and his directors had their hands on it they planned to make it profitable.

Seven more months and seven more companies. The Lear jet's turbo-fans barely stopped revolving between flights. In that short time Pattison bought three more trailer or mobile home manufacturers (United Trailer Company of Calgary; Otto Manufacturing Enterprises of Edmonton; and Manitoba-based Triple E Manufacturing).

He enlarged his trucking fleet to cover most of Canada with the purchase of Hunt Transportation of Vancouver. He bought TVS Group of Vancouver, which distributed Sony closed-circuit television equipment. And as he entered into a joint venture with Bigelow-Sandford to build a carpet manufacturing plant in Canada, he negotiated with the federal government to help pay for the factory.

Along the way, Neon Products' identity problem grew worse. In business circles, where the identity of a product is sometimes as important as the product itself, there was unease over a neon sign company getting involved in everything from helicopters to bingo supplies. In backroom meetings, Pattison and his advisers devised a new corporate identity and trotted it out for "shareholder approval." (The suspense was diminished since Pattison and his backers had more than half the votes at the meeting.) The new name was to be "Neonex International," Neonex being a contraction of "Neon" and "expansion." The reasons behind the new corporate name were easy enough to discern and signalled a future of more of the same. Neonex International was born at the shareholders' meeting of March 12, 1969, one of the largest corporate infants in Canadian business history. Only the communications and graphics division retained the old name, Neon Products.

The combination of Pattison's boosterism, a jazzy new name and Neonex' apparently rocketing sales attracted the attention of many small investors across Canada and some in the U.S. Their demand for Neonex shares drove the price to an all-time high of more than $45. For most of 1969 it floated above the $30 mark.

Because of the high price, Neonex shareholders approved a one-for-one stock split, a common business procedure whereby the company issues one additional share for every share outstanding. The new or "split" shares have exactly half the value of the old ones. A shareholder with 100 shares, each worth $40, would be issued another 100; each of the 200 shares is then worth $20. There is no gain in total worth, but the company benefits from a lower share price. Since shares are usually sold in blocks of 100 each, a lower price makes share blocks accessible to more investors. Stock-splitting also increases the likelihood that share values will rise.

With the name change and a stock split out of the way, Pattison turned his attention to management. He may have been able to parlay an initial $4 million investment into a $150 million a year empire, but he had realized that actually running the new smorgasbord of companies was a different matter.

Pattison scouted around for someone with experience in managing a conglomerate like Neonex, one which owned 100 per cent of the subsidiaries and was run by a small, tight-knit group at head office. There weren't many. Professional managers at giant conglomerates like Canadian Pacific and Brascan would hardly stoop to work for upstart Neonex. Neither would executives from those two eastern giants, Argus and Power Corporations.

Whoever was to fill the post had to have first-hand experience operating a vertically integrated conglomerate. As Pattison told countless financial wizards in speeches delivered across the continent, he wanted all of his companies to interlock with each other. His trucklines, for example, would carry his carpets to be installed in his motor homes. The parent company, Neonex, would pocket profits each step of the way.

Ironically, Pattison, whose empire was ever-expanding, found his new manager not three miles from

Neonex' headquarters. Genstar, a mega-corporation which was one of the leading practitioners of vertical integration, was parent to BACM Development of Winnipeg (itself a conglomerate of construction and building supplies firms formerly called British American Construction Materials). Pattison lured away BACM's executive vice president, Ross J. Turner, to manage the Neonex empire.

The six-foot-four Turner, described by business writers as "ruggedly handsome," joined BACM in 1962 when its annual sales were $16 million. When he left seven years later sales topped $100 million. Turner was Pattison's kind of guy.

The former accountant brought to Neonex the expertise that had helped turn the BACM-Genstar connection into a system of vertical integration second to none in Canada.

Genstar's housing division provides an outstanding example of vertical integration at work. Vancouver architect Donald Gutstein outlines the process in *Vancouver Ltd.* Wherever Genstar built a new housing subdivision, the land was bought and assembled by BACM. Standard General Construction, also owned by Genstar, was hired to install sewers, sidewalks, water mains, streets, etc. Access roads to the subdivision were built by BACM using Genstar's Ocean Cement ready-mix concrete and asphalt, and Ocean Construction's cement pipe.

Once the land was assembled and serviced, BACM sold the lots to builders or its own home building company, Engineered Homes. That company, in turn, bought building supplies including lumber, cabinets and windows from other Genstar subsidiaries. After the frame and windows were up, Truroc Gypsum Supplies, owned by you-know-who, installed drywall.

The proud new owners of their Genstar-built home received one of their first telephone calls from Genstar Chemical Ltd., offering them a deal on "Nutrite" brand lawn fertilizer for their new yard.

Ross Turner had no regrets about the change of employers. "I left one exciting company to join another exciting company," he bubbled. Before he had a chance to warm the seat of his presidential chair at Neonex, Pattison dispatched him on a series of pep talks to financial analysts.

Apparently Neonex still had an image problem. One of Turner's tasks was to fix it. Some investors pondered the hodge-podge of companies and doubted whether Neonex would last. By this time conglomerates had acquired a poor reputation, especially in the U.S., where many overspent on the companies they acquired and went belly-up.

Turner assured one audience that Neonex was not a conglomerate but a "multi-divisional company." "A diversified, growth-oriented, multi-product company" were the words used to reassure another assembly of potential investors.

Beyond finding a euphemism for "conglomerate" Turner had to assure investors that the people at Neonex knew how to run the show. He let them in on some of the company's management techniques. "Our job," he said, referring to himself and other Neonex executives, "is to determine the ultimate possibilities of these companies." Once their word emerged from the inner sanctums about what each company was expected to achieve, managers were charged with accomplishing or exceeding specific goals. (The high turnover rate among managers of Pattison-owned operations demonstrates what happens to those who fail.)

Turner's speeches never dwelt on the negative, only on the rewards awaiting the successful manager. "Each company must come up to the standards Neonex sets for it...and management will be kept motivated through profit sharing..."

Turner won over a sceptical financial community, including Pemberton Securities, whose boss by now had left the Neonex board of directors. Pemberton's glowing investment review of Neonex said the "multi-divisional company" had "demonstrated [its] ability to acquire profitable companies [and] is considered to have excellent growth prospects." Noticeably absent was any mention of the Imbrex difficulties, even though Pemberton played a leading role in setting up the Imbrex purchase.

Pattison basked in the comforting praise, and as the decade ended, he prepared Neonex shareholders for greater things to come. Playing on the rising awareness of foreign domination of the Canadian economy, he donned a nationalist costume and said he had done more to counter foreign investment in two years than Walter Gordon did in twenty years of writing about it. "In order to compete with foreign controlled business giants which dominate this country in almost every major field... we need strong Canadian companies," he said. But pragmatists cannot afford consistency and even Pattison could not escape the irony of his own remarks. In speeches all over the continent he had praised American interventionists and had even privately boasted to the president of Imbrex that his U.S. backers were "substantial people with substantial firms." In public he had to walk a fine line. The delicate balancing trick is evident in his closing remark. "Most takeovers," he said, emanate from that homeland of corporate giants, "our good and friendly neighbour to the south."

The good and friendly directors on Neonex' board had been very good to Pattison. A tiny note in one of the financial statements of 1969 revealed that in April Pattison had been granted an option to "purchase a total of 40,000 company shares at $17 per share." At the time, $17 was about 10 per cent below market price, a bargain not available to other buyers. But by late summer, it was only half the market value, and sometimes less than that, as Neonex shares vaulted toward $45. The option was good for five years, the only restriction being that Pattison could not buy more than 20,000 shares in the first year.

In theory, he could almost double his money. Had he bought all 40,000 shares in the first two years he would have paid $680,000 for them. At the same time, anyone else buying that many shares would have paid at least $500,000 more than Pattison.

No one, including Pattison, would say why he was given preferential treatment. No laws, rules, guidelines or traditions require that any reason be given. Outsiders can only conclude that it was one of the perks of being the boss.

The gainful stock option rounded off a very profitable decade for Jim Pattison. In just two years Neonex had become the largest consumer services and transportation company in Canada. As the seventies approached, he embarked on the largest, costliest and riskiest takeover of his career.

6 FLOUR POWER

> [*Pattison*] *discussed his plans to take over Maple Leaf Mills with the* [*Neonex*] *board, and then he went out and did the opposite. I didn't like the way he operated.*
> —former Neonex director Charles Brazier,
>   on why he quit the Neonex board in 1971

It is widely known that Jim Pattison almost bought Maple Leaf Mills, the giant Canadian agribusiness firm, in 1970. Less widely known is the sacrifice he was prepared to make. Not only would he have put up some $20 million of shareholders' money, but he was prepared to make a deal to sell out the controlling interest in the entire Neonex conglomerate to a U.S. businessman. Neonex would have owned Maple Leaf Mills, but Pattison would have had to answer to an American boss. Never in his climb up the billion dollar ladder did Pattison come closer to meeting his Waterloo.

In the lexicon of hunters and corporate marauders, Maple Leaf Mills was big game. And in the fall of 1969, as conglomerate hunting season got underway once again, Big Jim Pattison went on safari after the elusive beast.

He had many reasons for wanting to bag the Toronto-based agriculture and food company. During the previous eighteen months, he had jetted to interviews with about 300 company executives, and knew from first-hand experience that there were very few available companies that met his stringent takeover criteria.

What is more, he frequently ran into agents of Canada's good and friendly neighbour to the south who easily elbowed him out of the way in their rush to snatch up plump Canadian companies for their corporate masters back home. Pattison was so upset by this state of affairs that he sent a telegram to Prime Minister Trudeau claiming that in a two-week period Americans had bought two companies he was planning to buy, including the snowmobile maker, Skiroule of Quebec. Pattison complained that Americans had an unfair advantage because they could borrow money to buy a company and could claim the cost of borrowing as a tax deductible expense, while Canadian companies did not have this option available to them.

Complaints aside, Neonex had done better than any other Canadian company in a comparable period. It bought sixteen firms in as many months and entered into two joint ventures, including a mobile home park project with Dawson Developments of Vancouver. (Dawson president Jack Poole—a graduate of Genstar's Engineered Homes—used his land-assembly expertise to set up the sites for mobile homes made in Pattison's factories. Together they planned to build mobile home communities in five provinces and two states.)

But for Neonex, small acquisitions no longer made economic sense. They simply didn't add enough new profit to the overall operation.

What Pattison was looking for was a large, successful, stable company, preferably about the size of the "new" Neonex. In many ways the ideal company would have the same qualities that first attracted him to Neon Products, except that it would be ten to fifteen times larger than the west coast sign firm he first laid covetous eyes on.

Maple Leaf Mills was as close as he could get to that

ideal. It was the largest flour miller in Canada, and one of the largest agribusiness corporations, with 1969 sales of $150 million (about the same as Neonex) and, more important to Pattison, its shares were selling at less than their true value. He surmised that Maple Leaf's managers were not making as much money with the company's assets as he could, though he was impressed with what the company had accomplished.

The flour milling firm had done very well over the years, though not always with clean hands. A 1948 report by the Justice Department found that Maple Leaf Mills had, since as early as 1936, conspired with three other major millers (Ogilvie, Robin Hood and Quaker Oats) to control and fix prices for the sale of flour, rolled oats, millfeeds and coarse grains. (The Mackenzie King government refused to prosecute.)

Another of Maple Leaf's assets was its reputation, enhanced by its name, as a solid Canadian company. Its roots lay in the early part of the century when it began milling flour, but it was not until 1964, ironically under the part-ownership of a Chicago grain merchant, that Maple Leaf expanded rapidly into related industries. The conglomerate that emerged within the next five years would be familiar to any student of vertical integration: a loaf of McGavin's Toastmaster bread baked by the consumer foods division used flour from the milling division which bought the grain from the elevator division; oil in baked goods came from the oils division...and so on. This was Jim Pattison's kind of company.

The only problem was that the bulk of Maple Leaf Mills shares were held by two men and their companies. To buy out Maple Leaf, Pattison would have to make the two owners an offer they wouldn't refuse. Identifying the owners and their other holdings was relatively simple, because Maple Leaf was publicly traded and had to disclose who owned it (see Table 6-1).

In order to acquire a Canadian company, it is often necessary to leave the country. So it was with Maple Leaf, which was effectively controlled by the Chicago-

TABLE 6.1
OWNERSHIP OF MAPLE LEAF MILLS LTD.
DECEMBER 1, 1969

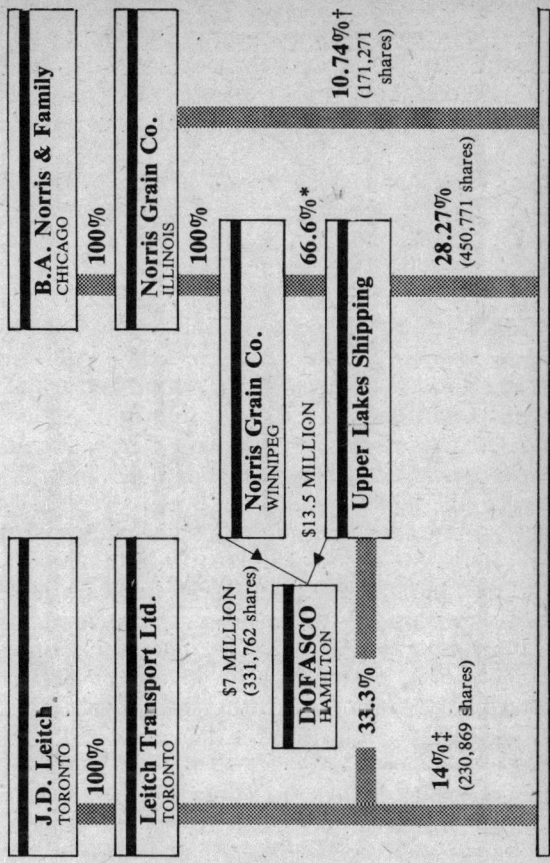

*235,728 preferred shares, 117,862 common

†Leitch, Upper Lakes and Norris owned a total of 52.5% of Maple Leaf. It was these shares that Pattison went after, plus 14% of the MLM shares on the open market.

‡balance of MLM shares are owned by individual shareholders.

TABLE 6.2
AFTER THE NORRIS AGREEMENT

- B.A. Norris & Family, CHICAGO — 100% → Norris Grain Co., ILLINOIS
- Norris Grain Co. — 10.74% → Maple Leaf Mills Ltd.
- Norris Grain Co. — 28% → NEONEX
- NEONEX — 100% → Norris Grain Co.
- NEONEX — 14.15% → Maple Leaf Mills Ltd.
- NEONEX — $7 MILLION → DOFASCO, HAMILTON
- Norris Grain Co. — 66.6% → Upper Lakes Shipping
- Upper Lakes Shipping — 13.5 MILLION → DOFASCO
- Upper Lakes Shipping — 28.27% → Maple Leaf Mills Ltd.
- Upper Lakes Shipping — 33.3% (to Maple Leaf Mills Ltd.)
- J.D. Leitch, TORONTO — 100% → Leitch Transport Ltd., TORONTO
- Leitch Transport Ltd. — 14% → Maple Leaf Mills Ltd.

TABLE 6.3

AFTER THE LEITCH AGREEMENT
(assuming closing of Norris agreement)

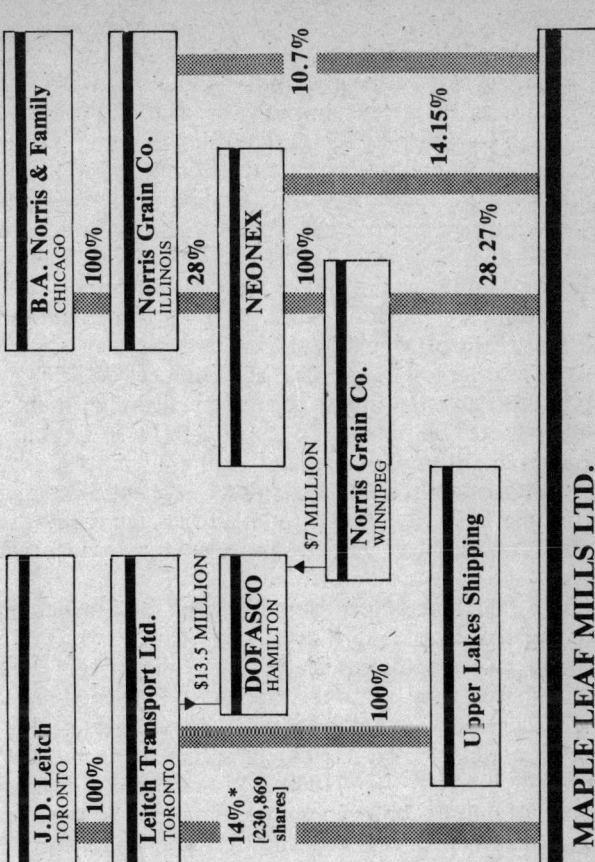

*Leitch can call on Neonex at any time to pay $30 for each share.

based Norris family.

Bruce A. Norris, the principal shareholder, was better known for his ownership of the National Hockey League's Detroit Red Wings than for the family's main sources of income, Norris Grain Company of Illinois and its subsidiary, Norris Grain Company of Winnipeg. The Winnipeg company in turn owned two-thirds of Upper Lakes Shipping. And Upper Lakes owned 28 per cent of Maple Leaf Mills. Besides this stepping-stone ownership, Norris Grain of Illinois directly held another 10.5 per cent of Maple Leaf.

The next largest Maple Leaf shareholder was its chairman (and, as these things go, he was also chairman of Upper Lakes Shipping), John Daniel (Jack) Leitch, a Toronto multi-millionaire and secure member of the Canadian establishment. Leitch's 14 per cent ownership of Maple Leaf gave him a toe-hold in a company that bought and milled plenty of grain, some of which was carried on his ships and stored in his elevators.

Both Leitch and Norris had inherited their ownership of Upper Lakes and Maple Leaf Mills from their fathers, who had been friends. When the fathers died, their shares were naturally transferred to their sons; their friendship was not so easily passed along. Jack Leitch and Bruce Norris barely spoke to each other, especially after the late 1960s. At that time it became apparent that Leitch, who was as committed to the shipping business as his well-known father, Gordon C. Leitch, was angry that Norris cared more about shots on goal than ships at sea. There was foundation to Leitch's anger since it was Norris who controlled Upper Lakes, with two-thirds of the shares. Leitch, who owned the other third, was the manager of the company. On at least one occasion Norris reminded Leitch that "you keep this job only at my pleasure."

Leitch, of course, knew it was true, and that he was helpless to change the circumstances unless Norris voluntarily sold his interest in Upper Lakes. So bad were the feelings between the two men that they did not even have a shareholder's agreement—a common document signed by two people or groups who control an entire company—which normally gives each party first refusal if the other decides to sell.

Although Leitch was under Norris' thumb at Upper Lakes, elsewhere in the Canadian establishment he wielded a great deal of power. What distinguished Leitch from dozens of other chairmen and thousands of other company directors was the way he was able to influence affairs far beyond the confines of his companies. Chronicler of establishmentarians, Peter C. Newman, lumped Leitch in with a handful of the most influential chairmen and presidents in a group he called "The Corporate Men."

In that elite group, Leitch rubbed shoulders with powerhouses like Argus' Conrad Black and Galen Weston of the bakery empire. A glance at Leitch's corporate directorships illustrates the scope of his wealth: besides chairing the boards of Maple Leaf, Upper Lakes Shipping and Leitch Transport Ltd., he sat on the boards of Massey-Ferguson, Canada Life, Dominion Foundries and Steel (Dofasco) and, coincidentally, the same bank that Pattison dealt with, the Canadian Imperial Bank of Commerce.

The intricacies of the attempted Maple Leaf takeover make Pattison's assault on Neon Products look like a stroll through a supermarket. Not that Pattison went through these corporate gymnastics just for the exercise. A circuitous takeover route for Maple Leaf was chosen, in part, to enable the Norris family to sell off their substantial holdings without having to endure the bother of paying tax on their profits.

The route was also chosen because Neonex simply lacked the profits needed to buy a company the size of Maple Leaf. The estimated cost of the takeover ranged from $20 to $34 million. Neonex' total profit that year was only $3 million.

On December 16, 1969, Pattison met with Bruce Norris in Chicago. In hurried negotiations, they and their respective lawyers hammered out two agreements.

The first, the "principal Norris agreement," committed Norris to sell his grain company in Winnipeg to Neonex for 2.55 million shares of Neonex stock. The market value of the stock at the time was about $25 million. Once this deal went through, Neonex would own Norris Grain Company of Winnipeg, plus the company's two-thirds share of Upper Lakes Shipping, plus Upper Lakes' 28 per cent of Maple Leaf Mills. At the same time, the price paid by Neonex, more than 27 per cent of its shares, would make Norris the single largest shareholder. Pattison later testified in court that Norris would have been, in fact, Pattison's boss had the deal gone through. Pattison, therefore, was entering into much more than a one-time deal. He was entering into a long-term partnership in which he would become the junior partner.

The second agreement with Norris, called the "Norris Option Agreement," gave Neonex the option to buy 171,271 shares in Maple Leaf (the block owned directly by Norris Grain), for a hefty $4.3 million cash. Part of the agreement stipulated that Pattison must put up a "good faith" down payment of $856,355.

A rough draft of the agreement was signed before lunch. Norris immediately telephoned Jack Leitch in Toronto and said he wanted to set up an urgent meeting that day. He refused to disclose the reason. As minority shareholder, Leitch had little choice but to agree. He soon found out what was in the works.

Norris climbed aboard Pattison's jet and in a few hours they walked into Leitch's office. Norris introduced Pattison to Leitch as the president of Neonex. Leitch had never heard of Pattison. Then Norris dropped the bombshell. Neonex, he said, had just bought out his two-thirds interest in Upper Lakes Shipping along with the underlying security of Maple Leaf shares.

Leitch was dumbfounded. An obscure western company was to become a controlling shareholder of both corporations chaired by Leitch, Upper Lakes and Maple Leaf Mills. And Norris was to be Neonex' largest shareholder.

Leitch quickly surmised why Norris was so eager to go through with this deal. Rather than give in to Leitch's vain hope and sell him all of Upper Lakes, Norris had set a course to oust Leitch and replace him with Pattison.

As Leitch anticipated, Norris insisted that Pattison make the same offer to Leitch as he had to Norris, namely, that he invite Leitch to sell his one-third interest in Upper Lakes in exchange for Neonex shares.

Leitch quickly rejected the offer. He explained that he did not want to get out of the shipping business, and in any event, he had no interest in the Neonex shares.

When the three men were unable to come to an agreement, the battle lines were drawn, or rather redrawn, in the same way they had been before the meeting began. Pattison and Norris were on one side of the bargaining table, Leitch on the other.

Pattison and Norris were disappointed at Leitch's refusal to sell, but still they were confident of getting their hands on more than half of the Maple Leaf shares. They knew that there was only one other place to buy Maple Leaf shares, and that was the stock market.

Before going to bed that night, Pattison telephoned Toronto and Vancouver newspapers with a press release saying Neonex had acquired control of both Upper Lakes and Maple Leaf. To show he meant business, Pattison even announced the appointment of three new directors to the Neonex board, Bruce Norris and two other Norris Grain officials.

The Canadian business establishment was uneasy. Some grumbled that this time the high-flying Pattison had gone too far.

The sequence of events that followed Pattison's announcement was rapid, often confusing, and difficult to follow without a scorecard. In this instance the most relevant scorecards are those which show patterns of "inter-locking directorships."

In attempting to take over Maple Leaf Mills, Neonex was tampering with some very big players. Leitch, for one, held directorships beyond those of Upper Lakes and Maple Leaf, including an all-important seat on the executive committee of the Bank of Commerce. The board of directors of Upper Lakes represented a cross-section of members of the boards of major Canadian corporations, but the one most pertinent to the Neonex deal was a Mr. H.H. Bawden, who was also a major shareholder and director of Molson's.

Bawden and the other directors of Upper Lakes were extremely loyal to Leitch. Although Norris was their "boss," they were prepared to do what they could to see Leitch continue at the helm. Their first act was to place a word in the right ear. Bawden must have acted quickly, for on Wednesday, December 17, Leitch received a call from Bud Willmot, president of Molson Industries, who expressed his interest in buying Maple Leaf. However, with Neonex apparently controlling about 38 per cent through the Norris holdings, Molson's would have to obtain, in addition to Leitch's Maple Leaf shares, the publicly traded ones, which represented about another 24 per cent of the company's outstanding shares.

Willmot decided to go after the public shares first. So did Pattison.

In Molson's, Pattison faced a head-to-head fight with one of the true giants among Canadian corporations. Molson's represented some of the oldest of Old Money in the country, a legacy traced back to its inception in 1782. In its early years Molson's built Canada's first steamboat, its first railway, its largest brewery and distillery. The company even founded its own bank and printed its own currency. In this century it broadened its scope considerably with a number of profitable takeovers. Its 1970 revenues were more than $700 million. It was this Goliath that aimed its firepower at Neonex, barely four years old.

In contrast to Pattison, the president of Molson's was the picture of establishment respectability. D.G. (Bud) Willmot had been so successful before he joined

Molson's that the brewing firm spent an unimaginable amount of money to win him over.*

It was December 18. Pattison heard that Molson's was going to fight him for control of Maple Leaf. Molson's made an offer for all publicly held shares of Maple Leaf. For each share, Molson's was prepared to pay $5 plus one Molson's share, then worth $20.

Pattison decided not to play Molson's game. Rather than make a competing offer, he began to buy up Maple Leaf shares for cash. Neonex "lent" $6 million to Overwaitea and instructed the grocery chain to buy all available shares on the Toronto stock exchange.

Trading was hectic, and the bidding war between Molson's and Neonex forced the price of Maple Leaf shares from $18 to $30 in a few hours. When it was over, Neonex had bought 14 per cent, Molson's only 10 per cent.

Business writer Alexander Ross spent that feverish day in Pattison's Toronto hotel room, ostensibly researching a story about the Maple Leaf Mills takeover but, as he later boasted, he was "rooting all the way for Pattison." Ross compared Pattison to an unknown boxer who wins the title against all odds (the movie *Rocky* had not yet been made). "He's big and has a long reach, but he's slow and *soft*," wrote Ross about Molson's, as he cheered Jimmy on to victory. (Oddly, Ross cheered Pattison's victory as a blow against foreign ownership, when Molson's was the more "Canadian" of the two competitors.)

When Neonex came out with 14 per cent, Pattison thought he had indeed floored the champ. He calculated that with the Norris agreement giving him 38 per cent, and this purchase, he would walk away with about 52

---

*Molson's paid $74 million to buy Willmot's company, Anthes Imperial of St. Catharines (a plumbing and heating supply firm) so that Willmot would be thrown in as part of the deal. In addition they gave him a hefty salary boost and $10 million worth of Molson's stock yielding $350,000 in annual dividends. Molson's investment in Willmot has proven very profitable.

per cent of Maple Leaf.

As Pattison savoured his apparent victory, Neonex and Molson's each received a telegram from Upper Lakes Shipping. It notified them that the ULS board of directors was calling an urgent meeting to decide who should buy the 28 per cent block of Maple Leaf shares held by Upper Lakes.

The fight for control was not over. The ULS board, rallying behind Leitch and openly defying majority shareholder Norris, was not ready to hand over their block of Maple Leaf shares on a platter simply because Neonex possessed two-thirds of Upper Lakes.

If that 28 per cent block was sold to Molson's, Neonex would end up in a minority position with 24 per cent of Maple Leaf; with the Upper Lakes block added to the 10 per cent Molson had acquired through the stock exchange, the brewery would wind up with 38 per cent and effective control.

The key to control would then lie with Leitch Transport, which owned a 14 per cent block of Maple Leaf. Leitch showed every indication of being loyal to Molson's, and had every reason to be hostile to Neonex. If the sale went through as expected, Molson's would own 52 per cent of Maple Leaf, the exact amount Pattison thought he had acquired after the open-market trading.

This is one instance in which Pattison's American advisers were stumped by the vagaries of Canadian law. Under American law, a board of directors must act in accordance with the wishes of the majority shareholder, period. Canadian law, however, stipulates that the board has a responsibility to all shareholders, not just the majority. Pattison and his friends were caught off guard when the Upper Lakes board remained loyal to the minority shareholder, Leitch.

The meeting called by the board of Upper Lakes began on the afternoon of Monday, December 22, 1969. Pattison walked in with his Toronto lawyer, Robert Davies, and an American lawyer, Sam Pryor. Norris wasn't there but was represented by his lawyer, Robert

Vincent. The Upper Lakes board was present, and Leitch and his lawyer, James Lewtas, rounded out the attending members of the legal and business fraternity.

The board met all day. In private, Lewtas advised the Upper Lakes directors to sell their block of Maple Leaf shares to the highest bidder. The board agreed, and Lewtas drafted a form of offer. Copies were distributed to the lawyers representing Pattison, Norris and Molson's.

The two bidding groups repaired to separate rooms to work out last-minute refinements to their offers. When they returned, the lawyers entered the meeting room to explain their bids. Pattison waited outside.

The meeting dragged on till 11 p.m., when the board made its announcement. Neonex' bid was the higher of the two—$30.25 a share for all 450,771 shares of Maple Leaf owned by Upper Lakes. Of course, Neonex didn't have the $13.6 million needed to complete the deal but the Upper Lakes board seemed unconcerned. Although its loyalties were to Leitch and other insiders, like Willmot of Molson's, those devotions were surpassed by a more fundamental consideration, the bottom line. The board voted to accept the higher bid.

That night Pattison issued a press release. Neonex, he said, had outbid Molson's and now controlled the majority of Maple Leaf shares.

But the next morning, as Lewtas read over the Neonex bid, he spotted a clause that was not in accord with the offer. There, in fine print, was a stipulation that the Neonex offer required approval by the majority shareholder in Upper Lakes. Thus, the bid would not go through unless Bruce Norris approved it. Lewtas hastily contacted Norris in Chicago. Norris was unequivocal—no, he would never approve the offer. Lewtas was stunned. He knew that Pattison would not have included the clause unless he could count on Norris' support. But Pattison must have known that Norris would reject the bid. Why submit the bid at all? Confused, Lewtas called the Upper Lakes board urging that another meeting be convened. As the meeting got under way, Pattison and his lawyers, Davies and Pryor, sat in an outer room awaiting the outcome. At one point Lewtas left the meeting for a drink of water. Pattison moved in. Taking Lewtas by the elbow, he suggested another way around the problem. He asked Lewtas for a private meeting with Leitch.

When Pattison told his lawyers what he had arranged, Davies objected. He did not want Pattison to attend the meeting alone. Pattison ignored the advice.

In the private meeting with Leitch, attended also by Lewtas, Pattison got right to the point. He proposed that Neonex sell Upper Lakes Shipping to Leitch (he was referring to the two-thirds of Upper Lakes that Neonex would own once the deal with Norris went through). This marked the beginning of the "Leitch agreement," which will be best understood after a brief look at Pattison's unorthodox bidding techniques.

It was not until this whole matter came up in court some years later that the full story behind the Neonex bid came out. When Pattison submitted the $30.25 bid for the Maple Leaf shares held by Upper Lakes, he knew it would not be accepted. It was a tactic he'd cooked up with his lawyers and Norris. Their objective was to get Molson's out of the bidding and to buy time for private negotiations with Leitch. As Pattison said later in court testimony, "I knew before the lawyers left for the Upper Lakes meeting—I knew it [the bid] was not to be accepted."

It was clear that Pattison was orchestrating a scam intended only to push Molson's out of the race, not to win it himself, at least not at that time.

The mastermind behind this strategy was not Pattison or his Toronto lawyer, Davies, but Sam Pryor, a New York corporate lawyer who had worked on some of the largest takeover deals in the United States. Pattison's new friends at Englehard had referred Pryor to Neonex earlier in 1969 because of his expertise in takeovers.

In court, where the judge attempted to dissect the complex deals surrounding the attempted Maple Leaf takeover, Pryor admitted that Norris and Neonex were acting as one in the deal—in other words, that Neonex knew before making the offer that Norris would turn it down. He further testified that the sole object of the phony bid was to preclude Upper Lakes from selling to anyone other than Neonex.

Pryor also knew on the evening of December 22, when Leitch accepted the Neonex bid, that neither Leitch nor his lawyers had spotted the "catch" in the fine print. And when they called the next morning, after they had discovered the catch, Pryor said he was not surprised. It had all been part of his strategy to drive Molson's out of the marketplace, and buy time. When Lewtas came out of the board of directors' meeting at eleven o'clock that night and said the offer had been accepted, Pryor made no attempt to say the offer had been misunderstood. "It struck me that if the letter was misinterpreted it would give me another twelve hours," said the unrepentant Pryor later in court.

Pattison admitted later he had full knowledge of the underhanded dealings. In court the judge made only one comment on the bad faith in which the deal was conducted: "One is entitled to expect a higher standard of behaviour from lawyers." He said nothing about Pattison, for whom the lawyers were misbehaving.

Regardless of ethics, the strategy worked. Pattison and his lawyers got the time they wanted. They got rid of Molson's. And they sat down on December 23 to work out a separate deal with Leitch.

That agreement was no less complicated than any of the transactions, real or supposed, in this tale so far. The essence of the new agreement had Leitch selling the 28 per cent block of Maple Leaf shares held by Upper Lakes to Neonex—the same block that Neonex and Molson's just "bid" on. In return, Neonex would hand over to Leitch the other two-thirds of Upper Lakes, giving Leitch full control of the shipping firm for the first time. In addition, Neonex would pay Leitch a further $3 million cash. One clue as to why Leitch went through with the agreement after being tricked by Neonex is, simply, money: besides getting all of Upper

Lakes and $3 million cash, Leitch gained possession of a block of shares in Dofasco, held by Upper Lakes, worth $13.5 million. There was more.

After the first phase of the Leitch agreement was completed, Leitch could call on Neonex to buy Leitch Transport's 14 per cent block of Maple Leaf shares for $30 per share—a further $6.9 million. Not bad for a share that had been trading only days earlier for $18.

It was only two days before Christmas and by this time everyone involved in the deal was tired and anxious to get home. Three of the lawyers headed back to the States and Pattison boarded his plane for Vancouver.

As he left Toronto, his only fear was that Molson's might rebound with another offer for Maple Leaf, after they realized the ruse that had been played on them.

It didn't occur to Pattison that there might be some danger in the fact that Norris and Leitch did not have their signatures on the same agreement, even though both men were now inextricably bound in the tangle created by Neonex. All three parts of the Leitch agreement hinged on Norris coming through on the promise to deliver 100 per cent of Norris Winnipeg along with two-thirds of Upper Lakes and its block of shares in Dofasco.

Neonex lawyers had been more nervous than their boss. They convinced him to ask Norris to sign an overall agreement with Leitch but Norris refused, apparently because he wanted to avoid paying taxes related to the deal. The most Neonex could get out of Norris was a "best efforts" letter, dated December 23, 1969. Norris wrote, "I shall devote my best efforts to ensuring that Norris Grain Company Limited duly carries out and performs the transactions on its part contemplated by the agreement..." (referring to the Leitch agreement).

In all, only three short documents existed to bind the parties in this complex and expensive agreement, which involved the transfer of ownership of a fleet of ships, several massive grain elevators, Canada's largest chain of flour mills and other agribusiness assets, and millions of dollars in cash and securities.

The schedule made the agreement seem even shakier. The earliest that the Pattison and Norris agreement could close was the morning of September 30, 1970. The latest that the Leitch agreement could close was the afternoon of the same day. The Leitch agreement could not possibly close unless the Norris deal went through first, but Pattison foresaw no hitches when he met with Norris on the morning of the last day of September in 1970.

When Pattison arrived back in Vancouver he set the Neonex financial whiz kids the task of coming up with the estimated $21 million needed to complete the whole transaction. Pattison's aides spent the holidays poring over the financial documents. When they surfaced they identified three likely sources of capital: the Dofasco shares held by Norris Winnipeg, worth $7, could be sold; another $4 million could be "generated from internal sources," meaning siphoned off the already stretched earnings of the Neonex companies; and a bank loan could provide the remaining $10 million. For some reason, Neonex decided to borrow the money from a U.S. bank instead of the Commerce, even though it had established a "line of credit" earlier in 1969 with the Canadian bank totalling $20 million. Of that amount Neonex had borrowed about $10 million, leaving exactly the amount needed. Instead, Pattison flew to New York and negotiated a $10 million (U.S.) loan from Marine Midland Grace Trust Company. He planned to pay off the loan with the $10 million line of credit from the Commerce when the loan came due the following March. (Subsequent events suggest one reason for the foreign loan was the opportunity to profit from the rising U.S. dollar.)

In keeping with the accounting practices outlined in the last chapter, Neonex lent $6 million of the U.S. loan to Overwaitea so it could purchase Maple Leaf shares. Neonex charged Overwaitea, its own subsidiary, 1.5 per cent more for the money than the U.S. bank charged Neonex. (If this looks like robbing Peter to pay Paul, remember that—as far as we can tell—neither Peter nor

Paul paid income tax. Neonex did, and shuffling income and expenses is one of the standard bookkeeping practices designed to capitalize on tax loopholes and to minimize tax payments.)

Meanwhile, Molson's president Bud Willmot conceded defeat and withdrew his offer. Pattison chalked up his direct hits: through Upper Lakes Shipping he got 28 per cent of Maple Leaf; through Norris Grain of Chicago another 10.5 per cent; through purchases in the open market another 14 per cent; and now, through Leitch, a final 14 per cent, for a total of 66.5 per cent of the biggest flour milling company in Canada.

"What we've done," said Pattison as Christmas approached, "is we've doubled our size in one move."

It may have been the season of "goodwill toward men" but that did not stop Pattison from unceremoniously dumping Jack Leitch from the board of Maple Leaf. His unfestive greeting to the former chairman was cold and crisp: "[you] will not be involved in the future of the company." Then Pattison moved swiftly to install his own people. On Tuesday, December 30, he appointed himself chairman and president of Maple Leaf, replacing Jack Leitch, and he nominated Michael Dingman, Lawrence Hoguet,* Ross Turner and Harry Dunbar as directors. Five former Maple Leaf directors stayed on, including Bruce Norris.

It was a strange way to close the decade, changing the board of directors of one of Canada's major agribusiness corporations a full nine months before the ownership could officially change hands...

New year's 1970 began inauspiciously for Neonex. It was exactly one year since the conglomerate had been shaken by Harding's unilateral cancellation of the carpet franchise which plunged Imbrex into great financial trouble.

---

*Again, interlocking directorships aided U.S. control of a Canadian business. Pattison was helping U.S. interests like Norris and Englehard (through Hoguet) to gain influence in Canadian businesses without having to buy them outright.

Now, with chilling deja-vu, came another unsettling new year's message.

Among Jack Leitch's many powerful directorships was a seat on the board and executive committee of the Bank of Commerce. Over the holidays, he had taken Commerce chairman Neil McKinnon aside and complained about the gauche behaviour of Jim Pattison. No further promptings were needed. McKinnon, considered at the time to be the most powerful banker in Canada and reputed to run the Commerce like a one-man show, issued the directive that when business resumed in January, every one of Pattison's and Neonex' loans were to be "called"—in other words, they had to be repaid immediately.

Not only that, but McKinnon slapped a freeze on Neonex' line of credit, cutting off the $10 million worth of unused credit which Pattison had counted on to repay the U.S. loan. McKinnon said he was cutting off credit because Neonex had borrowed the money from another bank without first getting permission from the Commerce.

Frantically, Pattison tried to arrange a meeting with McKinnon. He even bought a relatively conservative three-piece suit and flew to Toronto. He checked into the Royal York hotel and began calling McKinnon's office to arrange an appointment. Pattison got the same runaround every day for two weeks. In between calls to McKinnon he talked to Marine Midland in New York, pleading with them to understand his plight and reschedule the loan repayment date, coming up on March 17. The bank reluctantly agreed.

McKinnon was not so accommodating. In fact, he didn't return a single one of Pattison's calls.

The bank president's sudden actions meant Neonex would have to redirect "internal cash" away from the Maple Leaf acquisition to pay off the Commerce loans. As for new loans, the staff at the Commerce bluntly told Neonex to borrow its money elsewhere.

Even worse, Pattison knew that as word of the Commerce's action seeped out, the investment community would get jittery about Neonex shares, which would then plummet in value: few people want to invest in a company that the bank won't lend money to.

As Pattison jetted back to Vancouver his elaborately constructed house of cards began to teeter. Neonex, the darling of the investment community whose shares topped $45 the previous year, was now in danger of losing its largest acquisition. At the same time, it struggled to fill the broadloom gap created by Harding's pullout last January.

Word of the calamities was slow getting out. A January 1970 analysis of Neonex by Greenshields, a Montreal investment counselling firm, painted a glowing picture of the conglomerate. It predicted Neonex would experience 20 per cent growth in 1969 and 1970 and 10 per cent per year for the following few years. They recommended investing in Neonex for "capital growth," that is, investors should hold on to shares, which would yield a fat profit in the future. Ironically one of the growth areas highlighted by the report was Imbrex. It said nothing about the loss of Harding-brand carpets, but mentioned the construction of a new carpet manufacturing plant in Quebec, a joint project by Neonex and another giant carpet maker, Bigelow-Sandford of New York. (That factory got a healthy injection of taxpayers' money from the federal government.) At the time of the Greenshields report Neonex shares traded around $10.

By the middle of April 1970 the sales and profits figures arriving on Pattison's desk confirmed his fears. For the first time since he took over Neon Products two years earlier, profits did not increase. In the first three months of 1970 they dropped to barely one-quarter as much as the same three months of the previous year. (January to March 1970: $127,000; January to March 1969: $438,000.)

In a short news release Neonex blamed the drop on "the costs incurred...in changing our new carpet suppliers." No explanation of what happened to the old suppliers was given.

Rumours popped up in financial journals. They intimated that Neonex was in trouble, not just because of Imbrex but Maple Leaf too. Pattison attempted to "clarify and correct" the reports. He revealed for the first time some details about the source of all the cash needed to buy Maple Leaf. He said $10.7 million came from "a United States bank," and admitted that the takeover had not yet taken place and could not be completed until sometime later in the year.

Throughout the spring and summer he tried to bolster the Neonex image, assuring investors, somewhat lamely, that "most of our divisions are operating on a favorable basis." But any careful reader of the financial pages could see that Neonex was in trouble. Its stock was "falling outta bed," said one analyst. From its $10 value at the beginning of 1970 it had slumped to the $3.50 range.

Regardless, Pattison tried to complete the Maple Leaf deal. On August 17, he notified Norris in writing that he wanted to close the deal on September 30. More hints of trouble. Norris balked at the date, complaining about his "heavy market losses" and saying he would rather close later. Pattison, who was backed into a corner by his agreement to close no later than September 30 with Leitch, convinced the reluctant Norris to meet on the last day of September.

Wednesday, September 30, Norris met Pattison in Toronto. As agreed, he handed over all outstanding shares in the Norris Grain Company of Winnipeg and two-thirds of the outstanding stock of Upper Lakes Shipping. But he said he would need another 60 days to come up with the $7 million worth of Dofasco shares owned by Upper Lakes, and claimed that the wording of the agreement gave him the extra time. Had it not said, "Norris shall have 60 days to comply..."?

What Pattison's and Norris' lawyers had failed to include in the contract was a specific date at which the 60-day period would begin. Pattison assumed it began 60 days before September 30. Norris, obviously, thought it began on the closing date. Both men knew that without the Dofasco shares Pattison would not be able to complete the Leitch deal.

Pattison was under no illusions about Norris' motives. Under the agreement, Norris had to acquire 27 per cent of Neonex stock, 2.55 million shares. They were a lot more attractive at $10 each than after they fell "outta bed." But there had been no provision in the contract for a rapid decline in share values. That was considered to be one of the risks investors take. From Pattison's point of view, Norris found a loophole in the 60-day clause and squeezed through it.

Pattison was livid. He said Norris knew how important the Dofasco shares were to the overall deal. Neonex had sent him a detailed description of its plans to pay for the entire Maple Leaf takeover. He said Norris knew the details of the Leitch agreement, including the latest possible closing date of September 30. He said Norris knew from personal discussions that Neonex would need the Dofasco shares to pay for Maple Leaf, and in those discussions Norris had made it clear that he understood. He said Norris had promised to carry out the entire agreement in his "best efforts" letter. But he was powerless to get the Dofasco shares before the end of the day.

Up at Leitch Transport headquarters, Jack Leitch waited for Pattison to show up. But the Neonex chairman didn't show. Leitch told reporters afterward that Leitch Transport was "fully prepared to perform all its obligations but Neonex failed to deliver the Upper Lakes shares." The chairman said this default by Neonex meant Maple Leaf lawyers would soon decide whether to sue.

Pattison, back at his hotel, telephoned prepared statements to the newspapers. He wanted to make sure his version of the day's events got out first.

Thursday, October 1, the Vancouver *Sun* ran the headline, "Neonex fails in major takeover bid," and the following day, "Pattison blames Norris firm." The *Globe and Mail* stuck to more factual headlines like, "Neonex fails to acquire shares of Maple Leaf held by

Leitch." All the stories related substantially the same details, including the accusation by Pattison that "due to the failure of the Norris Grain Co. to deliver certain securities...Neonex was unable to complete the transaction with Leitch Transport."

Clearly, Jack Leitch had won. He would have preferred that no one take over Maple Leaf, or, if a takeover was inevitable, that the new owner be a company like Molson's. As for the brewing giant, its acquisitive president Bud Willmot had gone after more lucrative prospects and said it now "had no interest in Maple Leaf."

Another group that came out ahead was the corps of lawyers who piloted the ensuing lawsuits and countersuits through thirteen years of court battles. Neonex alone ran up a legal bill in excess of $260,000. In June 1971 Pattison launched a $32 million suit against Norris for breach of contract, and Norris countersued for $2 million in specific damages and $50 million for defamation (referring to Pattison's press releases which claimed the breakdown was "Norris' fault").

Leitch, too, sued Neonex for breach of contract and Pattison's lawyers concluded that Leitch had a good chance of winning. Almost $4 million was put aside to cover what they considered to be the probable loss.

In 1975, Norris and Neonex reached an out-of-court settlement. The two agreed that Neonex would sell its 213,100 shares in Maple Leaf to Norris for $7.3 million. Neonex needed the cash and Norris wanted the shares, as he was in the process of buying up all Maple Leaf shares and taking the company private.

In March 1978 Leitch was awarded $9.3 million in damages. Neonex thought the award was too high and appealed. Leitch who thought it was too low because the double-digit inflation of the 1970s had eroded the value of the dollar, also appealed. Ultimately, Leitch settled for $4,114,934. (Leitch would have been much better off if he had not appealed. The judge agreed with his argument that inflation had been higher than 3.5 per cent per year allowed in the original settlement. The appeal court awarded Leitch an additional $500,000 to cover added inflation. At the same time, however, the appeal court reviewed the rest of the settlement and concluded Leitch had been awarded too much under several headings, and reduced the total award from $9.3 million to $4.1 million.)

The legal scraps didn't end with the lawsuits. Loyal servants of Her Majesty's Ministry of National Revenue had been observing the fray through their field glasses. When the dust cleared they moved in and poked through the debris. They scoured the documents pertaining to the labyrinthine financial deals in search of evidence that someone had evaded paying his full share of taxes. Their search was not in vain. In 1977 Neonex was hauled into federal court on four counts of tax evasion. Two of the counts related directly to the Maple Leaf affair.

The first involved the $10 million loan from Marine Midland of New York. By the time Neonex paid back the loan, the foreign exchange rate had shifted enough to give Neonex a windfall profit of $305,007. The tax collectors viewed this as taxable income and wanted their bite. The arguments on either side are complex, but it is enough to report here that the verdict of the first judge required Neonex to pay tax on the money, and that his decision was overturned by the appeal judge. No tax was ever paid.

The second count concerned legal expenses. When accountants at Neonex filed the 1970, 1971 and 1972 corporate income tax returns, they deducted the cost of legal fees connected with the Maple Leaf takeover attempt, a sum in excess of a quarter of a million dollars. Both the trial judge and the appeal judge refused to permit this deduction. Their decision was based on the technical argument that the fees in question were not "operating expenses" but "capital expenditures," having been spent in pursuit of a capital gain—Maple Leaf Mills. The appeal court judges as much as called Neonex a liar, saying the company's explanations for the deductions were "so skimpy and unsatisfactory" that the court couldn't believe they were "correct and accurate."

Jim Pattison's day in court, a rare experience for him personally, is one which is familiar to seasoned officers of major corporations. There are a number of common elements in the courtroom scenario. One is the very high-priced legal talent employed to establish the innocence of the accused. Another common thread pertains to the main players and their motives—businessmen struggling to dominate sectors of the economy, to concentrate wealth in fewer and fewer hands. This practice runs counter to the philosophy of the founding fathers of "free enterprise," but the logic of capitalist expansion has led almost inevitably to greater economic concentration and lowered competition. The oligarchic structure of major economic sectors, in which a handful of companies wield very disproportionate degrees of power, is a fact which the courts have been unable and often unwilling to challenge. Corporate justice usually amounts to little more than a slap on the wrist.

Pattison's slap was added to the painful, drawn-out Maple Leaf Mills fiasco. He decided to cut his losses and consolidate.

7 THE POLITICS OF GREED

My wife and I took our savings and bought shares in Neonex for $5 each. Now we are told we must sell them for $3... Why is this so?
—Neonex shareholder William Kolasa

It was 6:30 on a bright, mid-July morning in 1971. Half a dozen sleepy sheet metal workers stumbled toward picket line duty at Neon Products Ltd. They stopped in front of the building on noisy Clark Drive, put down their lunch boxes and shouldered picket signs, just as they had done for the previous nine weeks since the strike began.

Soon after, when managers showed up for work, one of them muttered something about replacing the whole crew with non-union workers. A picketer responded by spitting at the manager, by this time out of reach.

The manager's threat was more than hot air. On the afternoon of July 26 Neon Products issued a press release warning its striking workers that they must either accept the company's latest offer or it would shut down sheet metal operations altogether and hire non-union workers for other jobs.

The threat was obviously aimed not only at the

striking workers, but at the painters, electricians, office employees and carpenters, who respected the picket line and effectively shut down all production at the plant. Each one of them received a letter from company manager John Gough demanding they be back at work in three days or be fired.

Neon Products and Jim Pattison's other companies were clearly in trouble in the early 1970s. The conglomerate, perched as it was on the rickety foundation of rapid expansion, and very dependent on unpredictable consumer spending, was more vulnerable than most industries to adverse conditions. In 1971, the adverse conditions were mostly of Pattison's own making.

They began with the ill-planned takeover of Imbrex and culminated with the Maple Leaf Mills fiasco. His conglomerate was in danger of coming apart at the seams, and his corporate henchmen, needle and thread in hand, were ready to stitch it together, union or no union.

Neonex was hemorrhaging money and was in danger of losing plenty more if pending Maple Leaf lawsuits didn't go its way. Members of the sheet metal workers, Local 280, had no way of knowing then, but their demands for pay increases couldn't have come at a worse time.

The union, which was just emerging from a five-year contract that left them lagging far behind other workers, had only one demand, to catch up with sheet metal workers in the rest of the industry. For 42 years they had been paid the same as all other sheet metal workers in B.C., currently $6.72 an hour, and that's what they asked for. They were turned down flat.

The company put forward its offer—substantially less than the industry-wide agreement signed by 130 other firms—and two-thirds of the union members voted in a secret ballot to reject it. It was not long before this union, with one of the lowest strike records of any in B.C., set up picket lines.

As the strike dragged on into the summer, the

company issued press releases calling negotiations "fruitless" and ultimately demanding the return to work of all employees. It is worth noting that management at no time directly accused the union leaders of negotiating in bad faith. They only implied that the union had not let their members vote in a secret ballot on company offers, a charge which was false. On the other hand, Neon Products didn't deny the union's charges—published in an advertisement in the *Sun*— that management had "failed to negotiate and talk in a serious manner for nearly ten weeks," and that they had put forward "facetious offers to the other unions involved, with the hope of killing 'four birds with one stone.'"

Further, the union said it was more than coincidence that a number of smaller firms in the neon sign business had delivered identical threats to their sheet metal workers: they would shut down sheet metal operations and hire non-union staff for the other jobs unless striking employees accepted a below-industry wage offer.

Neon's intimidation was two-pronged. Besides threatening to fire the workers, the company put the Clark Drive plant up for sale. Predictably, the sight of real estate agents erecting For Sale signs upset picketers, especially those who were not on strike but respected the picket line. One group, the 35-member Office and Professional Employees Union, Local 15, buckled under the pressure, and on August 5, crossed picket lines to return to work.

Management's simple-minded approach to contract negotiations incurred the wrath of most unions, and ultimately forced the provincial government to intervene. The Labour Ministry appointed a mediator who heard the arguments on both sides and proceeded to settle the strike by ordering Neon to pay the sheet metal workers exactly what they had asked for.

As the strike-weary crew returned to work for the first time in three months, they passed by the Sold signs on the front of the building. Neon, it turned out, had sold only the land and buildings, not the contents, to an investment firm, on the condition that they be leased back to Neon.*

Management's attitude confirmed the workers' worst suspicions. Now that Neon had become part of a conglomerate, good intentions and social conscience were enthusiastically sacrificed in the pursuit of profit. "Neon management used anti-union, anti-strike tricks on us," said Cy Stairs, business agent of Local 280 of the Sheet Metal Workers Union. In his view, Neon's 40-year strike-free record would soon be ancient history. The union may have won the first round, but its members knew their relationship with management would continue to degenerate. The previous owners of Neon Products had been no angels, but compared to the current crew they seemed positively benevolent.

The difference can be traced to simple "kitchen" arithmetic, i.e., how the pie gets sliced up. The former owners were content with an 8 per cent return on their investment in Neon Products. The current owners shot for at least 20 per cent. The 12 per cent had to come from somewhere.

Pattison, who often said he keeps tabs on every facet of the conglomerate's operations, was no doubt aware of the strike at Neon Products, but as he paced the powder-blue broadloom that covered his sprawling office floor and even some of the walls, he faced more pressing problems.

His second-largest problem in the summer of 1971 was Imbrex and the new carpet factory it had built in partnership with Bigelow-Sandford of New York. The two firms gladly accepted a $1 million federal grant to aid construction of the plant in Ste. Agathe, north of Montreal. There the $14.95 a square yard Bigelow Deaufield Colony Blue had been manufactured on which Pattison now padded nervously.

---

*A common business practice. Investment pools, like pension funds, put their money in a relatively safe commodity—real estate. The company that sells the property gets a quick influx of cash, and can write off the rent from its taxable income. In 1985 the registered owner of Neon Products' land was Pensionfund Properties Ltd.

The Bigelow joint venture was a band-aid solution, a desperate attempt to stem the losses at Imbrex after Harding Carpets angrily withdrew their franchise. Until then, Imbrex had been the largest carpet wholesaler in Canada with a string of warehouses from coast to coast.

Year-end results showed that even the Bigelow rescue failed. Imbrex lost $2.8 million in 1970 and Neonex wrote off another $1.4 million—the cost of switching from Harding to Bigelow carpets. Some cash was sacrificed while the new factory was under construction. Bigelow carpets had to be imported from Virginia at a loss. And some losses arose from the difficulties of introducing consumers to a new brand. For the impatient Pattison the profits were not worth the effort.

"We could have made it pay," he admitted later, "but it would have taken time and more money. We decided we could get a better, faster return in other fields than by hanging in." Once again, jobs and the community's welfare were not even taken into consideration (to do so would, in the long run, be suicide). Although the firm had made a profit, it was considered too small at that time to justify carrying on. With a stroke of the pen, the operation was wiped out, and Ste. Agathe joined countless other communities in railing against owners who drain the lifeblood of a town from thousands of miles away.

Pattison had other priorities. First, there was the $10 million U.S. bank loan he had to repay now that the Commerce had cut off his line of credit. He sold most of the Imbrex warehouses, plus his 50 per cent interest in the Ste. Agathe factory, and raised about $7 million cash.

He intended that money to reduce the U.S. loan (which had enabled him to buy hundreds of thousands of Maple Leaf Mills shares during the unsuccessful takeover bid). Maple Leaf, of course, was his largest problem. His attempt to grab a piece of the major league action had failed and cost Neonex dearly. Neonex lost at least $6 million, not including possible future losses from lawsuits. Coupled with the Imbrex losses, Neonex' net loss for 1970 was $8 million, compared to a $4.6 million profit the year before.

The rest of the conglomerate wasn't doing so well either. Disregarding the Imbrex and Maple Leaf losses, Neonex operations showed a surplus of $3 million, a 50 per cent decline from 1969 profits.

Pattison's next move, as he euphemistically put it, was to "clean house."

First he swept Neonex president and chief executive officer Ross Turner out the door. The dismissal of the conglomerate's top employee was as swift as it was secret. Neither Pattison nor Turner would comment on the reasons for the firing. Although it was widely assumed that he was fired because of the $1.5 million drop in Neonex earnings the previous year, neither man would confirm that. (Contacted in 1985—fifteen years after the fact—Turner still refused to say why Pattison fired him.) Turner immediately went back to that other "exciting company," Genstar, where he was appointed head of the western Canadian operations.*

Pattison appointed himself Neonex president in Turner's place, and continued his house cleaning. He pulled the plug on the two remaining directors from pre-Pattison days, Arthur Christopher and lawyer C.W. Brazier. The redecorated Neonex board included Pattison's hand-picked men, Lawrence B. Eberhardt (at the time a Neonex vice president) and M. Donald Easton, a senior partner in the Vancouver law firm Harper, Gilmour and Grey.

Having slapped a new coat of paint on the board room, Pattison took his shovel to the basement and tossed out those companies earning insufficient profit. Reimer Express lines of Winnipeg was the first to go. The rest of the divisional managers were put on notice that another one of their firms would be sold off before the year was out, not because they weren't earning profits, but because "we can show a greater

---

*Today he and Angus McNaughton are Genstar's twin chief executive officers. Among the top paid executives in the world, each man "earns" roughly $1 million a year (Canadian).

return on our money elsewhere."

Pattison let it be known that his goal was "to beat the averages, to show greater growth than those averages," and to dump companies that didn't measure up.

This sword of Damocles dangling over the heads of managers may explain the excessive behaviour of the Northern Paint Company's head man. He was summoned to a Winnipeg court on June 30, 1971, charged with false advertising. He had advertised that Northern Paint's paint had "no smell." When that advertisement was published, investigators from Consumer and Corporate Affairs sniffed trouble. They seized samples from local paint stores, and what they smelled landed the company in front of County Court Judge Thomson. The judicial nostril concurred. "While there might be different levels of smell in paint," said the judge, "this advertising said there was no smell, that the paint was odourless, and that is not a fact..." False advertising carried a maximum penalty of five years in prison, but his Honour was lenient: Northern Paint was assessed a fine of $800.

For two years Neonex International had lived up to the "ex" (for "expansion") in its title. Now came time to get serious about the "International" part.

As international ventures go, Neonex began modestly. It slid across the border and plopped a travel trailer factory down at McMinnville, 35 miles east of Portland, Oregon. Pattison said the purpose of this 50,000 square foot plant was to penetrate the northwestern U.S. trailer market. But later, when questioned by a reporter, he admitted that some of the U.S.-built trailers would be sold in Vancouver, adding that they were produced in the U.S. because it was cheaper to build them there.

The Oregon venture was not an isolated enterprise. It fit a broader scheme to give Neonex a higher profile in the U.S. and, incidentally, to legalize its share trading there.

Like many executives, Pattison spoke with a certain awe about the Mecca of capitalism, Wall Street. "After all, New York is the financial capital of the world," he said. "There is a big difference, if in the process of working out a deal, you can say you are listed on Wall Street instead of the Calgary Stock Exchange." Pattison adroitly avoided comparing Wall Street to the Vancouver and Toronto stock exchanges, where Neonex shares are traded, and chose as his example the cow-town exchange where they were never listed.

Comparisons aside, Neonex had been trying hard for years—with some success—to trade stock in the financial capital of the world. The negotiations to get Neonex listed on Wall Street dragged on for four years. Impatient, Neonex traded shares "under the counter" instead, without properly registering them with the official registry body, the Securities and Exchange Commission. When it came time for the SEC to rule on Neonex' application for a listing, the commissioners scolded the new kid on the block for disobeying the rules. The SEC said, in effect, "Admit to your wrongdoing and we'll list your stocks on the exchange." Under the gun, Pattison gave his *mea culpa*. It was not much of a penalty, if it could even be considered that, and it was Neonex' only obstacle to trading shares in the U.S. (Here is another instance of vast sums of money travelling in an environment virtually without laws, in contrast, for example, to employees' deductions at source being regulated to the penny.)

Pattison's buddies at Burnham and Company didn't get off quite so lightly. They were the agents who sold the unregistered Neonex shares and were ordered by the SEC to admit their wrongdoing. Their punishment: not to do it again for 75 days. Why the time limit, no one explained. Presumably Burnham could go back to the practice after that. Even such mild criticism ruffled feathers down at the trading house. Burnham agreed to go along with the order so Neonex could be listed, but refused to admit to any wrongdoing.

Crime and punishment were not mentioned on Monday, June 26, 1972, on the floor of the vast American stock exchange. Pattison, Dingman, a handful of Neonex officials and the head of the exchange looked up at the big board and witnessed the first (official) trade of Neonex shares in the U.S. As the 100-share block sold for $525.00, the governor of the exchange, Edwin Peterson, turned to Pattison and congratulated him on getting the company listed when it did. Four years earlier, when Neonex first applied, the entrance criteria were lower. "Your listing has been accepted on higher standards...," he shouted above the din of the trading. Neonex had joined that elite corps of 67 Canadian firms (mostly American-owned) whose shares were trading daily on the big U.S. exchanges—among them Vancouver-based Placer Development, Granby Mining and Westcoast Transmission.

There was a certain irony about the whole celebration on the Amex floor. Before a single share was traded there, Neonex was already more than one-quarter owned by U.S. residents (according to Statistics Canada's *1972 Inter-Corporate Ownership Guide*).

Before leaving New York, Pattison saw to another pressing piece of business. He made sure his lawsuit against Bruce Norris and the Norris Grain Company for $32 million was filed in U.S. District Court in New York. To no one's surprise, Norris countersued for $50 million.

The litigation would take years, Pattison knew. On the whole, he could forget the trauma of the past two years and focus on building a profitable conglomerate. In the cracker-barrel slang of rural Saskatchewan that Pattison was so fond of chewing on, he said, "We took our lickin' in 1970 and we started to clean 'er out." The "lickin'," of course, referred to Imbrex and Maple Leaf Mills. "Clean 'er out" meant five enterprises, most of them profitable, that Neonex had liquidated in the wake of its two unequivocal failures. The cash from selling its five subsidiaries enabled Neonex to show a profit of $2.8 million in 1971.

With the rapid reappearance of black ink at the bottom of the Neonex balance sheet, Pattison boasted that he was "on the acquisition trail again." His pace was not nearly so frantic as in the first round, when he picked up companies as fast as some people pick up pay cheques. In 1972 Neonex bought only three firms, including Fabco and Porta-Bilt, both involved in construction of industrial housing, which included items like trailers for work camps.

New companies were not the only acquisitions made by Neonex at the beginning of the decade. It raided the Bank of B.C., luring away its deputy general manager, Fred Vanstone. The young banker—only ten years out of university—had been in the deputy manager's chair only two months before announcing his resignation to become the top financial officer at Neonex.

As the new man with his finger on the pulse of the conglomerate, Vanstone was the first to feel the palpitations following the unexpected results in the August 1972 provincial election.

The "socialist hordes," under NDP leader Dave Barrett, defeated eleven cabinet ministers and picked up 25 seats throughout the province as they brought down two decades of Socred government.

Pattison was caught momentarily off balance. He heard businessmen grumbling in the wings about possible mass nationalizations, and he read the dire predictions about corporate head offices joining an exodus to the politically dependable east.

He waited until the first NDP budget to gauge the "danger." What he read reassured him. He told the Victoria Chamber of Commerce soon after the budget was released that there was "nothing in the new budget that should frighten any business out of the province... business [can] continue to thrive," he predicted, as long as the government stuck to its plans.

Nothing in Neonex plans for the immediate future indicated any fear for the survival and blossoming of capitalism under the province's first social democratic government. Its 1972 annual report, which showed record sales of $170 million and profits edging back up at $3.6 million, outlined spending plans totalling $8 million for the coming year.

If anything, Pattison spent more time arguing with the federal Liberals, not the provincial NDP, about improving the climate for capitalist endeavours. What particularly irked him was a section of the Income Tax Act assessing capital gains tax on share transactions. That hit close to home, for Neonex bought nearly all other companies with shares. Any capital gain (and there always was one, otherwise the deal wouldn't be worth it to Neonex) would be taxed at rates up to 32 per cent.

Pattison contended that the money simply wasn't there to pay the tax—a frank admission that Neonex really couldn't afford the companies it bought and that it bought them "on spec," usually in the hope that the new company could be made to pay for the takeover out of its earnings.

Even more enlightening are the consequences predicted by Pattison if the federal government failed to heed his warning. He said there would be "increased concentration of economic power and a reduction of competition in the marketplace...[and] an increase in foreign ownership of Canadian companies."

The ghoulish portrait Pattison painted of Canada's economic future was actually an accurate picture of Neonex' present. Neonex began with foreign capital. Its board was dominated by Americans. In four years it concentrated ownership into fewer hands. It limited competition through vertical integration and even conspiracy (which will be fully explained in the following chapter). And it was 25.4 per cent owned by foreigners. The only element missing in Pattison's analysis was an explanation of how removing the dreaded tax would reverse the trend toward increasing concentration of wealth.

Pattison's real objection to the tax was that it would be a drain on Neonex coffers and therefore on its ability to continue on the very path to which it piously drew the government's attention. His aim was to ensure that Neonex would continue doing business as usual. The new capital gains tax had to be fought. Pattison's arguments didn't have to make sense. They just had to be effective.

In summary, Pattison argued that unless the tax was removed, "growth-oriented" companies like his would acquire foreign firms rather than Canadian ones, which was precisely the course Neonex proceeded to follow.

In 1973, Pattison bought two more American companies, including the Pop Shoppes franchise for Texas, California and Hawaii. Neonex also established a new recreational vehicle plant within coughing distance of a Los Angeles freeway, which would soon carry a stream of Pattison's campers, trailers and other fun vehicles which get eight miles to the gallon.

It was a bit like old times, with Neonex back on the acquisition trail. But there were differences. The company's currency, its shares, were worth only one-quarter of their value in the conglomerate's heyday in 1968-69. And the "lickin'" the company had taken forced those in Neonex who survived the purges to sharpen their pencils before consummating new takeovers. The Pop Shoppes agreement, for example, involved the purchase of a franchise instead of a much riskier direct takeover.

In Canada, too, Neonex found cheaper and more cautious ways of extending its economic tentacles. Pattison, in public, portrayed his relationship with Pierre Trudeau and the Liberal government as adversarial. He regularly released copies of telegrams like the one about the right of the rich to live tax-free. But in private the two men were on cosier terms. In one instance Trudeau's ministers and Pattison negotiated a couple of lucrative deals for Neonex' eastern Canadian corporations. One provided a $1.4 million grant for the Ste. Agathe carpet factory. The other enabled construction of a mobile home factory in Moncton, N.B., built entirely with federal and provincial money.*

It was around this time that Pattison began to take more than an armchair fan's interest in sports. Professional sports, like other businesses, were in a boom period. Every major professional team sport was opening new franchises at a furious clip, either by expanding existing leagues or starting up new ones. The days of millionaire owners holding onto teams as a hobby were evaporating. As with other pleasures, sports was lucrative business, and a new generation of businessmen was eager to climb aboard.

Pattison, whose personal fortune was fattened by periodic purchases of Neonex shares when the price was low, became a sports entrepreneur like a true Canadian, in the field of hockey. He picked up the Philadelphia Blazers in the new World Hockey Association for $1.9 million and moved them to Vancouver.

It soon became apparent that Pattison knew about as much about owning a hockey team as he did about taking over a carpet business, and with comparable results. The Vancouver Blazers sunk like a stone to the bottom of the standings. The team's non-existent fans stayed home in droves from home games. Pattison needed 10,000 of them to attend each game just to break even. The average attendance was closer to 8,000.

Rumours that Pattison would dump the money-losing team from his private portfolio onto Neonex were dampened by vice president Vanstone. "Unless it...includes ownership of a sports arena and other assets,"

---

*Through subsidies like these, the federal and provincial governments unwittingly hurt established businesses. By paying "up front" costs of factories in traditionally high unemployment areas, governments made it cheaper for firms like Neonex to make mobile homes. Neonex didn't have to figure into its costs the interest on the money to build the plant. Therefore it was able to sell the homes cheaper than the firm, say, in Ontario which built the factory itself. In some cases old, established firms went out of business when new, subsidized industries undercut their prices.

said the company's top financial officer, "a hockey team would have no place in a public company."

His boss thought otherwise. After unsuccessfully trying to sell the team to other Vancouver millionaires, Pattison turned it over to Neonex. It was the first time the conglomerate knowingly bought a money-loser.

Entering the wide world of sports, Pattison came in contact with a new kaleidoscope of characters. One of the more unlikely was Tom Scallen, owner of the Vancouver Canucks, the National Hockey League's answer to the Blazers (and about as successful at putting the puck in the net).

Scallen, president of the Minneapolis-based Medicor Corporation, which owned Vancouver's Northwest Sports Enterprises Ltd., which in turn owned the Canucks, dealt with the team's negative cash-flow problem in an unoriginal but newsworthy way. He stole $3 million of it for himself, by "diverting" it from Northwest to Medicor.

It's difficult to hide a sum like that, even in a large corporation. Scallen issued phony documents to cover up his illegal gains but the bulge in his mattress was too big. He was caught and charged with theft. The judge released him on $25,000 bail, which was put up by... Jim Pattison.

An eager young prosecutor, Ray Paris, convinced the judge that Scallen was guilty. He was sentenced to two years in prison, of which he served only eight months.

For a man who wanted to be accepted by the business establishment Pattison wasn't backing the right people. Nor was he making the right business moves. He dabbled in hockey teams and soda pop stores. (Neonex got out of the Pop Shoppes deal only months before the entire company went belly-up). There seemed to be no overall plan or guiding principle. At times Pattison's empire seemed to be balanced on a toothpick.

Investors and others in the know steered clear of Neonex. Its shares, which once soared in the $22 (post-split) altitudes, now were grounded at $1.70. The Canadian Business Service of Toronto wrote the epitaph for Neonex: "It has all the earmarks of a has-been."

As evidence it pointed to an astounding error in the company's 1972 earnings which had gone unnoticed for two years. Neonex "overstated" its earnings for that year by almost half a million dollars. The $420,000 oversight resulted from "errors" in estimating the value of inventory belonging to the Acme Novelty chain.

The official explanation was that certain goods arriving at Acme warehouses just before Christmas were included in year-end inventories, but, according to Neonex vice president Guy J. Lewall, "due to an oversight the invoices for these goods did not show up... until after the books were closed [for that year].... The effect was that although 1972 sales were stated correctly, the cost of sales was understated and earnings were overstated."

All clear?

While this discrepancy could be an honest mistake, the potential short-term gains to Neonex are obvious. Inflated earnings could conceal the company's shortage of cash and seduce investors into thinking its shares are a better investment than they are.

The unanswered question in this case is whether the Acme Novelty incident was a mistake. The Neonex vice president said it was. But about the same time that the Acme inventory was over-valued, a former employee who worked at another Neonex subsidiary said he witnessed "a young chartered accountant being led around by the nose [by the firm's manager] being given vastly over-inflated values for inventory..."

He didn't know whether in his company's case the "mistake" would be spotted by the main accounting firm and "corrected." But in the Acme case, Neonex insisted that for almost two years no one at the local management level, or head office, or the independent accounting firm hired to audit the books spotted the $420,000 discrepancy resulting in a 14 per cent overstatement of the actual earnings. (The disappearance of large sums seems not to arouse much concern or curiosity.)

At best, the fiasco proved that Neonex had very weak management controls—in the end, it was the accountants and not Neonex people who spotted the error. *Financial Post* analyst Brian Roger accepted Neonex' version that it was an honest mistake. He blamed the half-million dollar error on "too rapid expansion; too little internal control; thin HQ management; too closely held control by top management and a wayward acquisition policy."

There is a larger context in which to consider these events, namely, an energy crisis in the western world, when energy shortages, real and contrived, and renewed fighting between Egypt and Israel, combined to catapult the price of petroleum to ten times its former value.

Suddenly, Canadians and Americans accustomed to cheap fuel fumed in gas station lines waiting for the privilege of paying $40 to fill a tank that once could be filled for $5. Many responded to the crisis by re-ordering priorities, not only by purchasing smaller cars or using transit or bicycles, but by using less energy in their homes and at work.

Among the first victims of the new energy consciousness were gas-guzzling behemoths like motorhomes and camper trailers that slurped up as much as a gallon of gas every six miles. The near demise of these homes on wheels badly shook the recreational vehicle industry, a major component of Neonex. Profits from sales of Pattison's RVs dropped 80 per cent between 1972 and 1973. Pattison sold the Alberta, Manitoba and Ontario camper factories and reduced inventories in the U.S. and other Canadian plants.

In 1975, the year that Neonex losses mounted to more than $1 million, Pattison and his U.S. directors desperately cast about for some way to revive the dying conglomerate. They looked to Harold Geneen, chairman of "the world's most successful conglomerate," ITT. It was said that Geneen controlled his vast holdings of telecommunications firms, hotels, insurance companies and forestry giants through elaborately programmed computers that monitored monthly cash-flows.

That there was blood on the underbelly of ITT's computer didn't trouble Fred Vanstone. (ITT had played a major role in toppling the elected government of Salvador Allende in Chile in 1973 and has been active in propping up fascist dictatorships there and elsewhere in the third world.) Vanstone was interested in how Geneen handled numbers, not dictators. He eagerly learned the "Geneen system" and adapted it to Neonex' situation. Every month, he and Jimmy and the others at head office pored over the computer printouts, which provided a far more accurate snapshot of the corporation's current position.

With the new accounting system in place, the news was still not good. Sales increased but profits didn't. The solution, familiar by now to followers of the Neon Products and Maple Leaf Mills capers, was to buy another money-making company.

With this in mind, Pattison began in 1975 a two-year behind-the-scenes takeover of the soft drink multinational corporation Crush International. Using other Neonex companies like Associated Helicopters as "covers," Pattison slowly accumulated thousands of shares in the company best known in over 60 countries for its sweet carbonated soft drink, Orange Crush. The "liquid" Pattison sought did not come in bottles, but in books and bank statements. Crush had plenty of both. No debts, $12 million in cash, plenty of fixed assets, and a relatively low share price. Just like the other targets. The difference this time was the edge of desperation—without Crush or a company like it Neonex would likely go broke.

How could Neonex, a company on the verge of financial ruin with a rock-bottom share value and internal problems (Acme and Northern Paint were losing money) take over a multinational money maker?

This is where Pattison's experienced U.S. advisers put him in the lead. Through a complex web of deals, he would use Crush's own money to take it over. Timing was all important. Pattison bought enough shares in Crush with borrowed money to use the dividends from the shares to pay the interest on the loan. His goal was to get 100 per cent of the company quickly so that he could use its considerable assets to pay for the deal and start making a profit for Neonex.

Crush shareholders who got wind of this were understandably nervous. Neonex had a reputation for taking over companies and stretching their resources to the limit. In some cases, the strain drove them out of business. Acme Novelty, for example, had operated with modest success for 40 years. In less than three years under Neonex ownership, after rapid expansion in an effort to grab a bigger share of the market, the company was broke. However imperfectly, Acme had provided a generation of workers with jobs and security, only to see the warehouses sold and inventory dumped at fire sale prices because of—there is no other word for it—the greed of its new owners. (It is greed but of a special sort. Wealth is acquired and disposed of so differently by the 95 per cent of ordinary people compared to the 5 per cent at the top that the two are like creatures from different planets, requiring separate vocabularies.)

In the words of Canadian Business Service, a Toronto investment firm, Neonex was buying Crush mainly to shore up its own deteriorating condition. "Neonex had $2.22 in short- and long-term debt for every $1 in shareholders' equity, completely out of line with any reasonable industry standard," growled CBS.

Pattison continued to buy Crush shares, mainly through private deals with large shareholders and also through the stock exchanges. By the end of 1976 he had bought 34 per cent of the company, was its major shareholder, and obtained a seat on the board of directors. He would not disclose how much he paid for the shares, although the educated guess at the time pegged it at $10 each, or about $14 million.

At the same time, he was quietly buying shares in his own company, Neonex. Between 1975 and '77 he became the major shareholder, buying enough from his U.S. partners to reduce the foreign ownership of Neonex to 9.4 per cent from 25.4.

That, though, was not the main reason Pattison bought Neonex shares. He announced his motive one mid-summer day in 1977. He told all remaining shareholders in Neonex that he wanted to buy all Neonex shares and turn it into a private company. No more shareholders' meetings. No more embarrassingly low-priced shares. No more annual reports. And most important, no more public disclosure of profits and losses. "We don't have to tell nobody nuthin'," was Pattison's shorthand summary of the advantages to him in taking Neonex private.

Pattison engineered the takeover of his own company like the takeovers of all the others—to be as advantageous to him as possible. That's the name of the game. There were two ways to take Neonex private. One was to offer to buy 90 per cent of the shares, at which point he could legally force the other 10 per cent to sell theirs—a form of legal expropriation.

But a legal loophole, passed by Parliament only two years earlier, gave him a much easier, cheaper takeover route. It permitted any person or group owning two-thirds of the company to merge it with another company. This meant that Pattison could merge Old Neonex (the public company) with his private holding company, and produce a new Neonex (a private company) with only two-thirds of the shares.

Pattison, who already owned 46.5 per cent of Neonex shares, wanted to maximize his clout. Although very few shareholders attend meetings to exercise their votes, Pattison wasn't taking any chances this time. The majority of Neonex shareholders lived in Vancouver or Toronto. The circular they received informed them that the meeting to vote on a merger would be held September 30, 1977—in Winnipeg.

Pattison ignored protests about the location and went ahead with the meeting. As Neonex director and lawyer Donald Easton banged his gavel to open the Winnipeg proceedings on September 30, scowling shareholders and their representatives took him on immediately.

Before any business could be transacted, Winnipeg

lawyer Alan Sweatman took the floor and read a prepared statement:

"I submit the [circular mailed to shareholders] is wrong in law—so fundamentally, in fact, that the meeting should be discontinued and the company should start over again." Others shouted that Sweatman was right. The chorus of protest swelled. Easton demanded order.

"I will take no further questions until the motion to amalgamate is put before the meeting," he said. The meeting eventually returned to order and the shareholders reluctantly cast their votes on the crucial merger vote.

The outcome was a foregone conclusion. Pattison alone held 62.3 per cent of the votes at the meeting. Of all the votes cast, only 5.6 per cent voted against the motion.

The dissenters were vastly outnumbered but not defeated. They immediately filed charges against Neonex in British Columbia Supreme Court.

Meanwhile, Pattison, who now had control of Neonex, still owned only 46.5 per cent of the shares. The rest were now "non-voting" shares although they still held their market value. Pattison offered $3 a share for every one of them, a figure most analysts called low. It was higher than the current price of Neonex shares but below the "book value" of $4.10. The offer failed to take into account the fact that the shareholders, who had received no dividends since Pattison took over, expected some additional compensation when they sold the shares. Most considered $5 a share to be an appropriate offer.

When the case was heard in Supreme Court early in 1978, it was not possible for the judge to rule on the merger itself because Pattison had stayed within the law. It was Parliament which greased his path to expropriate the property of the minority of shareholders who voted against the merger.

The shareholders also argued that Pattison had held the price of Neonex shares artificially low in order to take the company private for as little money as possible. Company officials denied this, and the judge said that this charge, too, was beyond the scope of the trial.

As the case proceeded it became clear how little power and protection the minority shareholders had. So far, there was no evidence to show that Pattison had done anything illegal, though in the words of Judge Bouck, who presided over the hearing, the "morality [of what he did] is for others to assess."

The only aspect of the case that came within the purview of the court was the $3 per share offer. Judge Bouck, obviously moved, commented on the emotional testimony of William Kolasa, one of the minority shareholders forced out by Pattison. Here is the judge's quote in full:

"William Kolasa appeared in person. He had no law books nor any particular legal point to make, but what he had to say goes to the heart of the matter. I can only paraphrase his comments since no court reporter was present. Nor can I reproduce on paper the deep sense of hurt which was evident in his remarks. He said: 'The leaders of this country have asked us all to invest in Canada as good citizens. My wife and I took our savings and bought shares in Neonex for $5 each. We are told we must sell them for $3. We seem to have little choice. Why is this so?'

"Why indeed?" echoed the judge. He noted that Parliament, after having passed a forcing-out regulation based on a requirement of 90 per cent ownership, went on to make the stipulation redundant. "The majority shareholder need not bother using that process when the same result can be obtained with a vote of only two-thirds of those present at a meeting."

Having demonstrated how the government made it legal (and easier) for the rich to get richer at the expense of the not-so-rich, Judge Bouck went on to illustrate how Pattison did it.

The books of Old Neonex showed that the company—that is, all the shareholders—owned $23.6 million under the heading "retained earnings." Yet when New Neonex was incorporated, its books showed retained earnings of only $7.9 million. The judge pondered both sets of books at length, concluding that the missing $16.7 million was probably untraceable. He went on to say, however, that "a number of unexplained accounting entries in the *pro forma* balance sheet of the consolidated companies left me with the impression that these retained earnings were used by Pattison to purchase the other 53.5 per cent of the shares of old Neonex.

"In other words," continued the judge for the benefit of the 90 per cent of Canadians who own no shares on the stock market, "the shareholders' own money in the form of retained earnings was spent to buy their shares. It looks as if it cost Pattison nothing."

This was a company which investors had called "a good capital investment." Of course, each investor knew the risk they were taking. They knew Pattison wouldn't pay more than five cents a share dividends. The rest of the profits were being invested for "future growth" and now those shareholders wanted their share of that growth. Instead, almost all of them came out with less than they invested. Investment counsellors, seeming unwilling to push the matter further, urged shareholders to "take the money and run."

The court, for its part, found the $3 a share offer was too low and ordered Pattison to pay "a fair price, set by the court" for any remaining shares. The price ranged from $4 to $5 a share, but by then most of the shares had been sold. Once again, Jim Pattison came out far ahead.

8 THE MOST EFFICIENT CONCEALER

> *...it is estimated that less than fifty men control $4,000,000,000, or more than one third of Canada's material wealth as expressed in railways, banks, factories, mines, land and other properties and resources.*
> —Gustavus Myers, 1914

> *I am the sole shareholder in this company and in the final analysis I don't really have to account to anybody but myself.*
> —Jim Pattison

On February 12, 1985, small articles appeared in the Toronto *Globe and Mail* and the Vancouver *Sun* about three billboard advertising firms that were fined a total of $700,000 for conspiracy to lessen competition. The *Globe* article mentioned only in passing that one of the three convicted firms was owned by Jim Pattison. The *Sun* noted the fact in its headline, "Pattison's firm 1 of 3 hit by fines," but the punch in the headline was watered down in the article by a quote from one of Pattison's employees. Ron Vandenberg, an ex-policeman who had worked for Pattison for years and who currently managed Seaboard Advertising, said, "Pattison was a minority shareholder of Neonex, which owned Seaboard" (at the time of the offence in the mid-seventies).

If that didn't get the point across, Vandenberg elaborated: "To be fair, it was in pre-Jimmy Pattison days," when the conspiracy took place. But if we follow Vandenberg's exhortation to be fair, a close examination of the facts reveals a very different story.

It was July 12, 1976. The receptionist sitting under the continuously blinking electric sign at Neon Products' Vancouver headquarters was startled to see what seemed like half the Vancouver RCMP detachment striding toward her desk. As the floor stopped quaking, the man who seemed to be in charge showed her his badge. He asked to see the manager immediately. She led him down narrow corridors and between rows of desks to a windowless fluorescent-lit office.

When the manager appeared he was ordered to direct the police to all company files. Gathering his composure, he set the open-mouthed staff to the task. The officers began wheeling out carloads of documents. By the time they finished there was barely a scrap of paper left in the place.

Over the next two or three days the scene was repeated across the country. The police raided HOAL Investments of Edmonton and in Toronto, Mediacom Inc., Gould Outdoor (Posters) Ltd., and J. C. Teron Company Ltd.

As bewildered staff at the billboard advertising firms pondered the impossible—how to carry on business without access to their files—officials were hard at work. Police and inspectors from the anti-combines branch of Consumer and Corporate Affairs photocopied reems of papers—anything remotely resembling evidence that could be used in court. That done, they obligingly returned the originals.

Federal investigators had been stirred to action by complaints from advertisers about the apparent monopoly held by billboard companies. Firms wanting their products advertised on the ubiquitous ten by twenty foot panels were virtually forced to buy space from Seaboard in British Columbia, HOAL in Alberta and Mediacom in the rest of the country. (Gould and J.C. Teron were never charged, but were named as "unindicted co-conspirators.") The restrictions applied especially to big-budget advertisers who wanted their ads to appear across the country. Not only was competition severely restricted, but the prices for billboard space seemed exorbitant.

In a two year period beginning January 1, 1974, all three companies increased their prices well beyond current inflation rates. Mediacom jacked up its prices 37 per cent, Seaboard 35 per cent and HOAL 46 per cent. These increases were implemented at exactly the same time, ensuring that no billboard advertisers would find rates cheaper in one city than another.

Federal government investigators, never ones to be rushed into these things, spent the following four years rifling through every page of evidence and tracking down one lead after another. To be fair, the feds knew that when the case came to court they were going to be fighting some of the highest-priced legal talent in the country. Their preparations had to be thorough.

One of the hardest tasks was tracking down corporate histories of the firms involved. Brian Linseman of Ottawa, one of the investigators, telephoned the company's branch in Victoria to get whatever information they had on Jim Pattison. It took one of their staff two weeks working full-time just to compile all the certificates of incorporation and other documents relating to the Neonex group of companies. When she finished, the files stood two and a half feet high.

By July 1980, investigators believed that enough material had been compiled to justify laying charges. The files were handed over to Jean Chretien, the Attorney General of Canada. The minster pondered the evidence another nine months; then, on April 2, 1981, he charged Mediacom, HOAL and Seaboard under two sections of the Combines Investigation Act.

The first, section 32, known as the "conspiracy section," alleged that from 1973 to 1981 the firms had conspired to "prevent or lessen competition unduly." The word "unduly" results in many conspiracy charges being dropped. It is one thing to prove that there was a conspiracy to prevent competition, but at what point does the reduced competition become "undue"?

The second charge was laid under section 33, the "monopoly" section. It alleged that during the same years, Mediacom had bought two-thirds of all billboards in Ontario and virtually all billboards in the rest of Canada outside Alberta and B.C. with the intent of monopolizing billboard space to the detriment of the public. In addition, the three firms were charged with conspiring to keep out competitors.

The body of evidence to back up the charges was impressive. The government claimed to prove that billboard owners had to belong to the Outdoor Advertising Association of Canada if they wanted to obtain national advertising accounts. And to become a member of the OAAC, they had to be voted in by its membership. Members had one vote for every billboard they owned (another definition of economic democracy). Since Pattison's Seaboard, Alberta's HOAL and Toronto's Mediacom had combined ownership of 85 per cent of all billboards in Canada,[1] the best one could hope for from the OAAC was a benevolent dictatorship.

By itself, this was not enough evidence to convict the companies of wrongdoing. There was one crucial question that would have to be answered first: "Could an individual seeking to reach the public through outdoor advertising find a suitable replacement medium if he concluded that prices being charged...were unreasonably high?"

At the outset, lawyers for the three accused tried to argue that anyone unhappy with their clients' rates could obtain equal exposure by advertising on radio, TV, in newspapers or handbills. But the industry's own propaganda contradicted this. When advertising their advertising space, the industry claimed that billboards were a medium for which there is no real substitute.

On the conspiracy charges, several documents introduced as evidence showed that illegal agreements had been signed by all three companies. However, the judge would not convict the firms unless the government could prove that the agreements lessened competition "unduly"—that is, to the detriment of the public.

The agreements revealed that Seaboard, HOAL and Mediacom divided Canada into geographic market areas. Seaboard (also operating under the names Jim Pattison Enterprises Ltd. and Neonex Consumer Group) got all of B.C.; HOAL (an acronym for Hook Outdoor Advertising Ltd.) took Alberta; and the rest of Canada was Mediacom's. The three free enterprisers agreed not to own billboards in each other's territory. They also agreed to prevent new billboard companies from setting up anywhere in the ten provinces (easily enforced through their control of the OAAC). Their only competition came from existing billboard firms, all of them relatively small and likely to get smaller since their ability to compete was severely hampered by the OAAC, which blocked them from getting national and regional advertising accounts.

Lawyers for the big three, including Jim Pattison's friend Jack Giles, a member of a prominent B.C. law firm and frequent worker for the Social Credit government,[2] were undaunted by the weight of the evidence. Rather than defending their clients from the charges, they invoked an obscure legal argument to "quash the information" (drop the charges) because, they held, the offences were "not known to law."

Nothing in the lawyers' presentation suggested that the companies had not committed the offences. The damaging evidence in the agreements seemed unmistakable. Instead, during the year following the initial court appearance on January 20, 1982, the companies tied up court time and spent large sums of money in court costs and legal fees trying to squeeze through a legal loophole.

At the preliminary hearing the judge refused to quash

the information. The lawyers collectively appealed to the Supreme Court of Ontario. The Supreme Court dismissed their appeal, so they appealed that decision to the Ontario Court of Appeal. In May 1982 that appeal was dismissed, so the three appealed *that* decision to the Supreme Court of Canada.

The justices of the highest court in the land looked at the record of appeals and dismissals and decided this case had gone far enough. They refused to hear the appeal. With no further legal recourse, Seaboard, HOAL and Mediacom were committed to trial. The evidence against them was presented in the Supreme Court of Ontario in February 1983, more than a year after the case first came to court and more than ten years after the alleged conspiracy began.

After the prosecution finished presenting its evidence, dates were set for the defence. Those dates, however, were postponed twice. No public reason was given, but in private the companies and the government were negotiating a deal. It amounted to plea-bargaining.

If the three firms pleaded guilty to the conspiracy charges and agreed on a suitable fine, the government would "stay" the monopoly charges and save themselves the expense of a lengthy court trial.

It was a deal.

The first step in formalizing the agreement required the court and the lawyers to sign an "agreed statement of facts" explaining in detail the illegal acts perpetrated by the companies. The next was for the judge to issue an "order" circumscribing the companies' future behaviour to ensure that the law would not be violated again.

The statement of facts revealed that the illegal practices went beyond the allocation of exclusive territories, the division of Canada into markets and exorbitant prices. The three companies had offered their customers "free production" in return for contracts of more than $50,000. In other words, the advertising firm was told that it would pay only for the billboard space and that the company would produce the posters "free." In fact, the cost of making posters was carefully calculated at 15 per cent of the total and was incorporated before a price was quoted to the customer. Not content to stop there, the three firms included rate increases in the total price without telling the customer.

The judge, instructing the companies to stop lying to their customers, and to stop using false advertising slogans like "free production" in their promotions, also issued a twelve-point order listing other offences that the firms must avoid committing.

Many of the points were obvious. Do not conspire to keep out competitors. Do not start price wars to force small competitors out of business. Do not carve up the Canadian market for your exclusive use. The judge then included an unusual clause: he ordered all three to furnish their directors, officers and managers with a copy of the Combines Investigation Act. Copies were also to be sent to members and directors of the OAAC. To ensure that the order was complied with, the court demanded a list of names and addresses of those receiving copies, and the dates they were mailed.

Then came the fines.

The court and the companies agreed that $700,000 would be a suitable punishment. Mediacom, the largest firm, was fined $400,000, the largest ever under the Combines Investigation Act. Seaboard was fined $200,000 and HOAL $100,000.

A clue to how they arrived at the numbers is contained in Jack Giles' comment that the $200,000 fine for Seaboard represented "five per cent of total sales... during the period of indictment." By Giles' account, Seaboard made $4 million during that time. Compared to such earnings, even a fine of this size appears to be little more than an operating expense.

To return to the comment by Seaboard president Ron Vandenberg to the effect that these offences happened in "pre-Jimmy days." He reminded us that Pattison was only a minority shareholder in those days and that he didn't buy Neonex until November 1977.

Both statements are technically true, but they ignore the larger picture. "Minority shareholder" Pattison was also chief executive officer, president and chairman of the board of Neonex, which owned 100 per cent of Seaboard during the eight years when the illegal acts occurred.

When I telephoned Vandenberg for clarification, he first claimed that the newspapers had misquoted him, "the way they always do." He then claimed that someone had given him the wrong information about the dates of the criminal acts. And finally, he admitted he might be mistaken. The exchange went like this:

> *Vandenberg*: The actual alleged wrongdoings took place prior to Pattison being involved in the company. The allegations that [the court] brought forth were in the early sixties.
> *RK*: No, I've got the judge's report on the case and they're talking about '73 to '76 as when the [first] conspiracy took place. [Are you] saying that you were under the mistaken impression that the charges related to...prior to '67, prior to Pattison coming on the scene?
> *V*: They [the newspapers] did that, I did not.
> *RK*: But you just told me that you were under the impression that the convictions were ten years earlier than they were...
> *V*: No, I'm not saying that. I'm saying part of the investigation took place over a longer period of time.
> *RK*: The judgment doesn't say anything like that.
> *V*: Well, you have that. All I can tell you is what I believe. Now, I could be mistaken.

Mistaken or not, the unchallenged remarks in the paper left the clear impression that Pattison was not involved. In reality, by 1973 his control of Neonex was highly public. He was personally credited with building Neonex up from a small sign firm to a massive conglomerate; he was the driving force behind the ill-fated Maple Leaf takeover; he was the one who hired and fired officers and directors; he was the one who embarked on quarterly tours of his offices and factories, supermarkets and showrooms, assuring even assistant managers that if there was any problem they were free to "talk to Jimmy."

Even the "minority shareholder" comment is misleading. At the time the conspiracies began, Pattison was one of the largest shareholders, with an estimated 10 per cent of Neonex stock. As the share price dropped he picked up more, until by 1977 he had almost 50 per cent. More to the point, Pattison himself said in 1968, "I'm fronting for nobody," in anticipation of questions about who really owned Neonex—U.S. investors or him. He referred to the Americans as "friendly money" who voted with him on major decisions.

For a man who went to such trouble to assert his authority over the company before 1973 when the conspiracies began, he was deafeningly silent about being the man in charge after the billboard debacle blew up. (He was unavailable to reporters after the fines were announced.)

As the president of Seaboard—a firm just convicted of one of the biggest conspiracy offences in Canadian history—Vandenberg showed scant familiarity with the details. The judge had explicitly ordered copies of the Combines Investigation Act and the written judgment from the trial sent to all officers, yet Vandenberg relied on second-hand information when trying to recall when the offences took place. But at other times in our talk he prefaced his responses to my questions with, "If you'll read the judgment...," but stopped after I told him I had the judgment on the desk in front of me. It stretches the imagination to think that Vandenberg, president of B.C.'s largest billboard firm, does not know whether it was his current boss or some predecessor who was in charge when the illegal practices began.

The newspapers did not provide many answers.

The *Globe and Mail* devoted front-page space to the story on February 12, 1985, but mentioned only parenthetically that Seaboard "had since amalgamated with other companies to become Jim Pattison Industries

Ltd." It appeared that no one attempted to discover whether Pattison had any connection before the amalgamation—a fairly obvious question given Pattison's high profile as head of Canada's first world's fair since Montreal. Tapping a few keys on the *Globe*'s much-touted "Info Globe" computer would have flashed up more than enough information. (Even as this story went to print, the *Globe*'s glossy new *Report On Business Magazine* was preparing its April edition, which featured a full-colour portrait of Pattison on the cover.)

The *Sun*'s coverage was even less excusable since the world's fair is happening in its own backyard. The newspaper's clipping library files bulge with stories about Pattison going back 25 years. No reporter should have let Vandenberg's statements go unchecked. A Supreme Court judge found that these three companies ran a sector of the Canadian economy "for which there is no real substitute" like their personal fiefdom, erecting barriers against outsiders, giving the boot to other insiders and ripping off advertisers.

The judge, and even the accused, agreed that the crimes were serious enough to warrant the highest fines ever levied under the conspiracy section of the Combines Act.

Not even the *Sun*'s headline accurately conveyed the importance of the story. "Pattison's firm 1 of 3 hit by fines." It sounded like an accident report—as if Pattison and two friends had been walking across the street and were hit by a fine.

Pattison being who he is, there were dozens of reasons to dig into the story—and just as many to drop it. Unmentioned was the fact that he was the head of a company which continually broke the law. There were no handwringing editorials about what damage this might do to Expo 86, now that its chairman was guilty...oh, of course, *he* wasn't found guilty of anything. One of the fancier provisions of Canadian corporate law is that corporations are granted the legal status of "persons." In one anthropomorphic move, the law found that an entity existing only on paper had deliberately broken the law. Jim Pattison *Industries Ltd.*, not Pattison or any officer in charge, was found to have committed the offence.[3]

From the point of view of the newspaper owners, it could be that the case struck a little too close to home. At the same time as Seaboard and the other firms were on trial, Pacific Press owner Southam Inc. (publisher of the *Sun* and the *Province*), Thomson Newspapers and F.P. Publications were also charged under the monopoly and conspiracy sections of the Combines Investigation Act. The charges followed the simultaneous closing of the Ottawa *Journal* and the Winnipeg *Tribune* by their respective owners, Southam and Thomson. The result was that each company eliminated competition in a "you-take-Winnipeg, I'll-take-Ottawa" deal. No conviction, however, was brought down in any of these cases.

Today, there is more potential than ever for one or more of Pattison's companies to drag him into another tangle with the combines officials. Said Combines investigator Brian Linseman, "We're keeping a close eye on the billboard business," which is now dominated by two, not three, firms. In 1981 Pattison bought HOAL Investments and now controls about 1,500 billboards in Alberta, roughly the same number as he owns in British Columbia through Seaboard. Mediacom of Toronto remains the country's largest billboard company.

The only evidence that competition is increasing is that Pattison also bought Gould Advertising of Brantford, Ontario, and now competes with his old acquaintances at Mediacom. However, the combines conviction is beginning to have the desired effect. In mid-1985 a small ad firm in Hamilton outbid Pattison and Mediacom on a contract to erect bus shelters in that city and to sell the advertising spaces on them. Still, it is too soon to celebrate any breakthrough for free enterprise: Pattison and Mediacom still own 85 per cent of all billboards in Canada. Unless they voluntarily sell some, that percentage will only decrease as newcomers erect new ones.

THE MOST EFFICIENT CONCEALER 163

The Jim Pattison Group makes it an article of faith to grab the largest market share in every sector in which it operates. Pattison's auto dealerships are now the largest in Canada, as any resident of the Lower Mainland can guess from having seen the myriads of "Jim Pattison" stickers on the backs of Toyota and General Motors cars and trucks.[4]

His airline, Air BC, virtually dominates west coast air service, aided by the provincial government's support in turning the airline into a near-monopoly.

He is Canada's second largest distributor of periodicals, annually selling 100 million copies of publications to 4,227 dealers. In the northern parts of B.C., Alberta, Saskatchewan and all of the NWT and Yukon, he has an absolute monopoly.

If you want to place an ad in one of the 2,500,000 ad spaces on Canada's buses, subways, streetcars, transit shelters or subway stations, you have to call Trans Ad, a Jim Pattison company.

He owns the world's largest electric outdoor sign company, and leases 38,000 signs, more than any other company in Canada.

He is already a dominant figure in the B.C. food industry, closing the gap on the province's number one retailer, Safeway. His supermarkets, Overwaitea and Save-On-Foods, control the largest share of the retail food market outside Vancouver. Save-On-Foods in particular is preying on competitors. Its North Vancouver store, opened in early 1985, forced a neighbouring Super-Valu out of business. Later in the year Save-On opened the province's first "mega-store" in Richmond; on opening day, the Safeway across the street was empty.

Pattison also controls a significant share of B.C.'s domestic food production. His Berryland canning factory in the Fraser Valley exports more canned fruit and vegetables than any other Canadian canner. The products show up in local stores under the Berryland and Glen Valley labels.

About the same time Pattison moved into agriculture

he also ventured into fishing, buying Canfisco's 91-vessel fleet and processing plants at auction. The company's Gold Seal canned salmon is sold all over the world.

By themselves, none of these near-monopolies are illegal under Canadian law. It is only when the government is able to and has the will to prove that the owner uses his dominant position to gouge the public or to keep out competitors that a company will be restrained.

But for every law aimed at increasing competition, there are ten more that help businessmen lessen it. In this regard, Canada is less willing to let the "free market" forces run their course than is the United States. There, the Federal Trade Commission requires that large, privately owned corporations disclose the financial statements of their various subsidiaries. If any particular category shows above-average profits for a long term, alarm bells sound and the company is investigated to see whether it employs practices to keep competition out. Canada has no similar law.

If such disclosure rules had been in effect when Pattison owned Neonex, he would have had to report the profits of every one of the 30 companies in the conglomerate. The benefits would flow both to competitors, who could see what "line of business" was worth competing for, and to investors, who would know which parts of the conglomerate were doing well and which ones were in trouble.

Line of business (LOB) reporting was one of the major recommendations by the Royal Commission on Corporate Concentration in its 1978 report. So far no Canadian government has acted on the commission's advice.

Another U.S. example highlighted by the commission was the Securities and Exchange Commission's reporting requirements. Larger companies, even private ones, are required to file annual "10-K" reports on the companies' finances, including salaries of the top executives. The closest Canada has come to this rule is a law requiring disclosure of the *combined* salaries of the top five officials.

The federal government also passed a law in 1970 requiring federally incorporated private companies to file an annual financial report, a Canadian version of the 10-K. Exempt from the law are all companies not registered federally. When Pattison bought out other Neonex shareholders in 1977 he immediately revoked the federal incorporation papers and registered Neonex as a provincial company. So far, all ten provinces have refused to implement disclosure rules similar to Ottawa's.

Provincial governments justify their protection of the privacy of companies with outdated arguments. The historical presumption is that if a businessman has enough money to operate an enterprise without relying on "capital markets"—that is, shareholders—then the financial affairs of the company concern only the owner and his bank. The public has no right to peek at the company ledger.

The argument held up well enough in horse and buggy days, but hardly today in the era of instantaneous worldwide communications and rapid transportation, when entire fortunes can be transferred from one country to another with the tap of a few computer keys. Not revealing profits, in the words of the 1978 royal commission, allocates resources "not to the most efficient producer, but to the most efficient concealer."

Some conglomerate owners openly flouted the laws of the land to conceal their methods of extracting wealth. When New Brunswick's Irving family, said to control "the most significant concentration of corporate power in Canada,"[5] was ordered to testify at the royal commission hearings, Irving lawyers thumbed their noses at the order and dared the commissioners to take them to court. The commission backed down, wary of an expensive court case.

The royal commissioners merely studied corporate concentration; Pattison perfected it.

A few months after the report was released, complete with its demands for more disclosure about the nation's

200 largest firms, Pattison vaulted Neonex higher up the ladder of corporate wealth with the purchase of Claude Neon of Toronto, and by increasing his ownership of Crush International. By the end of 1978 he held 63 per cent of the soft drink firm's stock; Crush's annual sales of $62 million considerably fattened the Neonex balance sheet.

In fact, now that the entire group of companies was privately owned by Pattison, earnings soared. His car dealerships, airlines, data processing company, and radio station were rolled into the new Jim Pattison Group along with the wagon full of firms from old Neonex. Together, they employed about 6,000 people who generated more than $500 million in revenue in 1979.

With Pattison more in control than ever, and hardly accountable to anyone but himself and his bankers, he underwent a kind of metamorphosis. While not a recluse, Pattison had not been the most accessible corporate boss, especially during his more embarrassing moments in the 1970s.

Then, in April 1979, like a butterfly emerging from a cocoon, Pattison's chamber of commerce smile showed up in a full colour photograph beneath an article in *Maclean's* magazine. He no longer had to answer tough questions about shareholders' dividends or dubious investments, or to explain awkward entries in the annual financial statements. Pattison could afford to be more "available."

The media, in turn, treated him like something of a celebrity. It is hard to find a critical word written about him. ("Some of Jimmy's acquisitions were just dirt dumb," the *Maclean's* article quoted one of Jimmy's admirers as saying—the only critical comment in the story.)

Pattison, once again, was intent on acquiring more companies, but he went about it with more polish than in the first binge of acquisitions a decade earlier. He showed he had more management capabilities, that he really "listened" to his newly acquired employees. In the jargon of the late seventies, he taught his company managers to "hear" what their employees were saying through the use of Japanese-inspired "quality circles."

North American companies which tried quality circles were considered innovative. In reality, they were pragmatic, having read reports like one in the *Globe and Mail* which said the real benefits of quality circles lay in "improved productivity, profits and competitiveness."

Pattison's quality circles consisted of five to ten employees drawn from all levels, and each circle was related to a specific area of work. During the meetings, all staff would identify problems, draw up improvement plans, and submit the recommendations to management for its decision.

Pattison's circles were promoted as "voluntary" but employees remember them being compulsory. One Air BC staffer recalls the frustration of airing complaints, recommending changes and then hearing that senior management had refused to act. In one circle, the staff said private owners of small, efficient aircraft were stealing charter business from the airline. They proposed regaining that business by replacing some of Air BC's old, large aircraft with smaller planes. Management said it was a good suggestion, but neither acted on it nor told the workers the reason.

Management sometimes used the circles for issuing directives. Office workers at one manufacturing plant were told not to talk to unionized blue collar workers, nor to have coffee with them, nor even to accept a ride home with them.

One manager at Fabco would walk into a clerk's office and, even though the woman was making a business call, put his finger on the receiver button and say, "I'm here now, and anyway they will just think you got disconnected. You can call them back later." The manager refused to change even after the matter was raised in his quality circle.

The Japanese model of quality circles are said to work best when the employees have profit sharing plans or other perks to motivate them to increase productivity.

Pattison did not go this far. The only perk employees got, other than the opportunity to improve their working conditions, was to see their name in print in the monthly newsletter, *QC Recorder*, put out by Pattison Group head office.

The newsletter allows employees nominated by members of the QC to write an article about how they solved one of their specific problems. The "lead" story in the August 1984 issue told how Overwaitea cashiers wasted time running from one till to another looking for customer service forms and bulk food prices. The circle calculated the time wasted in one store to be 534 minutes per week. At $15 an hour this translates to $6,942 per year. The QC designed a new "organizer" for each till, with pouches for the forms and a glass-covered shelf for the price lists, and a phone for trouble-shooting. The total cost of organizers for every till in the store was $688.80. That one-time purchase, by the workers' estimates, would save each store about $6,000 a year, or $300,000 a year for the 50-store chain.

Those chosen to write the QC reports seem to have undergone a course in cheerleading. Contributor Mike Jefferson of Seaboard chirped, "More Good News! We now have a new Quality Circle comprised of middle management folks who have selected the logical name, 'The Connector's' [sic]. This is really a FIRST."

In a recent interview Pattison estimated the total cost of implementing more than 70 quality circles in the Pattison Group was $1 million. He won't reveal how much the Group has saved as a result of the changes suggested by circles, but since Pattison hasn't dumped them, it's a safe assumption that they are cost-effective.

Pattison's top managers, the ones who work at head office and manage the various divisions, run in quality circles at a rather higher level. They were jetted down to Palm Springs, a desert hideaway for the ultra-rich, for an annual "Partners in Pride" conference. This was the royal jelly treatment for those Pattison counted on to keep the ordinary workers in a productive frame of mind. The managers were tanned, fed and entertained.

During their working hours their performance motivation was massaged in management problem-solving sessions. The neo-conservatives in the group must have imagined themselves in heaven, for they were addressed by giants on the right, including Ronald Reagan, then-governor of California, Henry Kissinger, Alexander Haig and Gerald Ford.

For Pattison, quality circles and management conferences resulted in plenty of public praise and favourable press coverage. Out of hundreds of articles written about him between 1968 and 1984, only one was harshly critical. It was a profile of Pattison published in the April 1985 issue of *Equity* magazine. The story quoted several unidentified former colleagues of Pattison's. One was particularly blunt: "[Pattison] may conform to the gospel and he may tithe and all that shit, but he'll sink you as soon as look at you. He's a ferocious competitor."

The unidentified critic continued: "Maybe he just carries to the nth degree all that business is all about. Maybe the rest of us are naive to think that in business we should be gentlemen. He realizes that's bunk and carries on right through to the end and wins. You know when you play monopoly with your friends, the objective is to wipe your friends out. Well, he's doing that every day."

One of the "friends" who got wiped out was former Social Credit Corporate Affairs Minister Rafe Mair. Pattison hired him to host an open-line show on CJOR after Mair resigned from politics in 1981. His salary, which topped $150,000 a year, made him the highest paid broadcaster in Canada. Mair said that when his contract was first negotiated, Pattison insisted he "never interferes in the decisions of his companies," but then promptly worked out every clause of the agreement with Mair, giving the finished contract to station manager Tiff Trimble to sign.

Once on the air, Mair used his insider's knowledge as a former senior politician to editorialize on diverse issues. He was, for example, strongly opposed to beer and wine advertising on radio and TV, something which Pattison was lobbying for in order to increase advertising revenue at CJOR.

Mair was an unceasing critic of Senator Jack Austin, a friend of Pattison's. "Word soon filtered down," said Mair in an interview beside his kidney-shaped swimming pool at his expensive North Vancouver home, "that it would be unwise for me to continue to editorialize on these issues." The irrepressible Mair told CJOR management "to go fuck themselves."

When his three-year contract was about to expire, Mair heard rumblings (and even read about it in the local gossip columns) that he was about to be replaced by former NDP Premier Dave Barrett. Mair asked repeatedly if it was true and he was assured it wasn't.

When the time came to renegotiate the contract, on Good Friday, 1984, the station's ratings were in the basement. Mair, however controversial his opinions, was not drawing a vast following of listeners. In Pattison Group jargon, he was "not performing." That didn't prevent Pattison from giving Mair a gentle Good Friday hug after his show that day. When talks got underway, then-manager Harvey Gold told Mair the new contract would include a $42,000 cut in pay. Mair gulped and asked for a couple of weeks to think over the prospect of living on $108,000 a year. Gold said no. The offer was withdrawn and, says Mair, he was fired on Easter Monday. Gold said Mair refused a six-figure contract and quit.

Whatever the truth, Mair later concluded he had been shafted by Pattison. He sued for alleged "breach of contract...defamation [and] deceit." But in November 1984, just before the trial was to begin, both parties agreed to settle out of court. Mair claimed that Pattison paid him a "handsome" settlement. Pattison's law firm would not comment. (If "handsome" is an accurate description—and we may never know because the agreement called for complete secrecy—Mair can be added to the list of top Pattison employees sent packing with a fat wad in their back pocket.)

By the early 1980s Pattison had acquired an air of respectability, even among the senators and other members of the B.C. establishment. He had accommodated them, partly by toning down his polka-dot, huckster image, and partly by holding onto new companies for longer than eight months. They had accommodated him by granting memberships in the province's upper class watering holes, the Vancouver Club, the University Club and the Terminal City Club. Aspiring to those perches is a drawn-out procedure, but Pattison stayed the course. "People with power like to check you out," he said sheepishly when asked why he had not been admitted sooner.

Pattison had been careful to craft a public image of himself as a devout and generous Christian. He let it be known that on one of the many Sunday services he attended at the Pentecostal Glad Tidings Temple on Fraser Street, he dipped into his considerable bank account and put a cheque for one million dollars in the collection plate.

Later, he coyly confirmed the "rumour" by insisting, "I'm sure others have given more, according to their ability." (He was probably right.)

B.C. Business magazine, in its April 1984 edition, devoted its cover story to "Born Again businessmen" who had made a personal decision to commit their lives to Jesus Christ and adopt the Bible as the authority for faith, ethics and lifestyle. "Pattison wears his born again label happily," wrote Lloyd Mackey, who added that Pattison had attended Glad Tidings for sixteen years—since 1968. But Pattison didn't talk much about his religious beliefs at work, said Mackey, "lest colleagues or employees think he is laying a trip on them."

Pattison's *laissez faire* attitude to religion annoyed other Christians, especially those who thought some of his open-line hosts on CJOR or the magazines he distributed "deviated from the Christian approach." That is the closest the article came to pinpointing the contradiction between Pattison's Christian image and his ownership of the country's second largest distribution network for pornographic magazines. (Ironically, the month of *B.C. Business*' article, that contradiction was exposed in very clear terms by women's groups, as will be seen in detail in Chapter 9.)

Pattison may have been the best known born again CEO in town but he was not alone. Besides brothers Clark and Robert Bentall, heads of Dominion Construction and seven other firms, Ken Stevenson of Pennyfarthing Development belonged to the group that prayed to God for guidance before making business decisions. (Stevenson's firm showed less-than-Christian concern for fellow beings when, in 1984, it openly flouted organized labour by enforcing non-union construction of its luxury $80 million Harbour Cove condominiums near Granville Island.) Stevenson chaired the fundraising committee for the fall 1984 visit by Billy Graham. Other committee members included Block Brothers president Arthur Block, Peter Dueck, Pattison's automotive competitor who also headed the Canadian chapter of the ultra-conservative Campus Crusade for Christ, and Trans-Canada president Arthur Skidmore.[6]

Like the good stewards of Biblical parables, these men set out to make the most of what God had "given" them. As a group they were undisturbed by religious conflicts between how they acquired their wealth and how they treated others in the process. Of all those interviewed, only Arthur Block, head of the $600 million real estate firm, attempted to reconcile his wealth with the idea that amassing riches means trampling on others.

The answer, he said, is to be a "servant-leader" with a desire to "share the production." When asked to say what he shared, Block recalled that during the recession all employees took a cut in pay, and the highest paid, including himself, took the largest cuts. (He avoided mentioning that 10 per cent off a secretary's $10,000 income cuts a lot deeper than 20 per cent off a CEO's

$200,000 salary.)

There were similar cutbacks at the Pattison Group once the reality of the recession hit home. But the rationale offered by Pattison was purely business-oriented. He made no attempt to invoke Christian ideals for the cutbacks. Sceptics labelled Pattison's belt-tightening "more show than substance." He ordered all top executives to "park your Cadillacs" and drive smaller, cheaper cars. He cancelled all first-class air travel, prompting columnist Allan Fotheringham to quip, "When Pattison flies economy, the Canadian economy is in trouble." In 1982 Pattison's major money-saving gesture was to cancel the annual Palm Springs getaway for executives and hold it at a Holiday Inn in Vancouver.

In addition to these well-publicized moves, Pattison complained loudly about how hard the recession had hit his automobile sales and leasing companies, his RV manufacturing firms, his airlines and real estate holdings.

The numbers tell a different story, however.

In 1978, after Pattison bought out the other Neonex shareholders and consolidated all the companies into the Jim Pattison Group, annual sales were $500 million. By 1982, in the depths of the worst recession in half a century, his group's earnings were up to $715 million. The Jim Pattison Group had risen to become the 103rd largest company in Canada.

Two years later, when B.C.'s unemployment rate still hovered around 15 per cent and the province recorded more business failures (2,000 bankruptcies in 1984) than any other province, the Pattison Group broke the $1 billion-a-year barrier.

The story of how Pattison soared beyond the reach of the recession's claws takes us on an odd journey from Vancouver to Dallas to Switzerland and combines elements of fundamentalist visions of the apocalypse with uncanny business acumen.

It began in 1978. Pattison, for reasons he describes as sound business practice tempered by gut instincts, sold off the "bottom" 20 per cent of all his companies—the "weakest producers." This happened at a time of rapid expansion in the economy, when the trend was toward takeovers. Consequently, there were plenty of buyers. His sale netted him about $30 million. He bought U.S. dollars with the cash, which were then cheaper than Canadian money.

In the fall of 1980 Pattison sold his largest single asset, the majority share of Crush International. Proctor and Gamble, one of the largest industrial giants in the world, paid $43.75 million (U.S.) for the share, and by this time the U.S. dollar was the higher of the two currencies.

Pattison continued selling off the other "poor performers" and investing the proceeds in the U.S. until, by 1983, he had accumulated $140 million cash in U.S. dollars. Pattison's gut instincts had netted him a sizable fortune, but others in his orbit fared less well. By cutting his losses, Pattison had laid off 1,000 workers, adding to Canada's already record-high unemployment. The closure of one of his Crush bottling and canning plants in Toronto alone put 300 people out of work.

Pattison's instincts may have been his prime motivator, but his actions bore a noticeable similarity to other events of the time. One of Pattison's fellow Christians was, as noted, busy recruiting students for God's work through the Campus Crusade for Christ. The CCC, an arch-conservative evangelical movement founded in the U.S. by Bill Bright, was part of the "Here's Life" movement.

Bright had convinced one of the world's richest men, Bunker Hunt of Dallas, to raise one *billion* dollars for Here's Life, a drive which the Texas industrialist began with religious zeal by donating $10 million from his personal fortune.

Here's Life, the CCC and Hunt all preached that an avalanche of evil was about to engulf the world. They pointed to rapidly increasing inflation, escalating acts of terrorism and unstable world politics, evidenced by developments like the Iranian hostage situation.

Hunt, during numerous fundraising events, urged other people of his class to find ways to protect their wealth from the coming apocalypse. Personally, he and brother Herbert decided to sell off many possessions and buy silver, which they planned to stash in a safe haven in Europe. That marked the beginning of the infamous "silver Thursday" when the Hunts almost cornered the world silver market.

It may be only a coincidence, but at the same time Pattison—against conventional wisdom—began "liquidating" his possessions, and then, in 1983, moved them to Switzerland, one of Europe's safest havens for capital. He actually set up a Swiss merchant bank in Zug, the Great Pacific Finance A.G., and hired an American Express executive, Guy Krug, to become manager. (Krug was a Swiss citizen, a requirement for bank managers under Swiss law.)

By world standards, the bank is small. According to the 1984 annual report of Great Pacific Industries, Pattison's bank employed only thirteen people. What it lacked in tellers it made up for in assets: $154,139,000 in May 1984, most of it in cash and most belonging to Jim Pattison.

In December 1985 Pattison owned 80 per cent of GPI (and the Swiss bank). Twice in recent years he tried to buy the other 20 per cent and fold GPI into his group of private companies. But the minority shareholders, led by stockbroker Stephen Jarislowsky of Montreal, refused to sell. Pattison's offers were $10 a share too low said Jarislowsky. "GPI is mostly cash and tax loss," he said. In other words, profits that would normally be taxed to pay for pensions, hospitals and schools ended up in the Swiss bank's vaults. (GPI's 1984 annual report said the company deferred payments of $866,000 in taxes in 1983 and 1984.)

About the same time, Pattison opened an arbitrage* company in the Cayman Islands, a Caribbean tax haven

---

*Arbitrage companies buy "liquid" assets like treasury bonds and foreign currencies in one part of the world, sell them in another, and pocket the difference.

favoured by the super-rich who dislike paying taxes or who seek to hide ill-gotten gains, or both. In the Caymans, bankers do not ask embarrassing questions about the origin of suitcases full of money, nor do they disclose to foreign governments the names of clients who fortunes fill their vaults.

Of course, the money seldom sits in vaults for long. Usually it is brought back to the country of origin in the form of a "loan" from the dummy Cayman company so it can be "put back to work" without the risk of having any siphoned off to pay for highways, health care and universities.

Both Pattison's bank and the arbitrage company were soon at work turning his huge fortune into an even larger one. The Cayman company bought and sold securities like U.S. Treasury bonds, turning big profits, often in the course of a few hours. Like the Englehard operation, it relied on accurate, fast "intelligence" to make, often in the course of a day, profits which exceed the lifetime earnings of an average Canadian.

The bank lent money to "high quality clients," usually millionaires interested in buying companies. Pattison had come full circle, beginning fifteen years earlier as a high-rolling takeover businessman and emerging now as a merchant banker, financing others' takeovers.

Whatever Pattison's motives—apocalyptic visions or greed—the results were the same. This man, who frequently said his contribution to society was providing 6,000 jobs, had found a way to take over the profits produced by those workers, lay off one out of six of them, siphon a lot of the money away from Canada and the Revenue Department, multiply his money without generating a single job, and leave the government to pick up the tab for the mortgages, rents and food bills of the people he'd laid off.

Commenting on Pattison's apparent foresight in selling when he did, Vancouver *Sun* financial columnist Der Hoi-Yin hailed his move as a "stroke of genius. He lowered his debt and diversified his assets in advance of the recession," she applauded, ignoring the negative consequences.

Scuttling whole companies the way he used to fire the worst salesman every month, then moving his assets offshore, were not the only reasons Pattison weathered the recession so well. He already dominated enough sectors of the Canadian economy to pick up business in one area when it slacked off somewhere else. For example, as unemployment increased and retail sales plummeted, many retailers cut back on expensive radio and TV advertising. They switched to less expensive transit ads and billboards. In 1983, Pattison's billboard and transit ad companies' earnings rose 22 per cent over the previous year.

Those stores which cut back on all media advertising often invested in better quality signs. Again the biggest sign producer in town—in Canada for that matter—is Jim Pattison. The various sign companies in the Group recorded increases in business.

Pattison also reported a jump in the sale of magazines—a cheap form of entertainment for those out of work, suffering from pay cuts or worried about economic doom.

The only two areas in which Pattison "got burned," though not in any serious way, were real estate and oil and gas. His real estate ventures were poorly timed because, in Pattison's view, he got in when the market was high and was stuck with over-priced office buildings and land. His unsuccessful foray into a gas pipeline venture in B.C.'s Grizzly Valley left him singed by the flames of public inquiry. In late 1976, some provincial civil servants took advantage of inside knowledge of major natural gas discoveries beneath the valley to make themselves a few thousand dollars buying penny stocks in companies exploring the area. Someone blew the whistle on them and a public inquiry into the affair began in early 1977. During the hearing businessman Barry Hemsworth said Pattison "influenced" two governors of the Vancouver Stock Exchange into letting him have a piece of the Grizzly action.

Hemsworth, then-president of Cheyenne Petroleum Company, which had exploration rights in the Grizzly Valley, said Pattison offered VSE governors R.M. Thompson of Pemberton Securties (a former director of Neon Products) and Peter Brown[7] of Canarim Investments (later appointed to the board of directors of Expo 86) $25,000 each to arrange the sale of 25,000 Cheyenne shares to Pattison (Vancouver *Sun*, April 25, 1977).

(Pattison couldn't simply buy the shares because the VSE had placed them "in escrow"—a practice designed to weed out unscrupulous owners who might otherwise sell shares to the public, then abandon the enterprise and skip town with the cash.)

As governors of the VSE, Thompson and Brown were in a position to influence the release of Cheyenne shares. According to the *Sun*, Hemsworth said they did just that. The deal, however, didn't go through "because Pattison didn't agree to the price."

That was the official explanation. Once Pattison learned of the public inquiry he may have decided to get out. Whatever the reason, his role in the Grizzly Valley controversy was obscured by the swirl of accusations that the Socred government's employees had taken advantage of inside information to make a fast buck.

In August 1984, when I interviewed Hemsworth, he said the amount of oil and gas under the Grizzly Valley was "no where near what I thought." It would appear that Pattison made the right move when he got out—if one ignores the questionable means by which he proposed to move in.

In an interview three months later Pattison refused to comment on the Hemsworth accusations but conceded that his ventures into oil and gas and real estate had been disasters, which he blamed on his lack of experience in those fields and on the incompetence of his business partners.

No matter who was to blame, the public image of Pattison is rarely tarnished. He sailed through the Grizzly affair just as he had the Neonex share controversy and the billboard conspiracy trial. If any thing, press coverage made captain Pattison appear every inch the smiling, energetic entrepreneur doing what he does best: making deals. It was Pattison's new acquisitions which made the headlines.

That remained true until the spring of 1984, when industrious researchers from a women's organization went gunning for pornography profiteers and threatened to blow Pattison out of the water.

NOTES

1. During the period of investigation (1973-76), the three companies received 85 per cent of all money spent on billboard advertising in Canada. Outside of Ontario, they were virtually the only game in town. The breakdown is as follows:
   Mediacom owned 65 per cent of all poster panels (billboards) in Canada, including,
     Nova Scotia: 99%
     New Brunswick: 99%
     Quebec: 96%
     Manitoba: 93%
     Saskatchewan: 86%
     Ontario: 66%
   HOAL Investments
     Alberta: 97%
   Seaboard Advertising
     British Columbia: 80%

2. Jack Giles' wife, Virginia, is also no stranger to government patronage. After serving a brief stint on the government's Community Colleges Board she was appointed in June 1985 to the B.C. Parole Board. In the last federal election, she worked on the Mulroney campaign.

3. To its credit, in July 1985, the *Sun* reprinted a column from the Los Angeles *Times* calling for criminal executives to be jailed when their companies commit crimes. The writer, Ernest Conine, noted that even large fines have little deterrent effect and anyway, "Such penalties are commonly passed on to consumers as just another cost of doing business." Conine also underlined the role of class solidarity when justice is dispensed to the rich. "One factor is the reluctance of most judges to put men of their own class behind bars for economic, non-violent crimes."

4. General Motors brass were reportedly miffed when they learned that Pattison planned to open Toyota dealerships. Pattison's attitude

was, "I already market the best-selling domestic cars, so why not the biggest selling imports?" So successful was he at selling their autos, that GM backed down.

5. The Irvings own more than 100 companies involved in oil refining, distribution and retailing, pulp, paper and timber products, ship building, newspapers, radio and television. They employ 10,000 people.

6. Skidmore and Pattison had more than Christianity in common. Trans Canada Glass was fined $4,000 under the Combines Investigation Act in September 1982 for forcing retailers to sell automobile windshields at TCG's "suggested" price. Retailers who attempted to sell for less were threatened with having their supplies cut off.

Trans Canada is also one of five companies currently appealing charges under the act, that it rigged bids on the glass contracts for major Vancouver buildings like the Daon building and, ironically, the Law Courts building in which the case was heard.

7. The same Peter Brown of Canarim Investments Ltd., who was involved in the "Pouilly Fuisse" scandal. In 1981, when he was still a governor of the VSE, Brown, his wife and another couple were the guests of Consumer Affairs Minister Peter Hyndman at an expensive Vancouver restaurant. The tab for the meal, including four bottles of Pouilly Fuisse wine at $37.50 each, was $347.57. Mr. Hyndman charged it to his government expense account.

The scandal erupted when a disgusted civil servant in the accounting department released the information. The uproar spawned a satirical bestselling poster showing a grinning piglet with its snout nuzzled between a glass of wine and a bottle of Pouilly Fuisse, over the caption, "So *That's* the B.C. Spirit!" Hyndman resigned a short time later.

9 HARD CORE CAPITALIST

The guys running our [magazine] distribution in Ontario—one is a deacon in a church and the other is a graduate of a Bible college. In Hamilton the police originally charged the deacon but I said, "don't charge him, just the company," and they did.
   —Jim Pattison

The unseasonably warm air was still heavy with the dampness of the morning rain as a woman clutching her briefcase walked along Georgia Street in downtown Vancouver. Donna Stewart, a member of the North Shore Women's Centre and long-time campaigner against pornography, didn't notice the traffic or heavy grey clouds scudding overhead. She had waited months for the occasion to reveal the information contained in the documents she carried. She was certain the revelation she was about to make would rock the city's business and political establishment.

It was April 3, 1984. Stewart walked through the large, bustling lobby of the Hotel Vancouver and up the thickly carpeted stairs to the meeting room where members of the federal government's Special Committee on Pornography and Prostitution were preparing to resume the day's hearing.

Stewart, one of several women scheduled to address

the committee that afternoon, was no stranger to the subject of pornography, which was as ancient as western civilization. It was the ancient Greeks who first named the practice, which consisted of drawing or depicting (graphos) the lowest forms of prostitutes (porno).

But it was not until the latter half of this century that pornography underwent a basic transformation. Technological changes made it possible to distribute the stuff cheaply and a new morality did away with the plain brown wrappers. Pornography mushroomed into a worldwide and very lucrative industry. With its emerging status as a "legitimate" business, pornography became the target of opposition and analysis by feminists.

What their research uncovered was a modern version of *pornographos*, which in its extreme versions depicted bestiality, incest, necrophilia, violent sexual acts, torture and even murder. A common message threaded through the pornographic material—whether in books, magazines, films or videos: the woman appears to find sexual pleasure in being physically abused. The conviction by feminists that pornography constitutes a form of propaganda hostile to women led to actions aimed at ridding communities of pornography.

Stewart, one of many local activists, was confident the brief she was to present at that day's hearing would further her cause of raising public awareness about links between big business and pornography. Stewart held no illusions that the committee would address the root causes of pornography. The Fraser Committee—named after its chairman, Vancouver lawyer Paul Fraser—owed its existence to the Liberal government of Pierre Trudeau. It was one response of a growing public outcry against the proliferation of pornography and prostitution.

No one disputed the enormous size of the pornography trade. By the committee's own estimates, "legitimate" Canadian businesses took in $437 million a year selling explicit photos of women and children, many depicted in degrading and dehumanizing poses, the victims of beatings, whippings and rape. This enormous industry ranked in size with the country's jewellery trade. Most of its money was generated by the legal distribution of magazines.

These ranged from "soft core" publications like *Playboy* and *Penthouse*, through the more explicit and violent *Hustler* ($3 to $5), to the "hard core" titles like *Sluts of Auschwitz*, *Mother's Little Lovers* and *Big Boobs in Bondage* (up to $20).

Ten years earlier, such titles would have been available only through the mail or in a handful of seedy stores where they would have been wrapped in plastic. Now they appear in eight out of ten retail magazine stores. One-third of these stores carry twenty or more titles.

Stewart knew there was little chance of the Fraser Committee recommending removal of the most offensive material from the shelves, which was one of her goals. And her fear was that the report would suffer the same fate as countless other government studies, becoming the focus of media attention for a week or so and then being shelved and forgotten.

She appeared before the committee for two reasons. She hoped that its report would influence governments to bring in stricter laws against obscene material. And in the short run she hoped to educate the public about who really benefits from the sale of pornography.

As she sat through brief after brief the air in the chamber grew stuffier. Members of the committee looked tired, the predictable effect of a gruelling cross-Canada series of hearings during which they heard 2,000 oral briefs and read more than 500 written presentations.

Another anti-pornography activist, Kit Stevenson of UBC's University Women's Club was scheduled to speak before Stewart. Stevenson read her brief to the committee in slow, measured tones: "Mainland Magazines, which distributes more than 250 pornographic magazines, including some depicting incest and rape, is owned by Richards Enterprises of Vancouver, which is wholly owned by Pattison Enterprises..."

It may have been the long afternoon sitting, or the muggy air, or the repititious nature of the presentations that prevented her listeners from grasping the significance of what she had said. No one stirred. There was no gasp, no sign of surprise or shock among those who had just been told that the man entrusted with running a $1.5 billion world's fair in Vancouver was also pocketing profits from the sale of pornography.

Stewart was distressed. Her friend had just broken a story—an important story based on months of research—and it had been met with a small yawn. Everyone appeared distracted or slightly bored. Half the committee had left for the day.

Stewart was next on the speakers' list. On her way to the microphone she decided to ad lib what she had to say, and not read from her brief. "It is the same Jim Pattison," she began, "who is *Chairman of Expo 86* who is the owner of a pornographic magazine distribution company." She almost pleaded with her audience to recognize the dimensions of the moral imbalance she was imparting. Suddenly, murmuring stopped, hands dropped from chins, faces turned towards her.

"As we dug deeper into this pornography stuff," she continued, "the RCMP warned us about Mafia elements involved in the pornography business. Well, there may be a Mafia element in this, but what we have to fear is when the chairman of Expo, who presents himself as a respectable businessman who is closely related to the Social Credit government, turns out to own a company that distributes this pornography."

There were now signs of life in the room. Stewart's audience jeered and hissed at her revelation. Television reporters elbowed sleepy camera operators, who began setting up their equipment for an interview with Stewart.

TV news reports and stories in the press jumped on the sensational aspects of the disclosure showing photographs of naked women in chains and linking the magazines in which they appeared to Jim Pattison, Chairman of Expo, and high-profile Christian. The stories carried comments and reactions from others opposed to the spread of pornography, but missing from all the reports was any word from Jim Pattison, who was "unavailable for comment." He would not even confirm that he sold pornographic material.

The women's expose did not get nearly as wide coverage as it otherwise would have because a strike had put the two daily newspapers out of commission. Vancouver readers got a reduced dose of local news in the *Globe and Mail*'s special "B.C." section which relegated the Pattison story to page BC-3, run under the headline "Expo chief's firm deals porn, women say."

The story virtually disappeared from the daily press as Pattison remained "unavailable" for weeks. It was revived when a half dozen women's groups pressured city council into asking Pattison to explain his position. They wanted him to account for the money he made from pornography. His conglomerate didn't reveal sales for individual companies, so they could only guess at the amounts, but statistics from similar magazine companies showed that 30 per cent of the revenue came from "adult sophisticate" magazines.

But they knew that in 1980 the top eleven bestselling pornographic magazines in Canada sold 13,500,000 copies, and they estimated that one in five of the magazines was distributed by a Pattison-owned firm.

City council had another large cause for concern: Expo. The world's fair began as a Vancouver centennial project, a relatively modest celebration of the city's 100th anniversary in the form of a $70 million Transpo 86 exhibition. Although Victoria soon took the thing over, blowing it up into a Socred mega-circus, the council still had a keen interest in the fair that was to rise out of the industrial muck on the shores of False Creek, just down the hill from council chambers. They wanted to know what Pattison was up to.

Pattison declined the invitation to the Community Services Committee meeting, scheduled for May 3, and persuaded his chief competitor in the magazine distribution business, Brian Brammal of Vancouver Magazine Services, known as Van Mag, to go in his place.

It was not until May 1, almost a month after the revelations at the Fraser Commission hearings, that Pattison called a news conference to make his first public statement on the issue.

It was a sombre and apologetic Jim Pattison who faced the hushed scribes that Tuesday morning. The message he conveyed was one of puzzlement: How could he, a devout Christian, have slipped so far from grace?

"I have been very troubled," he said plaintively, "to learn that some of the publications handled by Mainland...are offensive."

Then the capitalist Christian, whose reading normally included balance sheets and the Bible, confessed that he, too, had spent some time "examining" these publications. Lest anyone draw the wrong conclusion, he hastily added, "I, too, have been offended."

It may seem unusual that a man as compulsive as Pattison, who kept such a close eye on all of his companies, would be unaware of the estimated 480,000 copies of the offensive magazines he was peddling each year. But the most reasonable inference to be drawn from his news conference that day was that if Jimmy had only *known* what was in those darned magazines he would never have permitted his company to sell or profit from the pornographic flood that gushed through its hands. Nor would he have become Canada's second largest distributor of pornographic magazines (reflected in the combined sales of his companies in B.C., Alberta and Ontario).

Then came the *coup de grace*. "If it wasn't for Expo 86," said Jim Pattison, "I would attempt to bring together the church, women's groups, wholesalers and the government to see if we can improve the standard..." but because he didn't have the time and because "my position as a representative of British Columbia makes it difficult for me to continue to own a wholesale magazine distributing company, I will sell Mainland Magazine immediately."

Pattison's "solution" was widely criticized. Even Mayor Mike Harcourt of Vancouver said that selling Mainland wouldn't solve the basic problem. He wanted Pattison to keep Mainland Magazine and to drop the pornographic titles. As far as the North Shore Women's Centre was concerned, if Pattison wouldn't stop voluntarily they would attempt to bring the pressure of the law down on him.

With Pattison, and for that matter, other magazine distributors on the defensive, the centre marshalled its mountain of pornographic evidence and prepared to lay obscenity charges.

Bev Schroeter, chairwoman of the centre, along with Jancis Andrews, showed the committee copies of the letters and other documents the centre had sent to Attorney General Brian Smith. These had been prepared by Andrews, correspondence secretary for the North Shore Women's Centre. The "documents" included copies of articles from *Kinks*, *International Hooker*, *Swank* and *Samantha Fox's X-Rated Cinema*. Said Andrews, "These contain explicit descriptions of incest, rape, urination, bestiality... and the rape of a six-year-old girl by her father. Of all the forms of obscenity," she fumed, "surely kiddie porn is the most contemptible, the most socially dangerous."

Andrews then produced a computer printout, pilfered by sympathetic insiders at Mainland Magazine, showing that all the offending magazines were distributed by Mainland.

The women's centre wasn't alone in demanding that the chief law enforcement officer in B.C. do something to enforce the laws against obscenity and clean up Vancouver's image as "the porn capital of Canada." An Ontario police task force, called Project P (for pornography), claimed the majority of "hard core" pornography in that province came from B.C. "It is our view that the reason for this is that there have been few prosecutions in B.C.," said an exasperated member of the special force. He went on to point out that the lack of prosecutions had been explicitly incorporated into advertisements for pornography. Red Hot Video ads, which run regularly in Toronto newspapers, boast that what it sells and distributes is "legal in B.C."

If Andrews and the other women thought the uninterested authorities were protecting rich men from prosecution, they didn't say. Instead they preferred to give Attorney General Smith, a lawyer, a refresher course in obscenity law.

They sent him a brief in which they quoted from three simple guidelines, published by Smith's own department, outlining what material is "obscene" under the Criminal Code.

1. Material which depicts sexual acts coupled with violence (including masochism, sadism, and other similar acts);
2. Material which depicts bestiality;
3. Material which depicts juveniles involved in sexual activities. *Violence is not a factor to be considered in this context.*

Then they reminded the A.G. that section 159 of the Criminal Code states, "Everyone commits an offence...who distributes...obscene material." And in case he didn't remember his department's three guidelines for obscene material, Andrews included the Criminal Code's own definition: "...the undue exploitation of sex, *OR* of sex and any one or more of the following subjects, namely, crime, horror, cruelty, and violence..."

Lesson over.

Apprized of the law, Smith was expected by Andrews to begin laying charges against distributors of articles like "Animal Obsessions" (bestiality), "Daddy's Little Girl" (incest), "Why Urination Turns Me On" (kiddie porn), "Break-in" (rape and torture), "All in the Family" (father having sex with six-year-old daughter),

"Golden Showers" (urination), and "Busted and Balled" (rape).

Pattison, who had not seen the specific charges but knew the general nature of the North Shore Women's Centre's complaints, was being inundated with demands to do something about his sale of pornography. A coalition of women's groups, including the North Shore Women's Centre, the University Women's Club, Canadian Coalition Against Media Pornography, and a number of individual women and men wrote letters to the editor, appeared on media programs and phoned Pattison at his home. Their demand was not that he sell Mainland, but that he stop distributing pornographic magazines. Pattison side-stepped the demands, either putting the blame on others or pleading ignorance—a contemporary form, perhaps, of turning the other cheek.

To the charge that his company distributed obscene, therefore illegal, material, he replied, "It is my personal opinion that Mainland Magazine and other wholesalers in British Columbia are distributing material that should not be available for sale in British Columbia, *even though that material is cleared by the prohibited publications section of Canada Customs.*"

Hogwash, said Canada Customs: "We would need 50 times our present staff to check each and every title that passes through Customs." In Ottawa, assistant deputy minister in charge of Customs, Tom Grieg, said his department had only a five-person board which wades through advance copies of 60 imported magazines each month. (They also preview videotape movies.) But, he said, they see only a small fraction of the 540 imported pornographic titles coming into Canada. (He estimated that 90 per cent of all pornography sold in Canada originates in the U.S.)

Andrews echoed his comments. "[Pattison's] phrase 'even though that material is cleared by the prohibited publications section of Canada Customs,' lends the distinct impression that a government department has thoroughly viewed all materials. If, by some miracle, Customs were able to view all the materials, they would still not have the final word on what constitutes the obscene. Section 159 [of the Criminal Code] specifically mentions those who...distribute, circulate...any obscene written matter."

Undeterred, Pattison went on to blame the wholesalers who supply Mainland with its magazines, alleging that they sell "packages" of titles which cannot be broken up. In other words, if you want *Ladies Home Journal*, you take *Swank* too. In the trade this is known as "tied selling," which is illegal in Canada under section 31.4 of the Combines Investigation Act.

In addition, there is a section of the Criminal Code specifically dealing with obscene material. Under this section, a magazine wholesaler such as Mainland is in violation of the law for refusing to sell one publication (e.g., *Time*) to a retail store because the merchant refuses to carry an obscene publication.

"We cannot accept," sighed Andrews, "that magazine distributors are not aware of this law which so vitally affects their line of business." Continuing, she took issue with Pattison's next excuse. He pleaded that the government was at fault for "failing to produce any clear or precise definition of obscenity. Magazine wholesalers are forced to try to act as self-censors, a role for which they are not qualified, and which places them in an impossible position." (These claims are odd coming from Pattison since born again Christians are self-appointed experts at defining all manner of evils, including obscenity.) Andrews sarcastically pointed out that Pattison's statement "did not appear to fit the facts." She offered to send him the same guidelines she had sent the Attorney General, guidelines which the department claimed were so clear that "an average grade 10 student could understand them." It was so incredible that neither Pattison nor Mainland's executives or lawyers knew about obscenity laws. Andrews found it impossible to take his plea of ignorance seriously. His "surprise" at what had been going on, his "regret" that it had happened, his announcement that he would do something about it all rang hollow.

And it rang even hollower when the researchers-cum-detectives at the North Shore Women's Centre discovered two separate previous convictions of Pattison magazine companies for violating the very obscenity laws Pattison found so confusing. How could he insist he had been in the dark about Mainland's pornographic wares, Andrews wonders, "when, on not one, but two separate occasions, those products have caused a loss in profits totalling $22,000?"

To my knowledge, neither conviction was publicly reported in detail. Since the court cases are at the heart of the Pattison-pornography link, it is worth examining what happened to Pattison's company in the dank, steel-mill city of Hamilton.

It was January 1980. Assistant crown attorney Geoffrey Read of the Hamilton-Wentworth judicial district had heard enough complaints. Faced with a growing public outrage at magazines containing explicit photographs of child molestation, rape, torture and homosexual encounters, Read ordered a crackdown. He telephoned Staff Sergeant Fred Pawluk.

A few days later, on Thursday, January 31, Pawluck, dressed in plain clothes, entered Tabby's Variety store on King Street in Hamilton. He flipped through current issues of *Hustler* and found what he had been told to look for—graphic photos of adults fondling children. He paid for the magazine and left.

The next day, February 1, he returned to Tabby's, this time in uniform and accompanied by another officer. They produced a search warrant and seized nineteen copies of *Hustler*, along with invoices showing the distributor's name: Mountain City News, a Jim Pattison company.

The following day the two men returned to Tabby's, this time with a warrant to seize all copies of *Numbers*, a magazine about male homosexuals, also distributed by Mountain City. (Some feminists and gays object to the authorities lumping gay pornography together with violent, child and straight porn. All pornography depicts nakedness and often simulated sex, but defenders of gay porn emphasize that it does not advocate dominance of men over women and children, a common feature of other porn.)

A week later, a Hamilton police van pulled up at the Mountain City News warehouse. Police ordered the manager, Gordon Birk, to hand over all undistributed copies of the two magazines. They also demanded Birk's computer print-out of all magazines distributed and the list of customers. Birk, a church-going man, complied. With this information, police raided five other small stores and hauled boxloads of magazines to court.

During the ensuing trial, Crown counsel Read had to overcome a major legal hurdle common to all obscenity cases. His task was to show that the material distributed by Mountain City News was offensive to "community standards." He knew well that arbitrary interpretations by Canadian judges across Canada of what constitutes "community standards" had resulted in widely differing verdicts and sentences.

A Vancouver feminist group condemned the obscenity standards as "legal fiction" and demanded much clearer definitions of what they said amounts to hate literature aimed at women and children. In so doing, they argued that political judgments, not moral ones, should be applied to the whole issue of pornography.

Read was well acquainted with the arguments but as often happens when the rich are about to be drawn into court, the central charge gives way to lesser ones. The trial advanced to the stage where the nature of pornography could be argued. Instead, Read's major fight with the Pattison company boiled down to a legal technicality.

Pattison's legal dodge had its roots in the original police action, about nine months earlier, when Mountain City was first charged with distributing obscene material. In this case, the company didn't protest its innocence, but worked out a deal with the prosecution. If it would drop the charges against the manager, Gordon Birk, the company (legally a "person") would plead guilty. On May 14, 1979, Mountain City News pleaded guilty to distributing obscene material and was fined $10,000. No real person was punished.

The second time around, Mountain City's lawyers were not so accommodating. They reregistered the company under a new name, Jim Pattison International Ltd., and back-dated the name change six months. Then they argued in court that the charges should be dropped since the "wrong" company was named in the charge.

Read could play the same game. He responded quickly by back-dating the indictment to read "Jim Pattison International Ltd. *carrying on business as* Mountain City News." The judge allowed Read's change and proceeded to trial. Outmanoeuvred, Pattison's lawyers pleaded guilty on behalf of the company. Judge Joseph Sciny fined Jim Pattison International $12,000 for distributing obscene material.

The two convictions against Pattison's company were a small but significant part of wider efforts by Ontario police to enforce obscenity laws. In 1983 alone, over 500 charges were laid by Ontario police against producers and distributors of child and adult pornography. Most of those charged pleaded guilty, if for no other reason than it was the cheapest way out.

They had only to look west to the example of Red Hot Video in B.C. to appreciate how costly a court fight can be. Red Hot's lengthy trial, much of which focused on the exact meaning of "undue exploitation of sex," ended in May 1983 with a guilty verdict. Red Hot was fined a paltry $300, although its legal costs were an estimated $150,000. Still, the mounting legal fees hadn't broken the company's back, for it went on to appeal the verdict. By themselves, the fines could be paid out of petty cash.

News of the volume of Ontario convictions, and especially the fines against a Jim Pattison company, was slow reaching B.C. The first fine, $10,000 in 1979, was not even reported in Pattison's home province, possibly because his name did not appear in the charges. But the following year the name Jim Pattison International was read into the court record. There is no indication that B.C. papers picked up the story. Whatever the reason, it wasn't because Pattison lacked public stature. He was at that time the head of a $700 million-a-year conglomerate, the tenth largest private company in Canada, and had been annointed "Businessman of the Year."

News of the convictions may not have reached the coast at all had it not been for a rare coincidence of timing and shared ideals.

Donna Stewart visited Hamilton while on vacation in 1983. Her sister, who was also active in fighting pornography, knew the head of the Hamilton vice squad, who remembered the name Pattison and told her about the previous convictions.

News of Pattison's convictions landed in Vancouver during the Pacific Press strike, soon after he had promised to sell Mainland Magazines. The story first appeared under the byline of Alderman Harry Rankin in several neighbourhood weekly newspapers.

About a week later an industrious *Globe and Mail* reporter, Paul Taylor, included the information in a well-researched story about Pattison's promise to sell Mainland and divest himself of this offensive material. Taylor dug through dusty corporate records and found that the man named by Pattison as the potential buyer of Mainland, Fred Vanstone, had more than a country club acquaintance with Pattison. Vanstone, the former Bank of British Columbia boy-wonder, had, in 1979, been listed as "vice president of finance and a director of Mr. Pattison's company, Neonex," wrote Taylor, who might have added that Neonex was the same company that owned Mountain City News at the time of the Hamilton convictions. As financial officer, Vanstone would have been one of the first to know about the reason for the fines.

"As well," continued Taylor breathlessly, "in 1980 [Vanstone] was listed as a director of the Jim Pattison

Group and a director of Crush International Ltd., another company Mr. Pattison controlled at the time."

Vanstone was more than reluctant to meet the press. He did not return dozens of phone calls. A number of anti-pornography women even staked out the Burrard Street office of his company, Vandella Enterprises. They saw no one enter or leave. This only fuelled speculation that the "sale" of Mainland magazines was nothing more than a paper transfer that would still leave the company in the Pattison fold.

Reporters pelted Pattison with questions about the deal, but he continued to insist that everything was above board. To Taylor's specific allegations he said only, "Vanstone is no longer a director of any of my companies." This did little to silence the cries for a complete inquiry into the interlocking directorships of the Pattison empire, specifically as they pertained to the pornography question.

Away from the glare of TV lights Pattison engaged in another form of defence, one quite commonly practised by the powerful and well-connected: using contacts.

Like most pragmatic businessmen, Pattison didn't let his conservative political leanings interfere with his friendships with leading Liberals in the government of the day. He was a friend of Liberal Senator Ray Perrault. He was on a first-name basis with Liberal cabinet ministers like Lloyd Axworthy and Marc Lalonde. So in his hour of need, Pattison turned to another prominent Liberal, Maude Barlow, the special adviser to the prime minister on women's issues. He had met her before, and knew that she personally knew the anti-pornography activists who were demanding that he stop selling pornography. He expected that she would agree to ask those women to stop pressuring him. What he didn't count on was that Barlow's opposition to pornography would far outweigh any loyalty to Pattison as a friend of top Liberals.

The telephone in the Prime Minister's Office rang. "Hello?" It was a woman's voice. "Hello, is this

Maude Barlow?" asked Pattison. "Yes," she replied.

Pattison identified himself and launched into his appeal.*

"Will you speak to the ladies of the North Shore Women's Centre on my behalf?" he asked.

Barlow had not expected the appeal from Pattison, but she was already familiar with the Mainland Magazine situation. As a long-time campaigner against pornography, she was one of the first to hear about the North Shore Women's Centre's disclosures about Pattison.

"Mr. Pattison," she replied, "I don't see how I can be of any help to you. What exactly have you done to upset the North Shore Women's Centre?"

He said sheepishly that it was about "some magazines that I sell."

"I really don't see what I can do," continued Barlow, "but maybe the best thing I can do is to tell you the names of some of the magazines and what's in them." She recited from memory titles such as *Big Boobs in Bondage* and a few more before he interrupted and reminded her that he was a church-going man and he, too, was offended by this material.

The call had gone on long enough. "I suggest," said Barlow, "that your Sunday mornings could be spent more profitably reading the contents of the material you sell." Pattison hung up.

Barlow later recalled that there was no mistaking the abrupt end to the conversation. "I heard from a number of sources that he was upset at my position," she chuckled.

Shunned by allies, under constant pressure from women's groups, other Christians, individuals and the media, Pattison went on the offensive. He called a meeting of his own. In spite of what he had told reporters at his press conference, he made time to gather representatives of women's groups, the churches and city

---

*Details of this phone call have been confirmed to the author by Barlow.

hall for a mid-May meeting.

In the hectic days before the meeting Pattison's staff left nothing to chance. Donna Stewart recalled a phone conversation with Maureen Chant, Pattison's trusted executive assistant, "who seems to be a lovely woman. She told me that so-and-so from another women's group would be at the meeting and asked if I was going too. Now I'm not saying that Maureen Chant deliberately lied to me, but when I called that other woman she said she had given no such commitment. I think this indicates the tremendous pressure that Pattison puts on his staff to get results no matter what."

(This was not the most bizarre phone call Stewart received during the Mainland affair. On one occasion she was phoned by an angry woman who asked in cultured tones whether Stewart and her colleagues understood the harm they were doing, not just to Pattison but to the province. "Don't you know," she lamented, "that Jim Pattison wanted to be Lieutenant Governor of B.C. and all this publicity about pornography has ruined that?")

If one of Pattison's goals in calling the meeting was to split his opponents, he succeeded. Some women's groups refused to collude with Pattison. Others felt they had no choice but to show up. In the end, some women attended over the strong objections of others.

Those who went were joined by members of church groups and city hall staff. Besides Donna Stewart, there was Jillian Ridington, a former vice president of the National Action Committee on the Status of Women, Kit Stevenson of the University Women's Club and Karen Phillips of the Port Coquitlam Women's Centre. Among church representatives were Anglican Archbishop Douglas Hambidge of New Westminster and Dean Jim Cruickshank of Christ Church Cathedral. Pattison brought along his manager of Mainland Magazines, John Seebach. Also attending was a senior projects officer from the B.C. Attorney General's office, Linda Cronin.

Pattison persuaded all his critics present to agree to

participate in setting up a review board to screen all pornographic magazines coming into B.C. before they are distributed to retailers. Pattison said ten of B.C.'s eleven magazine wholesalers had agreed to the plan, in which they would also pay for the cost of setting up and running the board, in co-operation with the Attorney General's department.

Under the proposal, three people would sit on the board (with a fourth acting as alternate). For a nominal fee—$850 a month for the chair and $650 for each member—they would flip through thousands of pages of pornography searching for photographs and articles that they considered obscene under the Criminal Code definition. If two out of three board members objected to something, the distributors would agree to withdraw the magazine or at least rip out the offending pages.

No one other than Pattison and Seebach was totally in agreement with the plan. "People are being desperately hurt and someone has to do something," said Archbishop Hambidge when asked after the meeting why he supported the proposal.

Donna Stewart sought a middle ground between militant feminists opposed to the board and the magazine distributors promoting it. "I don't think [the board] is going to make a substantial difference to all the garbage out there," she said. "But at least the very worst things will be kept off the market, which is superior to the criminal prosecution system which is very slow and expensive."

Kit Stevenson was more cynical. "Pattison had questionable motives [in proposing the board] *after* his involvement in distributing pornography became public. Now he is doing something to rectify it so he can come out as a knight in shining armour."

Whatever Sir Jimmy's motives, he now had agreement in principle from some of his staunchest opponents to a plan which he had engineered. He also had the enthusiastic backing of people who had backed him all along. "A.G. Applauds Pattison on Porn," bleated one headline over a story which quoted Brian

Smith as saying, "The industry should be policing itself," and not, he might have added, leaving it up to the Attorney General to prosecute the offending distributors. Smith is quite particular about which laws are worth upholding. He saved his heavy-handed legal tactics for those opposing his current policies, like prostitutes in the west end or unionized construction workers at Expo (see next chapter).

The rest of the feminist community united swiftly in opposition to the board. Calling the proposal "a sleazy tactic of Pattison's," Regina Lorek of Vancouver Rape Relief and Women's Shelter denounced the magazine distributors for "reneging on their own responsibility and putting it on another group of people. The irony of this is that [the review board] will have to let some pornography go through, and because women will be on that board they will be giving the stamp of approval to that pornography. The distributors don't need a review board because the Criminal Code is very clear on this matter."

Jancis Andrews, who objected to the establishment of the board but remained correspondence secretary of the North Shore Women's Centre, said, "Distributors are trying to wriggle out of their legal responsibilities and [use the board] as a smokescreen, a safety belt."

Megan Ellis of the Women Against Violence Against Women rape crisis centre echoed the general sentiment. "It's a cheap alternative to prosecution," she said, and predicted that the board would be stuck in an untenable position, berated for what it withholds and also for what it lets through.

After analysing the proposal, Joni Miller and Lee Lakeman of Rape Relief noticed similarities between it and another Pattison initiative, the "quality circles."

"The theme [of quality circles]," wrote Miller and Lakeman, "is 'we're all in this together.' What gets hidden is the hierarchy...

"Similarly, the tone of the review board is of co-operation. Because the magazine distributors voluntarily submit to the rulings of the board, they get to appear to be concerned with community standards. They also avoid publicity for the consequences of the products. The Attorney General and the distributors benefit by avoiding prosecutions under the obscenity law."

While the debate went on, Cronin and Seebach and others who attended Pattison's meeting formed a steering committee and put together an application form. It said any resident of B.C. was eligible to become a member of the review board. It advised applicants that, if successful, they would be spending eight hours of every week for the next three years exposing themselves to some of the worst hate literature and exploitative pornography available.

"How to seduce your seven year old daughter." When Alderman Bruce Eriksen passed by the magazine headline on his way into an east end Vancouver corner store, he felt a contempt for pornography in general, and for Jim Pattison and Brian Smith in particular.

Eriksen—wiry, greying, in horn-rimmed glasses—had working class roots similar to Pattison's but any resemblance ended there. Born in Winnipeg and orphaned as a young boy, he came to the west coast at fourteen and worked at a string of low-paying jobs. Eventually, he qualified as an ironworker, but his work in that field was cut short by an injury. He turned to organizing the skid road community and helped form the Downtown Eastside Residents Association. DERA successfully wrenched several concessions out of city hall and greedy landlords on behalf of the city's poorest (and second most stable) neighbourhood. A few years later Eriksen was elected to city council.

In May 1984, as chairman of the Community Services Committee, Eriksen was seeking ways of using city hall's muscle to crack down on pornography. But city councils are not very powerful bodies—they are granted charters by the provinces and cannot change the charters without permission from the higher government. They cannot tax income, only property. Their subordination to the province was ruthlessly drilled home by the Social Credit government in mid-1985 when it fired two elected school boards which refused to submit to its cutbacks.

Eriksen's committee attempted to get a number of potentially far-reaching recommendations through council, which, if enacted, would go beyond even the power of the province and on into federal government territory.

The most controversial plan was to revoke the business licence of any store selling "sexually graphic" material. This proposal was in one sense at variance with the position of the women's groups. They were not opposed to *all* depictions of human sexuality or nudity, but to exploitative, violent and dehumanizing portrayals of women and children. This debate did not progress too far because the proposed bylaw was quickly thrown out by a court, which said the city does not have the power to legislate in this area.

Eriksen had no better luck with another recommendation, which was passed unanimously by city council, asking that Jim Pattison keep Mainland Magazine but stop selling pornography. Pattison ignored the request.

The rest of Eriksen's proposals did not even get full support in council. Among them was a request for a full investigation of the "interlocking directorships of the Jim Pattison Group International" for the purpose of laying charges under the obscenity sections of the Criminal Code. Even Mayor Harcourt, who generally voted with the left-leaning faction of council, opposed the motion.

The single bylaw that council was able to enforce encompassed a quickly thrown together set of regulations governing the display of pornography. Among the new rules were orders to all retailers to display "adult" magazines at least five feet off the floor (out of children's line of sight) and to block from view all but the magazine's title. Shopkeepers were given one month to come up with their own plywood and modify their magazine racks.

If Pattison was pleased with the regulations, which placed no burden whatsoever on the distributors, pornography opponents were far from satisfied. At the next Community Services Committee meeting, Bev Schroeter again presented evidence gathered by the North Shore Women's Centre to show that Pattison's magazines violated section 159 of the Criminal Code and the B.C. Attorney General's guidelines.

Her evidence, which included copies of all the offending articles and photographs, was handed over to the city's legal department for advice. On June 1, 1984, in a "Dear Sirs" letter to the women's centre, city lawyer Terrance Bland said he understood that the Attorney General was "prepared" to lay charges against Pattison's company in connection with the pornographic material. He instructed the North Shore women to take the original copies of magazines to Inspector John Lucy of the Vancouver police who would prepare the charges.

Schroeter immediately acted on Bland's advice. Then she waited. And waited. After repeated calls to the A.G., the women's centre was told that there were "difficulties in enforcing the Criminal Code provisions relating to pornography."

Both the women's centre and the Community Services Committee were enraged. On October 3, 1984, Eriksen dashed off a three-page letter on city hall stationery to Brian Smith.

"Why," asked Eriksen, "are you so hesitant to carry out the duties of your office and enforce the law? Is it possible that charges against Mr. Pattison's Mainland Magazine Company would be embarrassing to the government?

"That's the way it looks to me (different strokes for different folks) or a law for the rich friends of government and a law for the poor."

He went on to remind Smith that his counterparts in other provinces had successfully obtained convictions under the same provisions of the Criminal Code, including the two fines levied against Pattison's other magazine company in Hamilton. He also drew Smith's attention to a story in the October 2 Vancouver *Sun* about another one of Pattison's companies, Provincial News of Edmonton, which had just been charged with distributing obscene material. Eriksen wanted to know why B.C. couldn't accomplish what Alberta and Ontario had.

The October 1984 raid on Provincial News of Edmonton netted police "a couple of truckloads" of offending magazines. The company, which was bought by Pattison in 1968 when he was head of Neon Products, is the largest distributor on the prairies. (At this writing, a date for the trial has not been set.)

After proposing several other logical steps to stem the tide of pornography, Eriksen ended his letter to Smith with the words, "May I suggest that you forget who owns Mainland Magazine and get on with your job of enforcing the law without fear or favour."

Brian Smith never replied.

On Sunday morning, October 7, 1984, in the heaviest downpour of the fall, fifteen members of Rape Relief arrived just before services were to begin at Glad Tidings Temple. The fundamentalist house of worship was widely known as Jim Pattison's church. He had maintained a close link to Glad Tidings over the years, since he joined the congregation in 1968. Although it had been a while since Pattison played in the church orchestra, he publicly acknowledged that he regularly attended Glad Tidings.

Two women draped a banner over the wet railing facing busy Fraser Street. It read: "TELL PATTISON: NO PORN." The others stood quietly around the entrance and, as worshippers hurried in, handed out soggy leaflets entitled, "Tell Pattison to cancel his order for porn."

The women's goal was to enlist the help of members of the church—whom they correctly imagined would be unalterably opposed to pornography—in fighting Pattison. Feminists and fundamentalists may hold opposing views on most subjects but they agree on the need to ban pornography. However, their unity ends there. Megan Ellis of the WAVAW Rape Crisis Centre says the two factions have vastly differing reasons for their stand. Conservatives want to eradicate pornography because "the state has a duty to protect the moral welfare of its citizens," she says, but feminists' opposition is based on the view that "pornography is anti-woman propaganda."

All of the churchgoers who spoke to the protestors knew Pattison and some said they had already tried to speak to him about it. "Give it up—he never listens to anybody," sighed one elderly man. The church officials were in a more difficult position. Publicly, they would have to stand with their parishioners against pornography, but privately they may have been influenced by Pattison's generous financial support for the church, the most publicized of which was his $1 million cheque in the collection plate. Church officials politely took the offered leaflets and did not ask the women to leave. But later that week the pastor sent a letter to Rape Relief saying that Pattison "is not and was never a member of our church."

This may be technically true. People in evangelical circles say it is quite common for only 10 per cent of the congregation to be members of the church, and the rest may attend for years without becoming members. But the pastor's letter made a startling claim, designed as it was to disassociate the church from Pattison.

Why hadn't the same church leaders sent similar disclaimers to McClelland and Stewart ten years earlier, when Peter Newman's bestseller *The Canadian Establishment* claimed that Pattison tooted his trumpet there every week? Or to the *Globe and Mail*, or the *Financial Post*, or *B.C. Business* magazine (which devoted its April 1984 cover story to "born-again businessmen," including Pattison), or *Maclean's* magazine or several other publications which wrote, in glowing terms, about Pattison's diligent attendance at Glad Tidings? Even more puzzling is why Pattison himself confirmed on several occasions that he played trumpet there and regularly attended services.

The most plausible answer is that Pattison's membership (or attendance) at Glad Tidings was rapidly becoming a liability for both the church and Pattison. His widely publicized Christian credentials had already brought him into conflict with angry fellow-worshippers. On the same day that Donna Stewart was blowing the whistle on him before the Fraser Committee, a small group of elders and pastors hand-delivered a petition to Pattison's posh Eyremount Drive home in West Vancouver demanding that he stop selling pornography. Church leaders said they had been pressuring Pattison for two years, to no avail. (As an aside, we might note this casts further doubt on Pattison's defence that he had no idea that Mainland was selling offensive material.)

Pattison's Christianity was also the main reason for his receiving a probing phone call at his home one night in the autumn of 1984.

Nine-two-two, eight-eight-three-two. The number, listed in the Vancouver telephone book under "Pattison, Jim, 855 Eyremount, West Van," was dialed nervously by the young lawyer. He was surprised to hear a woman answer crisply, "Jim Pattison Group." She identified herself as Maureen Chant, whom he knew to be Pattison's assistant, and he guessed that the "home" phone number was also an extension of the office phone.

He went directly into his pitch. "I am a Christian, my sister was raped and murdered, and I have a young daughter whom I want to see grow up without being the victim of violence. So I'd like to speak to Mr. Pattison about his involvement in selling pornography, please," he said. Chant politely refused his request. "I'm sorry, Mr. Pattison is very busy right now." Still, she took the man's number and not ten minutes later Pattison himself phoned back.

The lawyer recapped the basic facts for Pattison and

went on to elaborate. Pornography, he said, was a direct danger to his sister before her death and is a danger to his daughter and wife. Pattison agreed, saying, "We're both on the same side." The man then asked him to stop selling pornography. What he heard next surprised him because it contradicted what had been reported in the papers.

"We're not going to sell Mainland...the deal fell through...I doubt very much that it will work out because the guy [Vanstone] doesn't have the money," said Pattison.

The caller argued that Pattison could still stop selling pornography, even if he kept Mainland. Pattison countered, "We've pulled about 82 titles out of the 200-odd titles that were on the shelf..." and then he tried to appeal to the caller's sense of business ethics. "We've had a 27 per cent drop in magazine sales because of videos. You know that the Mafia controls a lot of pornography—if I'm out they'll be in."

"But they may be easier to prosecute than you," said the man, alluding to the Attorney General's reluctance to press charges against Pattison.

"When I got into this [magazine] business there was no pornography except *Playboy*," lectured Pattison. "Now all magazine distributors get this porn, including *Playboy, Penthouse, Hustler*—in fact I met [*Hustler* publisher Larry] Flynt—he's crazy—and I asked him to tone down the Canadian version."

Pattison then tried to score some points on common Christianity. "The guys running our distribution in Ontario—one is a deacon in a church and the other is a graduate of a Bible college. In Hamilton the police originally charged the deacon but I said, 'Don't charge him, just the company,' and they did."

The man asked Pattison why he kept selling pornography in Ontario after the convictions. His reply: because the competition sold it. "Then," said the lawyer, "why do you continue selling it on the prairies? Your Provincial News Company has a monopoly there and in the north, why not [stop selling] it there?"

Pattison invoked a well-worn defence, which rendered all of his previous ones hollow. "I just came back from Russia where they don't even allow you to read Bibles. You can't control what people read if you believe in freedom of speech."

"Not even if you might be able to prevent rapes and murders?" Pattison side-stepped the question. "Listen," he said, the tension causing his voice to rise, "I get a lot of heat for this. Those leftist women's groups are after me. I can't spend all night talking about this," and he coolly ended the hour-long phone conversation.

A few weeks later, after I'd heard about Pattison's conversation with the lawyer, I telephoned Pattison's office and asked for an interview about Mainland. Pattison was out so they directed me to his number two man in the corporate hierarchy, Bill Sleeman. Sleeman manages the Pattison empire's day-to-day affairs in a brusque, authoritarian manner. In person he even bears a passing resemblance to General George Patton.

"Mr. Sleeman, is Mainland Magazine still for sale?"
"Yes."
"Is Fred Vanstone still the proposed buyer?"
"Yes."

The interview lasted only 30 seconds. I came to expect little more than monosyllabic barks in reply to my questions.

"Is there any deadline for the deal to be closed?"
"No."
"How long are you prepared to let this go on before the deal is closed?"

"These things take time." His inflection dropped at the end of the sentence like a guillotine, cutting off any further questions.

Less than a month later (November 4, 1984), during an interview with Pattison in his office, I asked him if he was still going to sell Mainland.

"Yes, but the deal isn't closed yet." He pointed his right hand toward the large, cluttered desk which filled the far corner of the huge office. "On that desk is the preliminary agreement to the sale. But you don't have a sale until the closing. We're having trouble agreeing on a price because of the increased competition from Van Mag."

Pattison made these comments more than a month later, after he told a fellow-Christian that Mainland was no longer for sale.

A few days later, in a *Globe and Mail* story dated November 9, Bill Sleeman was quoted as saying that the Pattison Group will reconsider its decision to sell Mainland. His comments came on the heels of the announcement that the first appointments to the new B.C. Periodical Review Board had been made.

The steering committee of the new board had trouble finding qualified people. After a lengthy search, Jillian Ridington was chosen as "chairman" and Karen Phillips as alternate. The others on the board were Graeme Waymark, a Vancouver school trustee, and Gwenith Ingham, a West Vancouver teacher.

The new board officially began work the third week of November 1984 and by December 1 had made their first recommended cuts. Already the pattern of the board's operations was being set. The names of the offending magazines were kept secret.

"We won't release the information on the magazines we think need some changes until the distributors have received that information," Ridington told the *Province* in her first interview as head of the board. However, as the weeks rolled by and the new year dawned it became clear that even after the distributors were notified, the names of the pornographic magazines would not be disclosed. The anti-pornography activists cried foul, blaming the distributors for muzzling the board.

Pattison's top executive at Mainland, John Seebach, who had played a leading role in getting the board started, danced around the question of publicity. Asked if the board's reports would be made public, he said, "They will be public in the sense that copies go to the Attorney General." Having, in effect, answered the question in the negative, he then denied that the distributors were exercising any control over the board, but hastily added, "I don't think it serves any great purpose to release the titles of every issue that they held or had a comment on...I don't see that it serves any purpose...what harm could it do [not to release the information]?"

The harm Seebach's myopia prevented him from seeing was clearly articulated by those who had expressed opposition to the board in the first place. Without the list of titles and specific articles deemed by the board to contravene the Criminal Code, the public could not watch for those titles and alert the authorities. The procedure was akin to keeping court records secret from the public and making them available only to the Attorney General, who was on record as favouring anything but "the prosecution route" to stem the flow of pornography into Canada, and who apparently ignored the opinion of Vancouver lawyers and police that there was sufficient evidence to prosecute Mainland. Now that the public was cut out of the process, he alone would be empowered to watch for and prosecute distributors who sold magazines not "passed" by the review board. (Ridington said later that Seebach was wrong—lists of the suggested deletions were sent to about 20 B.C. women's groups, but not to newspapers.)

The review board had an immediate effect on Seebach —it relieved him of his censorship duties.

Between the time women's groups fingered Pattison and the review board was set in operation, Seebach had been ordered by Pattison to screen Mainland's 200-plus pornographic publications. Suddenly, titles like *Jugs, Turn On Letters, Uncensored Letters, Fox* and *Mandate* hit the shredding machine. Entire flats of magazines, too voluminous for the shredders, were burned in huge bonfires behind Mainland's Langley warehouse.

What Pattison had called an "impossible task" because of "vaguely worded laws" suddenly became a simple administrative chore overseen by one man. Suddenly the Attorney General's obscenity guidelines assumed an amazing clarity that anyone with a grade ten education could understand. No longer was the "fact" that Canada Customs had allowed the material into the country trotted out as an excuse to peddle it.

Pattison's new morality reflected an abrupt turnabout in his attitude toward pornography sold by Mainland. He refused to discuss the matter, referring all questions to Seebach. But it is safe to assume that widespread public opposition to the chairman of Expo 86 selling pornography (including calls to his home by irate citizens) spurred Pattison to do something fast while he attempted to set up the review board.

Seebach took all the conversions in stride, but confessed a distaste for the nuts and bolts of Pattison's new orders. "It's an unpleasant task," he chuckled uneasily, "and that's one of the reasons that a review board was formed."

Seebach's last comment was an astonishing admission, especially coming from a man who had that fall at city hall meetings been reminded that it is the responsibility of those who "possess, distribute or circulate..." printed matter to check for obscenity. His comment lent credence to criticisms that the review board was really a way of co-opting opponents of pornography. Those responsible for distributing pornography got their critics to do the dirty work for them. Little wonder Seebach pondered building upon the initial success of the B.C. board and he wondered aloud, "Perhaps there should be a Canadian review board..."

One small example of what the new review board found unfit for circulation was made available to me in the course of researching this book by a co-operative Mainland Magazine employee and an intermediary. On page 63 of the December 1984 *Hustler*, a montage of photographs and cartoons highlighted the magazine's "achievements" over the previous seven years. The friend who showed it to me asked if I could spot the single item which the board said violated the Criminal Code.

At a glance I guessed there could have been two or three: the naked woman lying on her back, legs spread apart, with a giant boa constrictor winding between her thighs across her neck, as a depiction of bestiality? Or the trick photograph of the couple copulating inside a lightbulb? Or *Hustler*'s boast about the time it offered a "scratch-n-sniff" centrefold. As it happened, it was none of these. I had missed the small cartoon of "Chester the Molester" showing children in their underwear tied to a bed while Chester writes in his notebook, "Dear Kinky Korner..." As the Criminal Code states, *any* depiction of sex with children violates obscenity laws. Thus, page 63 had been ripped out of all 8,000 copies of *Hustler* distributed by Mainland and many thousands more by the other distributors.

Seebach couldn't estimate how much the company paid in extra time and labour to rip out the page, but admitted it was "expensive, but worthwhile, because if the review board finds a problem page and we take it out and notify the publisher, then they may not publish that kind of material again." Perhaps when Larry Flynt hears from Mainland he'll sit up and take more notice than he did when Pattison asked him personally to "tone it down."

According to Jillian Ridington, 50 to 60 per cent of the 350 magazines they reviewed in their first six months had "some amendments." That meant either that the magazine was removed entirely from distribution or, if it was a big seller, that pages had been torn out or parts of an article blacked out.

All board members were surprised to find that most of their objections were to written, not pictorial material. Karen Phillips cites as typical examples "an article about how wonderful it was to be gang raped, and another about how to break in a house slave." Ridington agrees. "The 'Letters' magazines are the worst. Like *Turn on Letters*."

"I tend to be stronger [against] 'positive outcome rape' stories [which promote such notions as 'you can convince a woman to go into a rape situation'],'' said Phillips, adding that when the article is borderline the board may let it through, but Ridington will write to the publisher saying, "if you keep this up we may hold or change your magazine."

The other party in this complex scenario is the U.S. publishers, who were hardly about to sit idly by while prudes in Vancouver tampered with their magazines. Some called Mainland and the other distributors to say that if they didn't stop removing pages or holding back the magazine, the publishers would find other distributors.

Nineteen eighty-five began with one of the coldest winters on record in Vancouver. The snow on the lawns and beaches didn't melt for six weeks. Only the return of interminable drizzle from grey skies marked the passage into spring.

A year had passed since the Fraser Committee hearings at which Pattison's pornography connection was publicly exposed. That information, which caused such a stir at the time, hardly rated a mention in the committee's 750-page report tabled in the House of Commons on April 23.

The release of the committee's finding caused the predictable flurry of news reports, almost all of which concentrated on the most controversial recommendations, about prostitution. The startling finding that pornography in all forms was estimated to be a $12 billion-a-year industry in North America and $600 million for Canada was given only passing mention, although this figure was almost double the previous estimates.

Eighteen months after the initial revelations about the connection between Mainland Magazine, Jim Pattison and pornography, Pattison still owns the company and shows no signs of selling it or of getting out of the pornography trade in B.C. or the rest of Canada. He has indicated that if he could expand his territory he would. When asked if his Ontario distribution area included Toronto, the most lucrative distribution territory in the country, he said, "No, but I wish it did."

While Pattison continues to sell pornography, he has "voluntarily" dropped about 80 of the more than 280 titles he had distributed. He regularly follows the recommendations of the periodical review board, which he and the other distributors established and continue to fund.

City council has ruled that every store must place opaque barriers in front of "adult" publications, and must put the magazines out of the reach of children.

Most lasting, perhaps, is the fact that the focus of the debate has shifted ground. Before the Pattison revelations, anti-pornography actions were aimed mainly at retailers. The coalition of women's groups has shown that, in Canada at least, most of the power to control and profit from pornography lies with the distributors, who buy the material from abroad and circulate it to retail stores. Because there are only a handful of distributors for hundreds of retail stores, anti-pornography strategies become simplified, more likely to succeed. When a distributor happens to be one of the richest and most powerful men in the community, especially one entrusted with public money, he is, in theory at least, more vulnerable to public pressure.

At this writing, six months before the opening of Expo, Jim Pattison's well-publicized profits from pornography have had little discernible effect on the world's fair. The scandal has not prevented his continuing as chairman, nor even his taking over as president after the previous officeholder departed in a cloud of his own scandal. There are very few indications that any pornography has stuck to Pattison's image, nor that any lasting damage has been done to his public or private future. In the fall of 1985, he was accepted as a board member of the Toronto Dominion Bank, one of the most prestigious directorships in Canada and a sure sign of acceptance into the Canadian establishment. Pattison has managed to cover his tracks. As Harry Rankin had said of him during the pornography debate, "Like the man who has been wallowing in a pile of manure, he tried to come out smelling like a rose." Pattison tried and, whether the odour is natural or artificial, he appears to have succeeded.

10 EXPO'S DOLLAR-A-YEAR MAN

You get 'em on the site, you feed 'em, you make 'em dizzy, you scare the shit out of 'em.
　—Michael Bartlett,
　　on his appointment as Expo president

For 100 years the False Creek site on which Expo stands was the home of sewage plants, steel factories, gas plants, paper mills, railway yards and sawmills. According to Bill Curtis, the city's chief engineer, environmental studies show that the entire site is contaminated with heavy toxic metals, including cadmium and lead.

The False Creek shoreline, said Curtis, contains "several feet of sediment polluted with oils, tars, creosotes, and raw sewage." The waters of False Creek generally, on which many sea-going Expo visitors are expected to drop anchor in the summer of '86, is hardly better. A 1983 test measured concentrations of between 800 and 2,500 fecal coliform per 100 millilitres. The acceptable maximum is 200.

The exposition rising out of this toxic muck was originally intended to be a relatively modest celebration of Vancouver's 100th birthday. At its inception in 1978, the idea was to hold a transportation fair called "Transpo 86" at a cost, in 1984 dollars, of $127 million. That sum, while enormous, is only one-twelfth of the projected expenditures on Expo 86.

Plans for Transpo got derailed late in 1978. About 8,000 kilometres from Vancouver, in a posh London club, then-Tourism Minister Grace McCarthy proposed to Patrick Reid, then-president of the Bureau of International Exhibitions (which licenses all world's fairs), that B.C. should be a candidate to host a world's fair in 1986. The two were so excited by the idea that they developed a theme—transportation and communications—between the entree and dessert. Thus was the legend, and legendary deficit, of Expo born.

McCarthy's boss, Bill Bennett, also liked the idea and signed an application for world's fair status. In the fall of 1980 the BIE granted B.C. permission to hold a world's fair in Vancouver. It was to be a "class two" fair, meaning all pavilions and exhibits had to conform to a specific theme. Expo 67 in Montreal—a class one fair—allowed the participants to design their own pavilions under the very general theme "Man and His World." Expo 86 pavilions must adhere to the more specific "Man in Motion—Man in Touch" theme.

Bennett and McCarthy cast about for someone to run the fair. The candidate had to be able to convince multinational corporations and ministries of foreign affairs to ante up several hundred million dollars for the privilege of sitting at the Expo table. The person in charge also had to have experience watching bottom-lines, and the ability to ensure that spending wouldn't get out of hand as it had in Montreal and at so many other taxpayer-supported fiascos, the New Orleans fair being the most recent. Equally important, the right candidate had to be a supporter of the Socreds, given the party's belief that a successful world's fair was the key to re-election.

Pattison, who is reported to have made large donations to the Social Credit party (second in size only to his much-publicized mega-contributions to his church) and who began voting Socred prenatally, was a prime candidate. He had a reputation as a hard-line businessman who not only believed, with Ronald Reagan, that "the profit motive is probably the greatest thing invented by mankind," but who had few reservations about taking on organized labour.

In addition, Bennett had something Pattison wanted. In spite of the multi-millionaire's vast commercial empire, his Swiss bank, his 80-foot yacht, his fleets of cars and memberships in posh clubs, Pattison was still considered an outsider by members of the Canadian establishment. (This was five years before his appointment to the board of directors of the Toronto Dominion Bank.) His poor beginnings and lack of formal education in the right private schools and a tendency to be rough around the edges were mentioned as reasons for his exclusion. Heading a successful world's fair may not change his background, but it could go a long way toward establishing his credibility among his near-peers. Rubbing shoulders with foreign dignitaries and others in a rarified atmosphere might serve to plaster another coat of respectability over Pattison's *nouveau riche* faults.

When Bennett called Pattison in 1980 and asked him to take the job, Pattison said yes. Later, when pressed for an explanation, Pattison invoked patriotic tones, saying, "When your premier asks you to do something, you can't turn him down."

During another interview, Pattison said the reason he took the dollar-a-year position as chairman of Expo 86 was because he felt it was a way to do something for the province and the country that had been so good to him.

Just what he was to preside over was not clear. The government created the Expo 86 Crown corporation to organize the fair, and B.C. Place corporation to develop the 74-hectare site once the fair was over. But it said little about the cost or scope of the affair. Early estimates of total cost began at about $200 million. Then $400 million. Then $750 million. By 1984, when construction was underway, the government admitted the exposition was going to cost at least $1.5 billion. But Expo officials insisted that almost $700 million of that would come from corporations and other governments. The B.C. contribution would be limited to just over $800 million.

Information about the fair was released in dribs and drabs. Apart from the theme and the growing list of participating countries and private companies, few details were revealed by Expo in the early days. Hoarding of information was part of the sales strategy, much as it was part of the Socred's campaign strategy in 1983. Make the people curious enough to buy their tickets, but don't tell them so much that they may decide that Expo is not for them.

Pattison, the super-salesman, was a master at the technique. He sold the public on Expo 86 the way he would sell a used car—emphasizing brand names and pushing statistics, drawing attention to the upholstery and chrome, steering clear of the motor and mileage.

Expo, we were told, would attract over 80 participants, roughly half of them foreign countries and international organizations. They would include controversial and exotic countries such as Cuba—with a hint that Castro himself might attend. And for the first time at a world exposition in North America the big three nations—the U.S., Soviet Union and China—would all have pavilions.

Few details of the interior of the national pavilions were released, although as expected the U.S. and Soviet Union planned to emphasize their space programs. Soviet designers set out to build a life-size replica of the Salut Space Station that was so big it would have to jut out one side of the previously constructed pavilion.

The only exhibit that was specifically identified long before opening day was the Ramses II collection from Egypt, a $50 million display of artifacts and ancient treasures. Some of the special events would include a flypast by at least 50 twin-engined DC-3s—one of the world's most durable aircraft—and a display of steam locomotives from all over North America.

As with other Expos, long lineups for the most popular pavilions was expected to be a problem. On any given day Expo expects 100,000 people on the site. Officials could do little to shorten the lineups but promised plenty of free entertainment—roving bands of jugglers, singers, musicians and clowns—to divert hapless visitors in long lines.

Compared to other world expositions, Expo 86 will leave Vancouver with few legacies. A roundhouse, and a theatre in the shape of a giant sequinned golfball are the only two buildings that will remain after Expo, but at this writing no government had agreed to pay for the upkeep of the structures after 1986. It is a far cry from the first international fair which graced London with its delicate Crystal Palace in 1851 or the famous Paris fair of 1889 which bequeathed to the city one of the world's best-known landmarks, the Eiffel Tower.

Instead, Expo 86 officials talked about the immediate benefits: 53,400 man-years (sic) of employment, $1 billion in wages and salaries and $2.8 billion additional output in the B.C. economy. (These estimates have been analyzed and disputed by a number of B.C. economists. See bibliography.)

Another aspect of Pattison's sales technique for Expo involved recruiting as much volunteer labour as possible. For example, the proposition of paying large sums for mailing lists was circumvented by an "Invite the World to Expo" program launched in B.C. Newspaper ads and flyers begged residents to fill out the names and addresses of three people they would like to "invite" to Expo. Expo then sent sales kits to those people, along with order forms for buying tickets. The technique proved more successful than Expo had hoped: B.C.ers scribbled out more than half a million names of friends and relatives who would be sent the direct-mail advertising kit.

In the year before the fair, Expo embarked on an even more ambitious plan to recruit 30,000 volunteers to work on the site and around the province creating interest and enthusiasm for the world's fair. Critics complained of lost jobs—citing Expo's earlier promises that the massive celebration would bring prosperity and jobs to B.C. Instead, most of the work associated with promoting the fair would be done by volunteers, and the 15,000 jobs at the fair itself would pay too little to support any but the most frugal single person.

Advance ticket sales also exceeded Expo forecasts, but that was a mixed blessing. Chairman Pattison gleefully reported in mid-November 1985 that "we have sold 6 million 'visits' or 44 per cent of our total," which was forecast to be 13.75 million. He was technically correct, but what he worried about in private and wouldn't say in public was that the dollar value of each visit dropped with every advance ticket sold. Maximum ticket revenue was derived from those who bought their tickets at the gate for the full admission price of $20. Per visit, far less will flow in from season passes, which holders will use an average of 12 times for less than $10 a visit. To a lesser extent, the three-day passes will similarly cut into gate receipts. Ironically, advance ticket sales which were to function largely as teasers, have been so successful that they have come to represent a potential net drain.

The size of the drain on Expo's budget can only be guessed at since Pattison has ordered fair officials not to release financial details. An educated guess was offered by the *Sun*'s Expo-watcher, reporter Gordon Hamilton. He tapped his calculator keys and estimated that Expo's revenues from advance ticket sales were probably only half as great as Expo predicted, even though sales were higher than expected. Hamilton resolved this apparent contradiction by comparing Expo's estimate of total ticket revenues with the volume of tickets sold. Expo said that it would earn $210 million from 13.75 million clicks through the turnstiles during the six-month fair. That works out to $15.27 per click. But so many season and three-day passes were sold up to six months before the fair opened that the average per click was close to $10. Thus, Hamilton concluded, the fair sold 44 per cent of its tickets but received only 22 per cent ($46.2

million) of total ticket revenues.

Expo's decision to hold back as much financial information as possible bore the unmistakable stamp of Pattison. Few high-profile businessmen had maintained such secrecy even about their business affairs.

Pattison's well-known dislike for regulatory agencies that demanded he disclose financial and related information was an attitude he carried over to Expo. Senior management soon drew the line between what was and wasn't "public information." "Personnel matters"—the firing or resignation of high-level staff, how much the golden handshake was worth—fell into the "confidential" category. So did financial information of almost every description. For a time, Expo did not even release attendance figures for the glittery preview centre which opened one year before the rest of the fair, even though attendance far exceeded expectations.

Another of Pattison's trademarks was his adversarial attitude toward unions—whether at Air BC, Neon Products or elsewhere in his empire.

One of his favoured tactics, threatening to shut the operation down if unions don't give in to his demands, surfaced at Expo. During the heated labour disputes in the 1984 construction period on the fair site, Pattison recommended to Premier Bennett that the fair be cancelled—an astonishing piece of grandstanding. Bennett, after a dramatic 48-hour pause during which the news of the threatened closure reached most of Canada, resolved to carry on despite the difficulties with construction unions. Bennett's "decision" caused no one to fall down in shock.

The opening shots of the labour-management war at Expo did not happen on the fair grounds but across False Creek at a luxury condominium project, known as the Pennyfarthing site. A Fraser Valley contractor, J.C. Kerkhoff and Sons, which hired only non-union trades people, was to finish building the condos after union workers had laid the foundation. The unemployed union members immediately threw up picket lines and declared the site "hot." Many bitter and sometimes violent confrontations ensued as non-union contractors tried to drive trucks and cars onto the idle worksite.

Willem (Bill) Kerkhoff himself brought the confrontation to a head one overcast day in March when he ordered one of his employees to turn a fire hose on the picketers. Men on the picket lines replied with a barrage of stones, one of which hit the hapless worker, breaking his nose. The unscathed Kerkhoff was satisfied. It was not his nose that was out of joint. The provocation worked and had been recorded for the nightly news. The stone throwing was justification for the courts to order the site cleared of picket lines. Non-union work soon resumed.

It was more than a symbolic loss for the union trades. Traditionally, work on a given construction site was either all non-union or all union, and in B.C.'s better economic times it was usually union. But the recession brought record unemployment, forcing 50 per cent of all carpenters and other trades people out of work. Many, desperate to support their families, opted to take a $5 to $10 an hour cut from union wages to work for a non-union outfit.

Expo was determined to exploit these circumstances (created partly by the government's intentional policies of reduced spending for jobs). There was speculation that Kerkhoff was acting at the request of the Social Credit government in return for promises of contracts at Expo. (Kerkhoff denied any deals. He said his contact with the Socreds went no further than making regular donations of money and votes.) Ultimately, Kerkhoff was among the contractors favoured with big contracts on the Expo site, including the important East Gate, which had to be ready a year before the fair opened.

In April, Bennett warned that Expo would not go ahead unless the site was "open"—open to non-union as well as union workers. Labour representatives met with Pattison and tried to work out a deal whereby the unions would give up their right to strike in return for union-scale wages for every worker—union member or not. Pattison agreed to the deal and took it to the Expo board and the premier. Both nixed it. Bennett was particularly vexed. First he denied that Pattison agreed to the proposal. Then he insisted that Pattison "went beyond his mandate." (Whatever the case, the incident bore a disturbing resemblance to several previous incidents in Pattison's own companies. In the CJOR "Good Friday" incident, Pattison hugged broadcaster Rafe Mair and told him what a good job he was doing. Easter Monday Mair was out of work.)

In Expo's case, Bennett refused to consider negotiations with the construction workers. Instead, he introduced laws that would force union and non-union workers to work side by side. The building trades were given a choice. They could either submit voluntarily to Bennett's will, or he would club them into submission. One union rep said it was like asking them where they would like to have their legs broken.

From then on, all workers were paid a minimum "fair wage" imposed by Expo. It was $15.25 an hour—$3.50 below union scale but still better than most non-union jobs. Some workers had to fight Expo to get even that amount, as their employers tried to pay them less than the contract wage.

The labour clashes were only one of a series of controversies swirling around the vast project. There were scandals involving allegations of conflict of interest, especially where Pattison's companies or his religion was concerned.

The religious scandal began in 1983. An ecumenical group, the Pacific Interfaith Citizenship Association, wrote to Expo asking for a chance to set up an interfaith pavilion at Expo. According to Interfaith president Aziz Khaki, Expo took almost six months to reply to their letters, and then would agree to only two meetings. It became clear during those meetings that the Canadian world's fair was not prepared to donate one square foot of space to exhibit the diverse ethnic roots of Canadians to the world. Expo required each religion to put up between $75,000 to $100,000, money that several churches felt would be better spent on social projects like supporting the province's mushrooming food banks.

In late December 1984 the Interfaith group withdrew its proposal.

In less than three months, Expo had lined up another religious group to construct a $3.2 million pavilion and the deal was signed without delay. The group—Crossroads Christian Communications Inc.—is best known in Canada for its national television show *100 Huntley Street*. It is headed by a Pentecostal minister, David Mainse, who has a TV style described as "unrelenting salesmanship on behalf of Jesus." More to the point, he represents the same religious views and practices as those of Jim Pattison and the man hired to co-ordinate religious activities at Expo, Gordon McDonald—himself a Pentecostal minister.

When news of the new deal emerged, representatives of the Interfaith group said they had been duped. Charles Paris of the Canadian Council of Christians and Jews accused McDonald and Pattison of stalling negotiations deliberately. "Their intention from the very beginning," he said, "was to put this kind of [evangelical] religious pavilion in place. They come out of that tradition; they knew very well what they wanted and come hell or high water that's what they got."

Pattison at no time responded to the charge. One of Expo's PR people in charge of red herrings said, with a straight face, "Mr. Pattison is not a member of any church." The *Sun*, which printed the comments, added parenthetically that Pattison had told the newspaper previously that he "sometimes attended Pentecostal services." The paper was overly unzealous in tying Pattison to the Pentecostal bosom. It failed to note the fact that almost every magazine and newspaper profile of Pattison over the past decade specifically mentioned his membership in Glad Tidings Pentecostal Temple. As noted in the previous chapter, his actual "membership" in the church was not the issue. He acknowledged a lifelong adherence to the religion.

When it became clear that the only religious pavilion at Expo was to be run by a sect that often maintains that other religious traditions, such as Islam, are "the purveyors of darkness," the Interfaith group took legal and political action. They appealed to the federal Multicultural minister to intercede. They also attempted to obtain an injunction to halt construction of the *100 Huntley Street* pavilion, where evangelistic programming would originate during Expo. Both actions failed.

Pattison and McDonald blamed the other churches for failing to agree on an interfaith pavilion. But the last word went to the Rev. Mainse, who said with a smile that his church represents "the majority culture of our country."

So far Pattison had more or less successfully separated himself from the scandals involving labour and the religious pavilion. It was more difficult for him to avoid the next round of controversies.

It was a puzzle. Pattison, in his single-minded pursuit of wealth, had once said he would not grant media interviews because they didn't make him any money. Suddenly he had agreed to give up all his social time and days off to work for Expo at one dollar a year.

Pattison's contribution to Expo, beyond the mere donation of his time, is monumental if we are to believe his estimates. He said he could have made $50 million in deals in the time he spent working on the world's fair. He also donated about $1 million of his own money to pay travel and entertainment expenses for Expo-related work.

On the other side of the ledger, there was almost no speculation about how much money Pattison's omnipresent empire was making *from* Expo. The man's image as public benefactor suffered a small dent when he announced that a magazine company he bought in 1984, *Beautiful British Columbia* magazine, had been awarded the contract to publish the official Expo guide book. Pattison acquired the profitable *Beautiful British Columbia* during the darkest days of the government's restraint program. In a flurry of privatizing and downsizing, the Socreds sold the magazine to their old friend. A clause in the contract required B.C. Hydro to enclose ads for *Beautiful B.C.* along with customer bills. No extra charge to Pattison for this service. Other businesses, envious of the advertising dream provided by Hydro, complained to no avail.

The Expo contract called for Pattison's company to solicit advertising for the guide—an odd contractual stipulation since *Beautiful B.C.* staff had no experience soliciting ads. The press run was to be 1,250,000 copies. The glossy, full-colour guide would sell for $5 each, but most of the revenue would come from the ads.

Pattison insisted his company's bid was the best one, although it was impossible to verify his claim because he refused to allow anyone outside Expo to examine all the bids. He also protested his innocence, saying he had stepped out of the board room when the guide book bid came up for a vote. Presumably, he left his subordinates behind to cast their ballots freely, immune from any just-outside-the-door influence.

Pattison's explanation satisfied the board and the Socreds, but not the NDP opposition or a growing chorus of public critics. The normally pro-business editorial writers at the two daily newspapers called Pattison's absence during the vote irrelevant and said his companies should not be bidding on Expo contracts, or at least the chairman of Expo should have severed all ties with his companies during the fair. (One wonders whether there are enough scissors in the country.)

Pattison, on reading this, was angry.

"Does that mean Expo should not spend money on any company because a member of the board is an Expo director?" pouted Pattison. "Does that mean Expo should not advertise in the *Sun* and *Province* because [Southam director] Norm Keevil is on our board? (The ethical reply to Pattison's rhetorical question is "yes." The consequence would be to grind the country to a halt.) He stormed away from reporters without waiting for an answer.

Analyst Marjorie Nichols was one of many writers willing to oblige him with a reply. "If a man is unwilling to give up his personal opportunities for making money in order to take a public service position," she lectured, "then he is the wrong man for the public service position."

The argument fell on deaf ears. In the course of construction of Expo several of Pattison's companies sold goods and services to the fair, although the exact amounts cannot be listed because Expo deemed the contracts were "confidential." However, it is known that Neon Products supplied most of the abundant neon tubing on the fair site, EDP Industries some of the computer software, and Pattison's car and truck leasing companies provided vehicles. Pattison also acknowledged the involvement of other firms, like Air BC, the Jim Pattison Sign Company, Trans Ad, CJOR, Mainland Magazine, Vanguard Automotive Products. In addition, most of his companies are amply suited to benefit from increased tourist spending during the fair, whether in his Overwaitea and Save-On-Foods grocery stores, flying his airline, renting his cars, or leasing his yachts. (In 1985 Pattison opened "Jim Pattison Yacht Leasing Ltd." offices just across False Creek from Expo to take advantage of the anticipated increase in demand for yachts during the world's fair.)

One businessman's attitude to the hullabaloo over the alleged conflict of interest could be captured in a statement made by marketing analyst Gary Altman. "You have got to understand that when you are a dollar-a-year man you have got to earn a dollar."

The comment might be seen as the height of arrogance were it not for the official conflict of interest guidelines at Expo which made it perfectly legal for Pattison to "earn a dollar."

The guidelines, drawn up in 1984 by retired B.C. Supreme Court Judge Ken Fawcus, were summed up in one sentence by the justice. "The rules do not prevent a conflict of interest from continuing, but where one does arise, a director is required to disclose it."

Under Fawcus' guidelines, Expo directors like Pattison, Ray Dagg of Target Media, Peter Brown of Canarim Investments, Vancouver businessman Herb Capozzi (a life-long friend of Premier Bennett), Southam director Norm Keevil, and Clark Bentall of Dominion Construction, all had to disclose the fact that they signed contracts with Expo. That's it. They did not have to disclose any details. Fawcus could only advise for or against the contracts, not block them. The guidelines were Pattison's idea, first suggested by him in 1983.

Under these rules, Bentall's Dominion Construction "won" the contract for construction work at the B.C. pavilion. The size of the contract was not disclosed. And in general the taxpayers of B.C. are not being told how much the businessmen entrusted with running the show are making from it.

By most standards of conducting public business these practices would seem ludicrous. In fact, they are the norm at Expo 86, backed all the way by the provincial government. For example, the government can keep Expo's books secret for up to a year after each annual report. Thus, although Expo will have to report by April 1, 1986, on its finances for the preceding year, the government can legally keep the lid on that information until April 1, 1987—well after the fair has closed, and, most likely, well after the next provincial election.

Even these procedures seem like minor aberrations compared to some Expo transactions. There were, for example, instances of the tendering process being abandoned altogether. (Tendering is a standard procedure used in arranging government contracts. Companies which have demonstrated their ability to carry out a given project tender bids. The contract is generally offered to the lowest bidder.) The most bizarre case happened to involve the largest single contract awarded by Expo—the $100 million souvenir deal.

Specialty Manufacturing of Burnaby, B.C., a wholly owned subsidiary of Ace Novelty of Seattle, convinced Expo to abandon the public tendering of souvenir bids and award a monopoly contract to Ace. The iron-clad contract assured Ace of $100 million in revenues, plus little perks like the exclusive right to use certain words and symbols on its products—"Canada," "World's Fair," "Expo 86" and even the eleven point maple leaf used on the Canadian flag. The contract gave Ace the exclusive legal right to use these slogans and symbols on souvenirs sold in 1985 and 1986.

In other words, every T-shirt, mug, glass, penant, flag, button, ring, cup, umbrella, jacket, place mat, coaster, ash tray, notebook, calendar, lighter, wallet, pen, clock, and stuffed animal—over 2,000 items in all—sold before and during Expo would ring up a profit for the American company. On the other hand, a court summons might greet anyone other than Ace who slapped the Expo logo on a T-shirt and tried to sell it.

Even after the scale of the give-away became public, few details of the deal were released. B.C. business owners called and wrote Expo demanding to know why they had not been given the opportunity to participate in the souvenir bonanza, especially following Expo's earlier promises to create jobs and prosperity for B.C. One wag noted that so much Expo business was going to U.S. companies that this was going to be the "largest American exposition held outside the United States."

Just when it seemed the news couldn't get any worse, it did. Ace Novelty was convicted in a U.S. court of defrauding the 1984 New Orleans world's fair.

The U.S. Justice Department disclosed that Ace president Benjamin Mayers had set up a dummy company in the eastern U.S. called East Coast Jewelry Specialty Manufacturing Ltd. which gave $25,000 to the merchandising director of the New Orleans fair. A short time later, Ace Novelty got a handshake and a $726,000 contract to print "New Orleans" on any damn thing they wanted to.

Later, when the case went to court, it was revealed that Ace had overcharged the fair $400,000, and the judge ordered Mayers to pay back the full amount. He also fined Ace the maximum under U.S. fraud laws,

$1,000. The indictment said Mayers set up the east coast company to conceal Ace's involvement in the fair.

When Mayers shifted his attention to the west coast, he and Expo finance director Peter Brown sat down to work out the deal. Mayers admitted that his company was in court but denied that the charge involved fraud and claimed the fiasco was the result of a misunderstanding. Brown looked no further into the matter. This is all the more surprising given Expo's treatment of local bidders. One small company, hoping to supply balloons to the fair, was given the third degree—Expo treated them like foreign agents. "Why would they do that, and then take the word of a convicted criminal that it was just a misunderstanding?" asked the *Sun*'s Gordon Hamilton. He didn't get an answer to his question. (After the *Sun* revealed a number of scandals involving Expo, finance director Peter Brown refused to talk to any reporter from that paper. "If he saw me coming, he would turn the other way," said Hamilton of Brown.) When Hamilton checked with the U.S. Justice Department* and officials of the New Orleans world's fair, he was told without much difficulty about the fraud conviction. Why Expo entered into a $100 million contract with a foreign corporation convicted of fraud is a question which permits of very few possible answers.

Pattison insisted all along that the Ace deal was Brown's responsibility. Brown attempted to justify the contract by alleging that Expo would net about $10 million more in royalties from sales of souvenirs through Ace than if it had parcelled out the contracts to small B.C. companies. He refused to release the figures that led to his $10 million conclusion, but even if his argument was valid, his explanation did little to placate

---

*The investigation was carried out by the organized crime division of the U.S. Department of Justice. A few years earlier in Alberta, a royal commission into the allegations of profit-skimming and bribery by carnival suppliers found that there were links between organized crime and the carnival business. Mayers was one of the witnesses called to testify at that inquiry because Ace supplied several western Canadian carnivals with stuffed animals and other toys.

local manufacturers. They complained that they had been eliminated before the race began. That was just plain fact.

One entrepreneur reminded the government of the glossy brochure it had sent to every business in B.C. promising that all provincial Crown corporations would use the public tendering process, that B.C. companies could expect some preferential treatment over outsiders, and that special consideration would be given to small B.C. companies—those earning $500,000 a year or less. In the case of Expo, a Crown corporation, every one of these promises was broken.

Brown's explanation only reflected the narrowness with which he, Pattison and the rest of the Expo oligarchy viewed its affairs. They ran Expo like a private corporation, in the interests of profit and patronage.

Just who was in charge of Expo—Pattison and his board or Ace—became a lively topic of debate in the summer of 1985. At the Canadian pavilion, federal employees prepared a souvenir booth to peddle keepsakes like mugs and key rings bearing the imprint of the maple leaf and other national symbols. This harmless Canadian activity was crassly interrupted by a not so harmless Canadian tradition. A U.S. company (with a checkered background and a fraud conviction) approached the employees of our national government and ordered them to stop selling our national souvenirs. To back up their demand they produced a legal contract which clearly stated that Expo 86 had ceded exclusive rights to Ace Novelty to sell Canadian mementos and just about everything else. With its monopoly souvenir sales at Expo and expected revenue of $105 million, Ace was seriously prepared to fight the federal government over the use of the country's national symbols.

Ace's audacity provoked a few wry snickers in Vancouver but no one in Ottawa found it amusing. The minister responsible for the Canadian pavilion, Don Mazankowsky, demanded a full explanation and said there would be no deals with Ace. Faced with the might of the national government, Ace Novelty of Seattle backed down and grudgingly agreed to let the government peddle its souvenirs in and around its pavilion.

As a scandal, it didn't rank with the original Ace contract, but it created one of the most embarrassing moments for Expo 86. The national media coverage made Expo management look as though the rain had rusted their brains. The contract, said *Sun* columnist Marjorie Nichols, may be "the dumbest business decision since the billion dollar white elephant known as Mirabel." In the end, like most B.C. scandals, nothing much changed and almost no one cared.

Some of the other hidden surprises in the Ace contract soon surfaced. One big surprise pertained to T-shirts, the most profitable of all souvenirs. Local textile industry officials were joyous over the prospects of producing millions of shirts and in the bargain keeping B.C.'s 10,000 textile workers busy. Their joy was based on Pattison's and Bennett's promise that Expo meant a bonanza for B.C. business.

But their visions of T-shirts turning to dollars vanished when Ace applied to the federal government for special permission to import 1.5 million shirts from Korea. The normal quota is 300,000. Ace said it needed the extra shirts because Canadian producers could not fill the large order, and because "it makes good business sense."

It made good business dollars, too. Ace stood to save about $700,000 by buying its shirts from Korea instead of Canada. As for the capacity of Canadian suppliers, the president of the Canadian Textile Institute, Eric Barry, said domestic producers were fully capable of handling the order. In fact, garment makers had been asking Expo for orders for over a year.

"We haven't had any replies, whether [our prices] are too high, too low or whatever. We have never officially been asked to tender," growled Michael Stanton of Dominion Textiles.

Ace and Expo let the producers complain. While the

federal government pondered the request to relax its quota on imports, Ace was not sitting on its hands. It was industriously circumventing the annoying little restriction by importing shirts through middle-men. It commissioned local wholesalers to import T-shirts through their suppliers in the Philippines and sell them to Ace. The plan was carried out with the knowledge and approval of Expo retail director Michael Joss.

While Jim Pattison was shutting the door on B.C. business, he was practising his legendary brand of management relations on senior Expo staff.

People who work for Pattison have been described as "dedicated and terrified," curiously similar to fundamentalists' attitude to their Lord. Pattison demands unswerving loyalty. On the other side of the coin, he can be ruthless toward those who don't carry out his bidding.

A list that began with the first car salesman fired for having a bad month is added to by Expo executives who didn't make the grade. At this writing, 23 top people have left Expo suddenly or have been fired. (The exact circumstances of their departures were seldom revealed by Expo or by those departing.)

Some were there from the beginning. Personnel director Cathy Caper was dumped after three years. Others hardly had time to get to know the Expo site. Alan Hewitt, the human resources director, was fired after only five and a half months.

They were all in middle or upper management—directors, vice presidents, managers. And in the most controversial dismissal in four years of planning and construction, the president himself got the sack.

Little or nothing of the Michael Bartlett story may have been revealed had it not been for a little incident dubbed "The Mercedes Affair."

One February morning in 1984, former and eternal car dealer Jim Pattison strode into the Expo executive parking lot and noticed a shiny new Mercedes. He made a few inquiries and learned that the new $48,000 import had been purchased by Michael Bartlett with Expo money, and had been registered in Barlett's name.

Pattison the moralist immediately demanded that Bartlett hand over the keys. He then ordered one of his car dealerships to sell the car, which it did for $7,000 less than Bartlett paid. Pattison made up the difference by paying Expo out of his pocket.

Barlett was Pattison's hand-picked man to run Expo. The 40-ish Cincinnati native was working north of Toronto, running a Disney-style, U.S.-owned amusement park called "Canada's Wonderland" when Pattison offered him the $140,000-a-year job at Expo.

After the deal was signed in 1982, Bartlett told a news conference that he was the best man in the country for the job. Apparently Pattison thought so, too. According to *Sun* columnist Pete McMartin, plans for the fair were in chaos before Bartlett appeared. "Two planning years had been lost over financial bickering; the Expo board comprised men who had no idea of how to go about setting up a fair; the number of exhibitors signed up was laughably small."

Bartlett was credited with turning all that around. He cut the budget, signed up cultural, corporate and national sponsors, and incorporated "frivolous" features like dizzying rides designed to draw crowds. (One of Bartlett's widely quoted remarks vividly illustrates the point. "You get 'em on the site, you feed 'em, you make 'em dizzy, you scare the shit of 'em.") But Bartlett's abrasive style of management coupled with his "hatchet man" image so common among senior Pattison managers may have been his downfall.

Barlett filled the role with zest, and it sometimes appeared as if he spent half his time firing top Expo executives (mostly Canadian) and the other half replacing them with his friends and former colleagues from Canada's Wonderland (mostly American). By summer 1985, fifteen directors, managers and vice presidents had left Wonderland for Lotus Land.

Like Bartlett, most subscribed to the American "make-'em-dizzy" style fair and it soon looked as if the only thing Canadian about Expo would be its address. Contracts for everything from ticket sellers to trinket makers went to Americans. Bartlett held an Expo executive conference at a posh spa in California, at a cost of $9,000. Canadian businesses, which justifiably wanted to take advantage of the promised Expo goodies, usually got the answering machine; through no fault of their own, they happened to be 1,500 miles north of where the action was.

There are hundreds of stories of B.C. businesses snubbed by Expo. Many of them were volunteered to the daily papers on the condition that names not be used.

A woman who owned a marketing agency and asked for an updated Expo directory was told that names and job descriptions of Expo officials were not public. When she said she already had an old directory and merely wanted a new one, she was grilled about the source of the classified document in her possession.

A Vancouver man had an idea for a board game to promote Expo. When he was finally allowed to meet with fair officials, they insisted that he put up $20,000 in front money. He told them to forget it. Soon he heard from Expo's lawyers, threatening to sue him if he went ahead on his own.

The anonymous complaints all blamed Bartlett or his hired guns for the trouble. But Barlett's arrogance was not confined to his dealings with budding entrepreneurs. *Globe and Mail* reporter Ian Mulgrew quoted "Expo insiders" as saying that Bartlett refused to take direction from Socred cabinet ministers, including a "suggestion" that Premier Bennett and some top ministers appear in Expo advertisements. Let it be said that the Socred government has no higher political priority than Expo. (Before 1985 was out, the stiff figure of Premier Bennett flashed across millions of TV screens inviting the world to the fair.)

On Friday, May 31, 1985, *Sun* columnist Marjorie Nichols revealed the Mercedes incident. The news sparked a public outcry over Expo corruption and the abuse of public money. The protests threated to balloon into a major embarrassment. Within a week, Pattison stepped in and took action. Bartlett was on his way out.

There are as many versions of what happened next as there are dollars in Expo's deficit. There is, of course, an "official" version, but it contains too many contradictions to be taken seriously. Pattison said that Bartlett "resigned" because the "construction phase" of the fair was almost over. Bartlett was not a construction manager, he was hired to run the fair, and his contract ran until December 1986.

Then came the startling news that Bartlett was to receive his full salary until his contract ran out, a deal worth $220,000 of public money. The obvious question was put to Jim Pattison: Why was Bartlett kept on salary if he had resigned?

Pattison was not available, but his chief PR man, George Madden, squirmed and said it was actually a case of Pattison and Bartlett "coming to an agreement" that Bartlett would leave. (At the risk of repeating the obvious, we see another example of how the rich live in a sea of money which is largely ungoverned by laws, even by rules. Imagine Michael Bartlett's financial— and legal—situation if he worked as a clerk in a hardware store and was caught taking $50 from the till to buy himself a used bicycle.)

The malleable "official" version only increased public curiosity about what really happened. A *Province* editorial pointed out another one of the many contradictions: "It was only after the public learned about Bartlett's profligacy with the taxpayers' money— many months after the fact—that the [Expo] board appeared to become exercised about it."

Editorial writers, under the pressure of daily deadlines, do not have the advantages of authors who can spend weeks sifting through facts to piece a story together. With the benefit of hindsight and the opportunity to conduct several interviews, I have assembled an unofficial version of the Bartlett affair which explains the facts more fully than other public accounts.

Bartlett had, as reporter Gordon Hamilton wrote, "pissed a lot of people off," ranging from small entrepreneurs to senior Socred ministers. It was this, and particularly his unwillingness to let the Socreds dictate how to advertise the fair, that sparked calls for his head. The Mercedes affair, while true, was not the reason he was dismissed. It was a red herring, leaked deliberately to arouse public opinion against Bartlett while drawing attention away from Socred attempts to use the fair for its own political purposes, namely, getting re-elected.

And Bartlett's $220,000 gold watch? Call it an insurance premium against Bartlett's temptation to spill the beans.

Not even Expo Ernie, the fair's mascot, escaped the flood of comings and goings. Ken Larson, the man who operated the space-helmeted, four-foot robot and supplied Ernie's voice, quit in August 1985. He said he wanted a change of jobs. Although Ernie is still officially employed, no one can recall the last time he was seen. In fact, when Larsen left, his faceless robot was already a far less familiar symbol of the fair than was the face of Jim Pattison.

11 CONCLUSION

> *No man ever made a million dollars without breaking the law.*
> —Cyrus Eaton,
>   Nova Scotia-born U.S. industrialist

Jim Pattison has accumulated more wealth in 25 years than most wealthy families do over many generations. He is the only Canadian whose gross income is over $1 billion a year and whose personal wealth is estimated at over $600 million.

His rapid ascent to the rarefied atmosphere of the ultra-rich is especially surprising because of his background. What other employer of 6,000 workers was born to an ordinary prairie family struggling to make ends meet during the Depression? What other owner of airlines, food processing plants and car dealerships started out selling lettuce seeds door to door? What other distributor of 100 million copies of magazines each year can recall peddling single copies of *Ladies' Home Journal* to neighbours? What other chairman of a world's fair helped his father earn scarce Depression dollars de-mothing pianos?

It is not only Pattison's checkered past that sets him

apart from others of his class. Where he seeks out publicity, they live in fortresses protected from the media and the outside world. The DuPonts and the Mellons are anonymous and faceless figures. Old Money does not list its home number in the phone book. Pattison subscribes to a different etiquette. His gravitation to the spotlight is rooted in a populism sustained by the gregarious instincts of a salesman.

Pattison is a culture hero to the right, a Willy Loman truly living out his own dreams. Do his dreams include a life in politics? This is a logical question and one that pops up with increasing frequency in letters to the editor columns. In one sense, Pattison has already provided an answer. Asked by the *Globe and Mail* whether he thought he'd been treated fairly by the press, he said, "When you get into politics—which this [Expo] is—I don't think it matters."

Pattison has denied having "real" political ambitions but as Expo chairman he fills one of the most political and sensitive public positions formally outside of government. If he harbours ambitions of crossing over the line, there is no springboard more perfect than Expo.

If there is to be a transition from chairman Pattison to candidate Pattison, it will likely occur in the months following Expo. Pattison will begin his race for public office with a background unmatched by his colleagues. Although the current crop of Socred MLAs includes many car dealers, none had erected a billion dollar empire before filing nomination papers. And none had authority over such an empire to put to use in the course of a campaign.

Pattison will bring to politics his PR department's tailor-made image of a hard working, decisive bottom liner. Added to that will be his reputation as the helmsman of a dazzlingly successful world's fair. Reality notwithstanding, the Socreds will ensure that history's judgment of Expo will be more than kind.

Does Pattison's record prepare him for public life? Does it suggest a desire to place public well-being above his own? Consider the facts:

He's had a reputation for declining interviews because they do not contribute to his companies' revenue.

He has used the same reasoning for refusing directorships on the boards of others' companies.

His concern for the welfare of his lowest-paid employees and minority shareholders has varied between little and none.

He has displayed no discernible compassion for the black miners who slaved under the South African veldt to enrich his mentor, Charles Englehard, and indirectly Pattison himself.

His attitude toward the victims of pornography can at best be called cynical.

While he has been chairman of Expo, his companies have reaped several million dollars from contracts with the world's fair.

There is almost nothing in Jim Pattison's past to suggest that the public good would be well served in his custody. Nor is there much in recent B.C. history to indicate that a track record such as his would harm his chances for election.

In fact, in enshrining the virtue of self-interest, Jim Pattison can be called a man of his times. It might be more accurate to say that the times have caught up with him. In the 1960s, when Pattison was laying the foundation of his conglomerate, people marched in significant numbers on behalf of civil rights and in opposition to the war in Vietnam and to the profits it was generating for arms manufacturers. By the mid-1970s, the mood of the times had radically changed. An aggressive neo-conservatism had taken hold. Self-improvement and get-rich-quick bestsellers like *Winning Through Intimidation* and *Profit Is Not a Dirty Word* epitomized the values and aspirations of the Me Generation. Collectivist values fell into disrepute. Evidence for the natural superiority of selfishness was found in everything from the Bible and theories of human nature to the philosophical pronouncements of Ronald Reagan. The sea change in political mood was a source of great pleasure to Jim Pattison. It gave words to the song he had been singing for years.

Pattison's future as a billionaire businessman seems assured. It is hard to imagine an empire as extensive and solid as his crumbling (like Nelson Skalbania's) or tottering (like Peter Pocklington's). Whether Pattison has his eye on a new career should be known soon after Expo dissolves away. The neo-conservatism of the eighties, which has been very kind to his economic fortunes, can only encourage any plans he might have to add the Legislative Buildings in Victoria to his scores of existing addresses.

All through 1985 as I researched and wrote this book, billboards and bus ads repeated endlessly a Pattison promotion: "Isn't it time you talked to Jimmy?" As I learned more about the roots of his power—in hate literature about women, lost jobs and depressed wages—the inane ad began to haunt me. As Pattison continues to enrich himself through the mass marketing of sexist and violent images of women, as he undermines unions and drives down wages, as he feeds at the public trough with the rest of the world's fair contractors and readies himself for the status of national hero for pulling off the empty spectacle called Expo 86, isn't it, finally, time we all talked to Jimmy?

APPENDIX 1:
FURTHER ACTION ON PORNOGRAPHY

The reader will have gathered that of all of Jim Pattison's blemishes, pornography evokes the strongest gut reaction from me. Several years ago I became aware of the emerging connections between pornography and violence against women. I was surprised and alarmed when it was revealed that Jim Pattison—the head of Expo 86, a leading businessman and a devout Christian—had been profiting from pornography for years. Was this, as Pattison claimed, a single oversight, a mistake committed by a businessman too preoccupied with the larger picture to keep tabs on every little detail? Or was it a hint of a depth of hypocrisy, of putting profits ahead of ethics (Christian or otherwise), of using power to engulf opponents?

The evidence, as I have argued, suggests the latter. Pattison did not volunteer information about his pornography sales, but waited a month before confirming what the North Shore Women's Centre revealed. Then he moved with increased speed to maintain his profit picture: he divided his opposition and convinced his more liberal opponents to serve on the pornography review board. He also left people with the false impression that he'd sold Mainland Magazine, when in fact he still owns it.

What to do? Tactics for change are difficult to arrive at under the best of circumstances, but are even harder to propose in books because the target of our protest changes with time. Businesses go under. New ones emerge. New information guides our actions. (That being said, I'll outline as best I can some strategies and tactics in the fight against pornography.)

Effective actions to challenge injustices often emerge from a combination of factors: the skills, knowledge and commitment to action on the part of people in the community; awareness of the injustice crossing a critical threshold for enough people—how close to home are its effects? Some successful actions are described in the chapters of this book.

There are, however, further actions I want to suggest here. They include personal decisions by men to stop buying and using pornography, and to speak up and ask friends to stop. Buying these magazines or video tapes puts money in the pockets of Pattison and other businessmen, and it keeps in circulation a form of hate literature that dehumanizes men's fantasies and behaviour and turns us against women.

It is also important to support organized groups. The feminists who have marched in the streets, leafleted in the rain and spoken out in public against pornography and the cascade of profits it generates need financial and other support. Phoning their offices will supply you with information on how to join in the battle.

Many of you belong to trade unions or other groups or organizations. These can be used as a forum in which to discuss what you know about pornography—for example, what you've learned in this book—how further information can be acquired and what actions can be taken. Your organization can get more information by inviting groups named in these pages to send you a speaker to one of your meetings.

There are many possible non-violent direct actions. For example, letters to the editor of daily papers and community papers protesting against Pattison's distribution and profiting from pornography will inform and remind people that he is still selling those magazines in B.C. and five other provinces and territories. The central demand—that he keep his magazine companies but stop them from distributing pornography—could be accompanied by a demand that he donate the profits from past sales of pornography to women's groups fighting porn. This would help the same women who exposed Pattison when they proceeded to challenge the businessmen who would inevitably pick up the pornography sales cancelled by Pattison.

Individuals could reinforce group actions by contacting Pattison (he's listed in the phone book): by phone (922-8832) or by writing to him at his home (855 Eyremount Drive, West Vancouver); his business headquarters are at 1055 West Hastings Street, Vancouver. As I noted in Chapter 9, Pattison is known to return calls, even when he knows the caller wants to criticize him.

Anyone who followed the Watergate scandal knows that public exposure of the wrongdoings of the rich and powerful is a potent weapon. But to be effective the exposure must take many forms. For example, I wear a protest button—"Save-On-Pornography, a Division of Jim Pattison Enterprises"—which sparks discussions with people on buses, in the lineup at the credit union, or in the grocery store.

During the height of the campaign to expose Pattison's pornography profits no one called for a boycott of any of his companies. The reason is not hard to imagine. Consumers cannot easily keep track of the myriad of brand names and trademarks owned by Pattison. It *is* difficult to live in B.C. and not put a buck in his pocket. But anyone with an idea for a boycott that might win consumer support should talk about it in their own groups or contact one of the organizations which have already spoken out publicly against pornography: the North Shore Women's Centre (984-6009); Vancouver Status of Women (873-1427); Rape Relief (872-8212); or my own group, Men Against Rape (255-7138).

The 1986 world's fair provides unprecedented opportunities for informing residents and visitors about the Expo chairman's porn profits (and about his strong ties to the Socreds, who have systematically cut back aid to B.C.'s poor while diverting hundreds of millions to this mega-circus). A hundred thousand visitors are expected to visit Expo every day. Creative protests and demonstrations which do not interfere with the visitors will send out messages that will travel far. The actions can take many forms: street theatre, information booths, slogans displayed on everything from T-shirts to balloons, banners flying from sailboats drifting along Expo's shoreline site. The messages should be simple and catchy and should convey a spirit which is the antithesis of the grimy, suffocating atmosphere of porn.

APPENDIX 2:
DIRECTORS OF NEONEX AND THE JIM PATTISON GROUP

NEONEX DIRECTORS, 1970

Jim Pattison	Chairman, Chief Executive Officer
Michael D. Dingman*	Vice Chairman
Charles W. Brazier	Director
Arthur B. Christopher	Director
Harry B. Dunbar	Director
Robert W. Halliday*	Director
Lawrence Hoguet*	Director
C.S. Mitton	Director

*U.S. citizens

Interlocking Directorships, 1970

Michael D. Dingman, New York
   Senior Broker   Burnham and Company, New York

Robert W. Halliday, Boise, Idaho
   Co-founder   Boise Cascade (fifth largest forest products company in U.S.)
   President   Greystone Corporation
   Director   Bank of Idaho
   Director   Air-Mac Incorporated

Director	Shareholders Capital Corporation
Director	Leckenby Company
Director	Health-Tecna Corporation
Chairman	Kensington Corporation
Chairman	U.S. Natural Resources Inc.

Lawrence Hoguet, New York

Sr. VP, Treasurer, Director	Englehard Minerals & Chemicals Corporation
VP, Treasurer, Director	American-South African Investment Company
President	Eurofund International Inc.
Vice President	Amersil Inc.
Vice President, Director	Connors & Hoffman Footwear
Director	Chappaqua Oil Corporation
Director	Neonex International Ltd.

Charles W. Englehard, New York (1917-1971)*

Chairman, Chief Executive Officer	Englehard Minerals & Chemicals Corporation
Chairman	South Africa Forest Investment Ltd.
Chairman	Rand Mines Ltd., South Africa
Chairman	American-South African Investment Corporation
Chairman, Director	Eurofund International Inc.
Director	Thomas Barlow & Sons, South Africa
Director	Anglo-American Corporation, South Africa
Director	Charter Consolidated Ltd., London
Director	Hudson's Bay Mining and Smelting Ltd.
Director	Boart & Hard Metal Products, South Africa
Director	Rand Selection Corporation, South Africa
Director	Foreign Policy Association
Director	Council on Foreign Relations Inc.
Commissioner	New York Port Authority

*Not a director, but a major shareholder in Neonex

DIRECTORS OF THE JIM PATTISON GROUP, 1985

Jim Pattison	Chairman, President
Robert W. Halliday*	Director
Mark N. Kaplan*	Director
Eward H. Meyer*	Director
William J. Sleeman	Director

DIRECTORS OF GREAT PACIFIC INDUSTRIES, 1985
(80 per cent owned by Jim Pattison Group)

Jim Pattison	Chairman, President
William J. Sleeman	Vice Chairman
John H. Coleman	Director
Robert W. Halliday*	Director
Mark N. Kaplan*	Director
Hugh H. MacKay	Director

*U.S. citizens

Interlocking Directorships of Jim Pattison Group and GPI, 1985

Hugh H. MacKay, St. John, New Brunswick

Vice President, Director	Maritime Beverages Limited**
Director	Ducks Unlimited Canada
Director	McChip Resources Ltd.

**formerly owned by GPI under Pattison

John H. Coleman, Toronto

Chairman	United Group of Mutual Funds
Chairman	Lehndorff Corporation
Chairman	MICC Investments Ltd.
Chairman	Mortgage Insurance Company of Canada
Chairman	Maritime Steel and Foundries Ltd.
Chairman	Central Trust Company Advisory Board
Vice Chairman	Cameron Corporation
Director	CKR Inc.
Director	Colgate-Palmolive Ltd.
Director	Hunter Douglas Canada Ltd.
Director	Inter City Gas Corporation
Director	International Minerals and Chemicals Corporation*
Director	Serem Inc.
Director	Standard Products (Canada) Ltd.
Director	Thomson Newspapers
Director	Westburne International Industries Ltd.

*Canada's largest chemical fertilizer company, based in Esterhazy, Saskatchewan; owns subsidiaries in South Africa.

Mark N. Kaplan, New York
- Director — Drexel Burnham and Company
- Director — American Biltrite Inc.
- Director — Elgin National Industries Inc.
- Director — Grey Advertising Inc.
- Director — REFAC Technology Development Corporation
- Member — Council for National Policy Review Advisory Council
- Director — Marcade Group Inc.
- Director — Unimax Corporation
- Director — Duty Free Shoppers Group Ltd., Hong Kong
- Director — New Alternatives for Children Inc.

Edward H. Meyer, New York
- President, Chairman, Chief Executive Officer — Grey Advertising Inc.

NOTES

My primary sources for the material in this book are the daily and weekly press: the Vancouver *Sun*, the Vancouver *Province*, the Toronto *Globe and Mail*, the New York *Times*, the *Wall Street Journal, Canadian Business Magazine, Marketing, Executive, Monetary Times, Canadian Dimension, Impetus, B.C. Business* and *Equity*. Unless otherwise cited, quotes in the text are taken from the foregoing. The epigraphs for the book opening and for Chapters 3 and 4 are taken from *Equity*, April 1985. The three speakers are not named but the clear impression given in the article is that each of these is a different speaker.

Chapter 1
The Richmond epigraph is from the *Sun*, June 6, 1985. Events in the Air BC hangar are reconstructed from press reports and interviews with some participants. Statistics covering the growth of consumer goods and service industries after the war are taken from Robin (see bibliography for references). The account of Pattison's takeover of the small airlines is taken from press accounts and interviews with union officials connected to the airlines.

Chapter 2

Much of the material about Pattison's home town was obtained in interviews with Luseland resident Val Finlay, and in the two-volume history of the town which she edited. Anecdotal material was gathered in interviews with Mac and Thearn Finlay (who baby sat young Jimmy) and Lois and Art Meier (who now live in the old Pattison house). Background details of the Depression years are taken mainly from Broadfoot and Robin.

Chapter 3

Outlines of the provincial economy and B.C. political history during these years are contained in Robin, Marchak and *Time* magazine. The historical background of Neon Products is from the company's annual reports 1946-1968, and press reports. Anderson's conflict of interest is summarized in reporter Pat Carney's dispatch on Pattison's takeover of Neon Products, *Sun*, August 27, 1968.

Chapter 4

The Goldfinger anecdote and other background material on Englehard are found in Fay, Moskowitz and Lundberg. His company's South African connections are documented in Moody's, and Standard and Poor's corporate directories.

Chapter 5

The Hamilton epigraph is from an interview with the author, 1985. Details of Neon Products' takeovers are contained in press reports and are verified in the company's annual reports, 1968-70. Information about directors' fees and foreign directors on Canadian boards can be found in Stewart and in Aubin. The account of the Imbrex takeover and subsequent court battle is taken from *Green vs. Charterhouse Group Canada Ltd., Ontario Supreme Court Reports*, 1973, Vol. 2.

Chapter 6

The Brazier epigraph is from a telephone interview by the author, January 1986. The corporate tables and the account of the Norris, Leitch agreements are based on *Leitch vs. Neonex, Supreme Court of Ontario Reports*, 1978. Historical background on Maple Leaf Mills is drawn from Warnock and from the company's annual reports. Details of the $10 million loan from the New York bank are found in *Neonex vs Federal Court of Appeal, Canada Tax Cases*, 1978.

Chapter 7

The Kolasa epigraph is from testimony given in B.C. Supreme Court, 1978. The account of the Neon Products strike is contructed from press reports supplemented by an interview from Sheet Metal Workers' business agent Cy Stairs. Pattison's purchase of all Neonex shares in 1977 is based on *Neonex vs Kolasa et al.,* Supreme Court of British Columbia, 1978, and press reports.

Chapter 8

The Myers epigraph is from *A History of Canadian Wealth,* 1914 edition. The Pattison epigraph is from *Equity,* April 1985. Statistics Canada's *Directory of Inter-corporate Ownership,* 1982 was used to establish the number of companies owned by Pattison. The account of the prosecution of Seaboard, HOAL and Mediacom is based on Supreme Court of Ontario records, including: *Regina vs. Mediacom et al.,* "Agreed Statement of Fact," February 6, 1985, and "Order," February 11, 1985. Discussion of the seriousness of the billboard conspiracy case is based largely on interviews with Consumer and Corporate Affairs investigators Brian Linseman, Ottawa, and Craig Fulton, Vancouver. The Hunt Brothers' religious beliefs and fundraising activities are outlined in Fay and in Hurt.

Chapter 9

Bev Schroeter's evidence for laying charges against Pattison is taken from minutes of the Community Services Committee meeting, Vancouver City Hall, May 31, 1984. Stewart's revelations to the Fraser Committee are based on an interview with her by the author. Press reports on the periodical review board were supplemented by interviews with Ridington, Phillips, Mainland Magazine president John Seebach, Linda Cronin of the Attorney General's Department, Megan Ellis of WAVAW and Regina Lorek and Lee Lakeman of Rape Relief.

Chapter 10

The Bartlett epigraph first appeared in 1982 in *Vancouver* magazine and was reprinted in both the *Province* and *Sun,* June 14, 1985. The analysis of the costs of Expo follows Blackorby. Background on Ace Novelty and Benjamin Meyers can be found in the *Report of the Royal Commission into Royal American Shows* (Alberta, 1978).

Chapter 11—Conclusion

The Eaton epigraph is taken from an interview by the author in Yarmouth, N.S., 1969.

BIBLIOGRAPHY

Aubin, Henry, *City for Sale* (Lorimer, Toronto, 1977). Although primarily about Montreal, this book contains rare glimpses into how South African and European businessmen control large sectors of the Canadian economy.

Blackorby, Charles, Glen Donaldson and Margaret Slade, *Expo 86: An Economic Impact Analysis* (The University of British Columbia, B.C. Economic Policy Institute, August 1984). A thorough, sometimes technical, evaluation of what Expo 86 will cost B.C.

Broadfoot, Barry, *Ten Lost Years* (Doubleday Canada, Toronto, 1973). Oral histories highlight the Depression years, a period in Canadian history dismissed by conventional historians.

Fay, Stephen, *Beyond Greed* (Viking, New York, 1982). A critical account of the Hunt brothers' attempt to corner the market on silver in 1979-80.

Government of Canada, *Report of the Royal Commission on Corporate Concentration,* (Minister of Supply and Services, Ottawa, March 1978). Some findings are outdated, but the overview of the structure of Canada's economy is still valuable.

Gutstein, Donald, *Vancouver Ltd.* (Lorimer, Toronto, 1975). A carefully researched argument for a strong citizen movement to develop Vancouver for the majority, not for a few developers.

Hurt III, Harry, *Texas Rich* (Norton, New York, 1981). A critical biography of the Hunt family of Texas, perhaps the world's richest "born again" capitalists.

Josephson, Matthew, *The Robber Barons* (Harcourt, Brace, New York, 1934). One of the early examples of "muckraking" reporting on the rich.

Lundberg, Ferdinand, *The Rich and the Super-Rich* (Lyle Stuart, New York, 1968). A carefully reasoned, densely documented interpretation of who owns the United States.

Magnusson, Warren et al., *The New Reality* (New Star Books, Vancouver, 1984). The first book-length examination of Premier Bill Bennett's "restraint" policies of 1983-84.

Marchak, M. Patricia, *Green Gold* (University of British Columbia Press, Vancouver, 1983). A critique of the management of B.C.'s forest industry.

Myers, Gustavus, *History of Canadian Wealth* (first edition 1914; reprinted by James Lewis & Samuel, Toronto, 1972). Canada's history to the end of the nineteenth century through the eyes of a pioneering muckraker.

——*Great American Fortunes* (first published 1907; reprinted by Random House, New York, 1937). Lays bare the corruption, fraud and swindling behind U.S. wealth.

Moskowitz, Milton, Michael Katz and Robert Levering, eds., *Everybody's Business* (Harper & Row, New York, 1980). An almanac of of contemporary U.S. companies, written for community activists.

Newman, Peter C., *The Canadian Establishment*, Vol. I, (McClelland and Stewart, Toronto, 1975).

——*The Acquisitors* (*The Canadian Establishment*, Vol II), (McClelland and Stewart, Toronto, 1981). Portraits of the Pattisons, Skalbanias, Pocklingtons and others who are rich and powerful but outside the establishment.

Persky, Stan, *Son of Socred* (New Star Books, Vancouver, 1979). A lively, irreverent account of Bill Bennett's first three years as premier.

——*Bennett II* (New Star Books, Vancouver, 1983). Sequel to *Son of Socred*.

——*The House That Jack Built* (New Star Books, Vancouver, 1980). An account of Vancouver city politics which anticipates the rise of the left at city hall.

Robin, Martin. *The Rush for Spoils* (McClelland and Stewart, Toronto, 1972). The first of a two-volume political history of B.C. from 1871-1972. A scholarly but readable account from a left wing perspective.

——*Pillars of Profit* (McClelland and Stewart, Toronto, 1973). Volume II. With *Rush for Spoils*, perhaps the best political history of B.C. available.

Stewart, Walter, *Towers of Gold, Feet of Clay* (Collins, Toronto, 1982). A lively account of the oligopolistic banking community in Canada.

Warnock, John W., *Profit Hungry* (New Star Books, Vancouver, 1978).

INDEX

Ace Novelty, 228-233
Acme Novelty, 86, 96, 144, 146, 147
Acton, Lord, 19
Air BC, 21, 22, 24, 25, 28, 32, 163, 167, 221, 227
Alexander, Ted, 89, 91
Allen, Julia, 38, 42, 53
Allende, Salvador, 146
Altman, Gary, 227
American Stock Exchange, 138
Anderson, Rose, 13
Anderson, William, 62, 70, 73, 75, 76
Andrews, Jancis, 199
Argus Corporation, 59, 99
Associated Helicopters, 87, 96
Austin, Jack, 170
Axworthy, Lloyd, 27, 195

BACM, 100

Bank of B.C., 29, 139
Barlow, Maude, 195, 196, 196n
Barrett, Dave, 139, 170
Barry, Eric, 232
Bartlett, Michael, 16, 215, 233-237
Bata, Thomas, 18
Bawden, H.H., 114
Beautiful B.C. magazine, 17, 225, 226
Belzberg, Samuel, 57
Bennett, Bill, 16, 27, 216, 217, 221, 222, 223, 228
Bennett, W.A.C., 46, 52
Bentall, Charles, 57, 172
Bentall, Clark, 57, 228
Bentall, Robert, 172
Berryland, 16, 163
Bigelow-Sandford, 96, 98, 124, 133, 134
Birk, Gordon, 192, 193

INDEX 257

Black, Conrad, 111
Bland, Terrence, 202
Block, Arthur, 172
Boise Cascade, 84, 85, 86
Born Again (Christian) businessmen, 171
Bouck, Judge, 150, 151
Bowell-McLean Motors, 45, 49, 50, 51
Brammal, Brian, 186
Brascan, 59, 99
Brazier, Charles, 104, 135
Bright, Bill, 174
B.C. Business magazine, 171, 172, 204
B.C. Hydro, 226
B.C. Lions, 49
B.C. Place, 15, 217
B.C. Tel, 18
Brown, Fred, 57, 84
Brown, Peter, 178, 180n, 228, 230, 231
Buckerfield, E., 60
Bureau of International Exhibitions, 216
Burnham and Company, 63, 64, 84, 85, 87, 137
Buston, John, 33

Calgary Stock Exchange, 137
Campus Crusade for Christ, 172, 174
Canada Life, 111
Canada's Wonderland, 234
Canadian Business magazine, 51
Canadian Business Service, 143, 147
Canadian Coalition Against Media Pornography, 189
Canadian Council of Christians and Jews, 224
Canadian Establishment, The, 56, 204
Canadian Fishing Company, 17, 164
Canadian Imperial Bank of Commerce, 111, 114, 121, 123
Canadian Pacific, 99
Canadian Transport Commission, 23, 26, 27, 32, 33
Canadian Textile Institute, 232
Canarim Investments, 178, 180n
Capozzi, Herb, 228
Cayman Islands, 175, 176
CBRT & GW, 25, 26, 29, 30
Chant, Maureen, 27, 197, 205
Chaston, John G., 88, 89
Cheyenne Petroleum, 178
Chile (ITT), 146
Chretien, Jean, 154
Christopher, Arthur B., 60, 69-75, 80, 135
CJOR Radio, 17, 56, 83, 169, 170, 171, 223, 227
Claude Neon, 16, 166
Clyne, J.V., 57
Coleman, John H., 85
Combines Investigation Act, 155, 158, 160, 161, 162, 190
Community Services Committee, 185, 187, 200, 202
conglomerates, 58, 59
Consumer and Corporate Affairs, 136, 153
Co-operative Commonwealth Federation, 43
CP Air, 18
CPR, 59
Craig, Al, 30, 34
Criminal Code, 188
Cronin, Linda, 197, 200
Crossroads Christian Communication Incorporated, 224
Cruickshank, Dean Jim, 197
Crush International, 146-151, 166, 174, 195
Curtis, Bill, 215

Dagg, Ray, 228
Davies, Robert, 116, 118
Dawson Developments, 105
Dawson, Graham, 57

Depression, Great, 19, 40, 238
Der Hoi-Yin, 176
Dingman, Michael, 63-65, 68, 71, 78, 80, 84, 87, 91, 122, 138
directorships, rules governing, 84-85
Dominion Foundries and Steel (Dofasco), 107-109, 111, 120, 121, 125, 126
Dominion Construction, 172
Dominion Textiles, 232
Dueck Chevrolet, 60
Dueck, Peter, 172
Dunbar, Harry, 122
Duponts, 239

Easton, M. Donald, 135, 148, 149
Eaton, Cyrus, 238
Eberhardt, Lawrence B., 135
EDP Industries, 17, 227
Ellis, Megan, 199, 204
Employers' Council of B.C., 76
Engineered Homes, 100, 105
Englehard, Charles, 63-68, 84, 122n, 176, 240
Englehard Incorporated, 63-68, 84, 85, 87
Equity magazine, 169, 250
Eriksen, Bruce, 200, 202, 203
Everybody's Business, 66
Expo 67, 216
Expo 86, 18, 161, 178, 184, 186, 199, 210, 215-237, 239, 241, 243, 245
Expo Ernie, 237
Eyre, Alan, 60, 84

Fabco, 139, 167
False Creek, 215, 221
Farrell, Gordon, 57, 60
Fawcus, Ken, 227, 228
Fay, Stephen, 64
Federal Trade Commission (U.S.), 164
Financial Post, 76, 145, 204
Finlay, Margaree (Mac), 38

Fleming, Ian, 64
Flynt, Larry, 211
Ford, Gerald, 19, 169
Fotheringham, Alan, 54, 173
FP Publications, 162
Fraser Committee on Prostitution and Pornography, 181, 182, 183, 186, 205, 212
Fraser, Paul, 182
Fraser Valley Frosted Foods, 16

Geneen, Harold, 145, 146
Genstar, 18, 100, 135
Genstar Chemical Limited, 100
Gerard, Walter, 38
Giles, Jack, 156, 158, 179n
Giles, Virginia, 179n
Ginter, Ben, 55
Glad Tidings Church, 51, 171, 203-205
Globe and Mail, 72, 152, 160, 161, 167, 185, 194, 204, 208, 235, 239
Godbout, R.G., 88-93, 96, 97
Gold, Harvey, 170
Gold Seal (salmon), 17, 164
Goldfinger, 64
Gough, John, 130
Gould Advertising, 16, 153, 154, 162
Granby Mining, 138
Great Pacific Capital, 17, 175
Great Pacific Industries, 17, 175
Greene, Arthur, 88n, 93, 97
Greenshields, 124
Grieg, Tom, 189
Grizzly Valley, 177, 178
Guinness Tower, 13, 23, 31
Gutstein, Donald, 100

Haig, Alexander, 18, 169
Halliday, Robert W., 84, 86
Hambidge, Archbishop Douglas, 197, 198
Hamilton, Bill, 76
Hamilton, Gordon, 80, 220, 230,

237
Harcourt, Mike, 187, 201
Harding Carpets, 91, 92, 96, 122, 124, 134
Harper, Gilmour and Grey, 135
Harris, Iain, 30, 33
Harris, W.R. (Rusty), 28
Haughton Group, 87
Hemsworth, Barry, 177, 178
Hoguet, Lawrence, 67, 80, 84, 86, 87, 122
Hook Outdoor Advertising (HOAL), 16, 153-158, 162, 179n
Hotel Vancouver, 181
Hudson's Bay Company, 59
Hunt brothers, 67
Hunt, Bunker, 174, 175
Hunt, Herbert, 175
Hunt Transportation, 98
Hunter, Jim, 30
Hustler, 183, 191, 206, 208, 209
Hyndman, Peter, 180n

Imbrex, 87, 88-93, 96-97, 102, 131, 133, 134
Income Tax Act, 140
Ingham, Gwenlth, 208
Institute of Chartered Accountants, 76
Inter-Corporate Ownership Guide, 138
International Association of Machinists (IAM), 25, 26, 29
Irvings (New Brunswick), 165, 180n
ITT, 145, 146

Jarislowsky, Stephen, 175
Jim Pattison Enterprises, 184
Jim Pattison Group, 13, 16, 17, 163, 166, 168, 170, 173, 201, 205, 208
Jim Pattison Industries, 162
Jim Pattison International, 193
Jim Pattison Sign Company, 227

Jim Pattison Yacht Leasing, 227
Jordan-Knox, Charles, 90, 93, 96
Jordan-Knox, Trevor, 90, 93, 96
Jordan Rugs Limited, 90
Joss, Michael, 233

Kaiser, Edgar, 57
Keevil, Norm, 226, 228
Ker, R.H.B., 79, 84
Kerkhoff, Willem, 221, 222
Khaki, Aziz, 223
Kissinger, Henry, 18, 169
Kitsilano Boys Band, 43
Kolasa, William, 130, 150
Krug, Guy, 175

Laidman, R.H. (Dick), 28
Lakeman, Lee, 199
Lalonde, Marc, 27, 195
Larson, Ken, 237
Leitch, Gordon C., 110
Leitch, John D. (Jack), 107-114, 116-123, 126-128
Leitch Transport, 107-109, 111, 116, 120, 122, 126, 127
Lewall, Guy, 144
Lewtas, James, 117-119
Linseman, Brian, 154, 162
Llobet, Josep, 78
Lorek, Regina, 199
Los Angeles Times, 179n
Lucy, Inspector John, 202
Luse, J.F., 37
Luseland, 35, 37

Maclean-Hunter, 18
Maclean's magazine, 166, 204
MacMillan Bloedel, 18, 47
MacMillan, H.R., 57
Madden, George, 236
Mafia, 206
magazines (Pattison's), 17, 163, 171
Mainland Magazine, 16, 183, 186, 187, 189, 190, 191, 194-196, 201, 202, 206-212, 227,

243
Mainse, David, 227, 255
Mair, Rafe, 169, 170, 223
Malkin, J.D.P., 60
Manhattan Project, 37
Maple Leaf Mills, 18, 104-111, 129, 131, 134, 135, 146, 159
Marine Midland Grace Trust Company, 121, 123, 128
Martin, Collin, 77
Massey-Ferguson, 111
Mayers, Benjamin, 229, 230
Mazankowski, Don, 231
McCarthy, Grace, 216
McConica, Edith, 40
McConica, John, 38
McConica, William, 36, 38
McConica Brothers and Pattison, 37, 39
McDonald, Gordon, 224, 225
McGeer, Gerry, 41
McKinnon, Neil, 123
McMahon, Frank, 57
McMartin, Pete, 234
McNaughton, Angus, 135n
Mediacom, 153-158, 162, 179n
Medicor Corporation, 143
Meier, Art, 38, 41
Mellons, 239
Men Against Rape, 245
Mike's News Stand, 95
Miller, Joni, 199
Mississippi Bubble, 91
Molson, Harold E., 60
Molson's, 114-120, 122, 127
Mountain City News, 16, 191, 192, 193
Mulgrew, Ian, 235
Murphy, Thomas A., 50
Myers, Gustavus, 152

National Action Committee on the Status of Women, 197
National Hockey League, 143
Neon Products, 16, 44, 54, 60-62, 64, 65, 68-72, 75-79, 80-83, 85-91, 94-97, 105, 111, 130-133, 146, 153, 221, 227
Neonex International, 98-106, 112-115, 118-122, 124-128, 134-150, 153, 158, 159, 160, 164-166, 173, 178, 194
"New" Neonex, 148-151
Newman, Peter C., 56, 111, 204
New York Stock Exchange, 40
Nichol, Senator John, 69, 79, 84
Nichols, Marjorie, 227, 232, 235
Norris, Bruce, 107-109, 110, 112, 114, 116-122, 125, 126, 138
Norris Grain, Illinois, 107-109, 110, 112, 120, 121, 125, 127
Norris Grain, Winnipeg, 107-109, 110, 112, 120, 121, 125, 127
Northern Paint Company, 81, 83, 136, 146
Northwest Sports Enterprises, 143
North Shore Women's Centre, 181, 187, 189, 191, 196, 199, 202, 243

Ocean Cement, 100
Office and Professional Employees Association, 132
"Old" Neonex, 148-151
Olson, Clifford, 31
100 Huntley Street, 224, 225
Oppenheimer, Harry, 18
Ottawa *Journal*, 162
Otto Manufacturing, 98
Outdoor Advertising Association, 61, 155, 156, 158
Overwaitea, 17, 81, 82, 115, 121, 163, 168, 227

Pacific Interfaith Citizenship Association, 223, 224, 225
Pacific Press, 162, 194
Palm Springs, 168, 173
Paris, Charles, 224
Paris, Ray, 143

INDEX

Partners in Pride, 18, 168
Pattison, Chandos (Pat), 35, 42, 44, 53, 60
Pattison, Jim, 14, 15, 20, 24, 26, 28-34, 49, 52, 54-65, 73, 74, 76, 78-80, 83, 85-87, 94, 95, 99-106, 131, 133-136, 139-141, 145, 154, 155, 163-166, 173, 181, 184, 189, 190, 195-202, 204-214, 216-220, 239-241, 243-245;
  Air BC shutdown threat, 22-23;
  buys airlines, 24-25;
  and American directors, 84, 87;
  billboard conspiracies, 156-162;
  birth, 38;
  born again Christianity, 171, 172;
  first car dealership, 51;
  children, 46, 50;
  buys CJOR Radio, 56;
  companies owned by, 16-17;
  Crush International takeover, 146-147;
  sells Crush, 174;
  Expo—Ace Novelty scandal, 228-231;
  Expo—Bartlett firing, 233-237;
  Expo guide controversy, 225-228;
  Expo labour disputes, 221-223;
  father dies, 53;
  Grizzly Valley scandal, 177-179;
  buys WHA hockey team, 142-143;
  Imbrex takeover, 88-93, 96-97;
  and Lalonde, Axworthy, 27;
  fires Rafe Mair, 169-170;
  fires senior managers, 84;
  Maple Leaf Mills takeover, 111-129;
  Neon Products takeover, 68-72;
  takes Neonex private, 147-151;
  Northern Paint takeover, 81;
  odd jobs, 43-44;
  Overwaitea takeover, 81-82;
  pornography charges (Edmonton), 203;
  pornography convictions (Hamilton), 191-194;
  admits to pornography distribution, 186-187;
  quality circles, 167-169;
  avoids recession's effects, 173-177;
  and religion, 42, 171, 223-225;
  fires worst salesmen, 45-46;
  posts bail for Tom Scallen, 143;
  sole shareholder, 152;
  South African connections, 63-68, 84;
  Swiss bank, 175;
  moves to Vancouver, 41;
  Wall Street lists Neonex, 137-138;
  personal wealth, 17-18, 238;
Pattison, Julia (Allen), 38, 42, 53
Pattulo, T.D., 41
Pawluck, Fred, 191
Pemberton Securities, 73, 88, 89, 101, 102
Pennyfarthing Developments, 172
Penthouse, 183
Periodical Review Board, 208
Peterson, Ann, 33
Peterson, Edwin, 138
Philadelphia Blazers, 142
Phillips, Karen, 208, 211, 212
Placer Developments, 138
Playboy, 183, 206
Pocklington, Peter, 241
Poole, Jack, 57, 105
Pop Shoppes, 141, 143
pornography, 15, 19, 181-214
Porta-Bilt, 139
Pouilly Fuisse scandal, 180n
Power Corporation, 59, 99
Proctor and Gamble, 174

Project P (pornography), 187
Province, 162, 226, 236
Provincial News, 16, 95, 203, 206
Pryor, Sam, 116, 118, 119

Q.C. Recorder, 168
quality circles, 167-169, 199

Rankin, Harry, 194, 213
Rape Relief, 199, 203, 204
Read, Geoffrey, 191, 192, 193
Reagan, Ronald, 18, 169, 217, 240
Red Hot Video, 188, 193
Reid, Patrick, 216
Reimer Express Lines, 87, 135
Report On Business magazine, 161
Richards Enterprises, 184
Richmond, Claude, 21
Ridington, Jillian, 197, 208, 211, 212
Ripley's Believe It Or Not!, 17
riots in Vancouver, 41, 42, 43
Roger, Brian, 145
Rogers, D.P., 79, 84
Rogers, Forrest, 57
Ross, Alexander, 115
Rothman's, 18
Royal Commission on Corporate Concentration, 164, 165

Save-On-Foods, 17, 163, 227
Scallen, Tom, 143
Schroeter, Bev, 187, 188, 189, 190, 202
Seaboard Advertising, 16, 60, 70, 77, 78, 153-162, 168
Securities and Exchange Commission, 76, 164
Seebach, John, 197, 198, 200, 208, 209, 210, 211
Sheet Metal Workers Union (Local 280), 133
silver scandal, 67, 175
Skalbania, Nelson, 241
Skidmore, Arthur, 172, 180n
Skiroule, 105
Sleeman, Bill, 207, 208
Smith, Brian, 187, 188, 199, 200, 202, 203
Smith, Harvey, 61, 70-72, 78, 82, 83
Smith, Ray, 43
Southam Incorporated, 18, 162
Specialty Manufacturing, 228
Stairs, Cy, 133
Standard General Construction, 100
Stanton, Michael, 232
Steeves, Ralph, 32
Stevenson, Ken, 172
Stevenson, Kit, 183, 197, 198
Stewart, Donna, 181-184, 194, 197, 198, 205
Supreme Court of B.C., 149
Supreme Court of Canada, 157
Supreme Court of Ontario, 88, 157
Sun, 72, 73, 75, 78, 132, 152, 161, 162, 176, 178, 179n, 203, 220, 224, 226, 230, 232, 234, 235
Sweatman, Alan, 149
Sweny, George, 60
Switzerland, 67, 175

Target Media, 228
Taylor, Paul, 194
Teamsters, 25, 26
Terminal City Club, 171
Teron, J.C. Company, 153, 154
Thompson, R.M., 178
Thomson Newspapers, 162
Thomson, W.E., 73, 74, 84, 89
Time magazine, 55, 190
Toronto Dominion Bank, 213, 217
Toronto Financial Analysts Society, 95
Toronto Stock Exchange, 115, 137

INDEX

Trans Ad, 16, 163, 227
Trans Canada Glass, 180n
Travelaire Trailer Company, 95
Trimble, Tiff, 169
Triple-E Manufacturing, 98
Trudeau, Pierre, 105, 141, 182
Turner, Ross J., 100, 101, 122, 135
TVS Group, 98
Tyee Air, 24, 25

Union Gas, 79
United Trailer Company, 98
University Club, 171
Universport, 95
Upper Lakes Shipping, 107-109, 110-114, 116-120, 122, 125

Vancouver Blazers, 142
Vancouver Canucks, 143
Vancouver Club, 171
Vancouver Limited, 100
Van Mag, 186, 208
Vancouver Status of Women, 245
Vancouver Stock Exchange, 55, 137, 177, 178
Vandella Enterprises, 195
Vandenberg, Ron, 152, 153, 158, 159-161

Vanguard Automotive Products, 227
Vanstone, Fred, 139, 142, 143, 146, 194, 195, 206
Victoria Chamber of Commerce, 139
Vincent, Robert, 116-117

Walburg, Weldon, 31
Wall Street, 137
Wall Street Journal, 55
Watergate, 245
WAVAW, 199, 204
Waymark, Graeme, 208
Westcoast Transmission, 138
Weston, Galen, 111
Whittle, Stanley, 83
Williams, Allan, 31
Williams, Bryan, 45
Willmot, Bud, 114, 115n, 117, 122, 127
Wilson, James, 29
Woodward, C.N.W. (Chunky), 57
Woodward, W.C., 60
World Hockey Association, 142
World War I, 35

Young, Maurice, 57

Russell Kelly has worked as a disc jockey, open line show host, CBC radio morning show host and news reporter in Nova Scotia. He left the CBC six years ago to become a journalist and writer. He has been a regular contributor to the *Globe and Mail* and other publications. When not writing or helping to raise his three year old son, he is active in organizing and fund-raising to stop violence against women.